The Bedside
'GUARDIAN'
32

The Bedside 'GUARDIAN' 32

A selection from The 'Guardian' 1982–83

Edited by
W. L. WEBB

With an introduction by
John Fowles

Cartoons by

Hector Breeze
Les Gibbard
Bryan McAllister
Marc

COLLINS
Grafton Street, London
1983

William Collins Sons & Co Ltd
London · Glasgow · Sydney · Auckland
Toronto · Johannesburg

British Library Cataloguing in Publication Data

The Bedside guardian.—32
1. English essays—Periodicals
082′.05   PN6010.5
ISBN 0-00-217072-8

First published 1983
© Guardian Newspapers 1983

Photoset in Linotron Plantin by
Rowland Phototypesetting Ltd, Bury St Edmunds, Suffolk
Made and printed in Great Britain by
William Collins Sons & Co Ltd, Glasgow

Introduction

When I consider and weigh in my mind all these commonwealths, which nowadays anywhere do flourish, so God help me, I can perceive nothing but a certain conspiracy of rich men procuring their own commodities under the name and title of the commonwealth. They invent and devise all means and crafts, first how to keep safely, without fear of losing, that they have unjustly gathered together, and next how to hire and abuse the work and labour of the poor for as little money as may be. These devices, when the rich men have decreed to be kept and observed under colour of the commonality, that is to say, also of the poor people, then they be made laws.

In my view that passage remains a judgement on human society that time has not (alas) staled. Translated into modern terms, it continues to ring painfully true, both East and West. It is not really a political statement, but a biological description of how the privileged will always behave – exploit their own luck, then make such exploitation the law and also, through the media they control, the social norm. At any rate, I hope the *Guardian* will not mind me thinking of it as the one voice in modern Fleet Street that Sir Thomas More might have approved. Apart from anything else, I cannot imagine any other of our present major newspapers daring to print him, were he writing today.

Of course constantly questioning the prevailing system must mean becoming a chief butt not only of the system itself, but also of its more extreme opponents. To those on the right such an attitude, with its implicit idealism, or utopianism, is only too easily attacked; while to those on the left it is too cautious (why doubt when you can hate?), too much of an eternal Gironde temporizing between the clear evil of the sworn reactionary and the supposed pure good of the Jacobin militant.

To both sides, in short, doubting is pre-eminently wet. That is why the sour and selfishly illiberal streak that characterizes so much of contemporary British journalism delights to mock and despise everything about the *Guardian*, from its supposed do-gooding priggishness to its famous printing gremlin. Only the other day I heard it damned for being 'so boring'; but judging things on the boring/amusing scale has, all through history, been a prime sign of the sick culture. Nothing suits More's conspiracy so well as declaring all serious content a yawn.

In any case this collection proves, like its predecessors, that the charge is absurdly unjust. There can seldom have been a time when such a dry and civilized voice was more needed than over this last year. The 'rich men' have never had it so good. Not only is their welfare a declared policy under Thatcher, but the electorate at large apparently welcomes it. Well may Salman Rushdie say, in his piece here, that 'dark goddesses rule'. I suspect a major psychological change has taken place in Western man: everywhere now he gains a survivor mentality. As long as Jack's inboard, all the rest may drown. The Labour Party's great mistake in 1983 was to assume that there was a discontented majority waiting in this country. There is not, despite unemployment and public spending cuts, and for the very simple reason that those who have 'survived' in job terms remain the majority. The fact that you still have work, when so many haven't, is a kind of perverse, if idiotic, proof that things can't be too bad.

All through history Tories have exploited such perversity, secure in the knowledge that the privileged will always want higher personal rewards from existence than natural justice or a true common weal allows. This ancient biological trait lies far deeper, I am afraid, than outward political belief; and here I do have a quarrel with the *Guardian* – or with that half puritan, half pagan favourite of the sociologists, the *Guardian* reader.

What would surely puzzle a visitor from outer space most about contemporary Britain is what educated conscience likes to say in public, and how it actually lives. It is as if semiology had never happened. We are virtuous in one (much over-valued) sign-system, that of words, and liars in so many others that mutely speak our real creed – or deep attachment to the *status quo*. As liberals we may denounce unfair public privilege (or what we see as selfish government); yet increasingly we dread and resist any diminution in the traditional personal perquisites of belonging to the educated cream of society.

Yet this seems to me precisely where the *Guardian* is such a valuable newspaper, because it does so well reflect, both consciously and unconsciously, this central dilemma, or contradiction, in 'liberal' Britain. When we read the arts or 'living' pages in the *Times* or the *Telegraph*, we know where we are: in a world where privilege and gross inequality in wealth is taken for granted, along with the conviction that some form of the 'conspiracy of the rich' is both necessary and desirable in society. But such juxtapositions in the *Guardian* – between, say, the committed political pieces and those on good restaurants, or wines, or holiday places, or other 'worlds' reserved to the fortunate minority – always disturb me.

The clash of value-systems and their vocabularies (between that needed to demonstrate social injustice or political folly and that to 'sell' private pleasure) is often revealing. In one column the need for a fairer society is proven; in the next, the enemy within stands plain. No English paper deconstructs itself so visibly – shows the inherent contradictions in its (or us its readers') hierarchy of values. That is why I sometimes find the *Guardian* an uncomfortably naked creature. Yet even this is at least partly because it does firmly set out to be a kind of contradiction in terms: a morally good and 'concerned' journal, as well as a plain good one in literary ones. Any fool can sneer at it for its virtuous side; but then is reduced to explaining why being selfish and feeling nothing is any better . . . indeed, not a great deal worse.

The *Times* is indeed the right paper for Top People, since it is dedicated to their preservation and the corollary axiom that they must in no circumstances be led to question the system – or conspiracy – by which they have become top. By employing modern versions of More's 'means and crafts', its main function must be to conform and to petrify – a sadly easy ambition in middle-class Britain. The *Guardian* has to satisfy a much harder and more fastidious readership.

This new anthology will show why it does so often bring off the trick. The main clue to its literary good lies, I think, in the cunning blend of staff regulars and a wide variety of outside occasionals. If the cost of such catholicity must sometimes be the clash of value-systems I spoke of just now, a very great virtue – and an increasingly important one in Thatcher's Britain – is that lively openness, that naturalness, that sense of *not* being editorially controlled, the paper so often displays.

This open-forum quality, inside the general context of a liberal humanism, seems to me the prime distinction of the *Guardian*. It keeps alive one of the most attacked and yet central traditions in European thought and feeling, that of intellectual scepticism, or indeterminacy. It stays open and unsure, where more and more its rivals are shut, turned prison cells by their own – or their owners' – determination to perpetuate the conspiracy. They stink of the externally managed machine, and so do their journalists. For all its faults, the *Guardian* remains freedom and fresh air by comparison.

That is why I think of it (perhaps not least because *peccavi et pecco*, I know I share those puritan-pagan faults) as 'my' paper; and why, in this age of a media pollution that is just as bad as that of the air and water, we all need it.

JOHN FOWLES

Woadicea rides again

I returned to England only recently, after spending two months in India, and was feeling pretty disoriented even before the general election was called. Now, as successive opinion polls inform us of the near-inevitability of a more or less enormous Tory victory, my sense of alienation has blossomed into something closer to full scale culture shock. ' 'Tis a mad world you have here, my masters.'

Have they been putting something in the drinking water while I've been away? I had always thought that the British prided themselves on their common sense, on good old-fashioned down-to-earth realism. But the election of 1983 is beginning to look more and more like a dark fantasy, a fiction so outrageously improbable that any novelist would be ridiculed if he dreamed it up.

Consider this fiction. A Tory Prime Minister, Maggie May, gets elected on the basis of her promises to cut direct taxation and to get the country back to work ('Labour isn't working'). During the next four years she increases direct taxation and contrives to add almost two million people to the dole queues. And she throws in all sorts of extra goodies: a fifth of the country's manufacturing industry lies in ruins, and (although she claims repeatedly to have vanquished the monster Inflation) she presides over the largest increase in prices of any British Prime Minister. The country's housing programme grinds to a halt; schools and hospitals are closed; the Nationality Act robs Britons of their 900-year-old right to citizenship by virtue of birth; and the great windfall of North Sea oil money is squandered on financing unemployment. Money is poured into the police force, and as a result notifiable crimes rise by twenty-eight per cent.

She constantly tells the nation that cash limits are tight, but finds untold billions to spend on a crazy war whose legacy includes the export of drinking water to the South Atlantic at a cost to the British taxpayer of 5p a pint; and, speaking of peace,

16 May, 1983

she earmarks further untold billions for the purchase of the latest weapons of death, although common sense, not to mention history, clearly indicates that the more such weapons exist, the more likely they are to be used.

So far, the story of Prime Minister May is almost credible. The fictional character does come across as unusually cruel, incompetent, unscrupulous and violent, but there have just occasionally been Tory politicians of whom such a description would not be wholly inaccurate. No, the story only falls apart when it gets to the end: Maggie May decides to go to the country, and instead of being hounded into the outer darkness, or at least Tasmania, like her whoring namesake, it seems that she is to receive a vote of confidence; that five more years of cruelty, incompetence, etc., is what the electorate wants.

The hapless novelist submits his story, and is immediately submerged in a flood of rejection slips. Desperately, he tries to make his narrative more convincing. Maggie May's political opponents are presented as hopelessly divided. The presence of alleged 'full-time Socialists' amongst her foes alarms the people. The leader of the Labour Party wears a crumpled donkey-jacket at the Cenotaph and keeps falling over his dog. But still (rejection slips point out) the fact remains that for Mrs May to hold anything like the lead that the polls say she holds, the unemployed – or some of them, anyway – must be planning to vote for her; and so must some of the homeless, some of the businessmen whose businesses she has destroyed, some of the women who will be worse off when (for instance) her proposal to means-test child benefits becomes law, and many of the trade unionists whose rights she proposes so severely to erode.

At this point, our imaginary novelist (compromising the integrity of his vision for the sake of publication) would, in all probability, agree to rewrite his ending. The trumpets sound, the sleeping citizenry awakes, *le jour de gloire* arrives, and Maggie May gets, in 1983, the same sort of bum's rush given to her hero Winston Churchill in 1945.

Is it not passing strange that this, the plausible and happy ending, is the one that looks, in the cold light of real-life Britain, like the one in which it's almost impossible to believe?

I find myself entertaining Spenglerian thoughts, about how there can be times when all that is worst in a people rises to the surface and expresses itself in its government. There are, of course, many Britains, and some of them – the sceptical, questioning, radical, reformist, libertarian, non-conformist Britains – I have always admired greatly. But these Britains are presently in retreat, even in disarray; while nanny-Britain, strait-laced Victoria-reborn Britain, class-ridden know-your-place Britain, thin-lipped, jingoist Britain is in charge. Dark goddesses rule; brightness falls from the air. 'The Ancient Britons,' says the best of history books, *1066 and All That*, 'painted themselves true blue, or woad, and fought heroically under their dashing queen, Woadicea.' The Britons are even more Ancient now, but they have been fighting once again, and that blue dye takes a long time to wear off. Woadicea rides again.

What an achievement is hers! She has persuaded the nation that everything that goes wrong, from unemployment to the crime rate, is an Act of God or someone else's fault; that the forces of organized labour are actually the enemies of organized labour; that we can only defend ourselves by giving the United States the power of life and death over us; that to be an 'activist' is somehow far worse than being an inactivist, and that the left must once more be thought of in Latin, as sinister. She propounds what is in fact an ideology of impotence masquerading as resolution, a con-trick, and it looks as though it's going to work: Maggie's sting.

And it was as recently as 1945 that the British people, politicized by their wartime experiences, threw off the yoke of the true-blue ruling class . . . How quickly the wheel has turned, how quickly faith has been lost in the party they forged as their weapon; how depressingly willing the nation seems to be to start touching forelocks once again. The worst thing about this election is that nobody seems really angry about what has happened, is happening, and is sure to go on happening if Mrs Thatcher is standing on the steps of No. 10 on the morning of June 10. (What will she quote from this time? St Francis of Assisi again? St Joan? The Hitler Diaries?)

I believe the absence of widespread anger matters enormously, for this reason: that democracy can only thrive in a turbulent climate. Where there is acquiescence, cynicism, passivity, resignation, 'inactivism', the road is clear for those who would rob us of our rights.

So, finally, and in spite of all the predictions and probabilities, I refuse to accept that the cause is lost. Despair brings comfort to one's enemies. And elections are not, at bottom, about reasoned arguments; they are about passions. It is just conceivable that even now, in this eleventh hour, a rage can be kindled in the people, rage against the dying of the light that Thatcherism represents. The electorate, we are told, has never been so volatile; so maybe the miracle can still be worked. Maybe, on the day, real life will turn out to obey the same laws of probability as fiction, and sanity will return.

If not, we can look forward to five more years of going to the dogs. *Guardian* readers will no doubt remember these unappealing canines; a few years ago, they used to be known as the running dogs of capitalism.

23 May, 1983   **Salman Rushdie**

Kinnock

So he believed that the one great asset of the Labour Party was people's fear of Mrs Thatcher? 'Absolutely,' said Neil Kinnock, who is one of Labour's great hopes. He said she represented the politics of intimidation. She made people malleable and deferential. But her confidence and assertiveness were starting to be seen as arrogance and ruthlessness. Her pride should have been seen as vanity for some time past.

So this fear of her, rather than any policy of its own, was Labour's greatest strength?

Oh no; Mr Kinnock said Labour had its policies too but put it this way, the reason Mrs Thatcher was Labour's greatest strength was that she was thought of as being the greatest strength of the Tory party too.

And that was why he thought her Cabinet were placemen, court jesters, and wets? Surely some of them were their own men?

'And what do they do about it? Sod all. Spineless wonders.'

I named a few names. Well, he said, Carrington had got the bloody heave-ho, hadn't he? And there was Keith Joseph, who felt, when he saw Mrs Thatcher, the pride of a patron and the affection of a soul-mate, but didn't say a damn word. As for Pym, he might be biding his time but was utterly ineffectual.

Mr Whitelaw, then. 'Poor old Willie, isn't it?' I'm absolutely sure that as one of the squirearchical Tories he loathes the position in which he's so frequently put. But he puts up with it. Mr Prior had copped out and was a doormat, and, as for Mr Walker, who Mr Kinnock believes should be the focus of opposition within the Cabinet, he hardly stuck his head above the parapet, and then it was only to make speeches in New York.

Mr Kinnock then summed up. 'They're bloody useless, the lot of them. And I really think a prime minister who has his or her own way is damn dangerous.'

Now this liberal helping of abuse laced with perception wouldn't be at all significant except that Mr Kinnock, as Shadow Education Secretary, would have a large part to play in the passionate levelling of any Labour administration and has, moreover, been seriously talked about as a future deputy leader of the Party.

Even then, the abuse is only one side to him. For the most part he's a reasonable man. In a long conversation at the Commons only one flash of plain, downright, cherished intolerance showed itself. And a lot of quick-wittedness.

We met in the strangers' coffee room at the Commons. The place is a noisy, squalid, bear garden. It is amazing what MPs put up with which they could perfectly well remedy, and yet still want to put the world to right. Mr Kinnock queued up for coffee for us, with energy, chatted up the woman serving it, also with energy, and then turned his mind, with inevitable energy, of which he has a lot, to an account of his political beginnings and his childhood, which are the same thing.

The family tradition is exemplified by his mother's father, who was a miner in Mr Llewellyn's mine. Llewellyn was

17 May, 1983

running against Keir Hardie for Merthyr Boroughs, and accosted his men at the pithead, inquiring how each might vote. 'You going to vote for me, William Howells?' 'No.' 'Why's that?' 'You don't do anything for me, do you?' Next week William Howells was sacked.

His grandson, the young Neil, went to Lewis grammar school where the uniform was black and white and the assembled school, he says, looked like the Waffen SS. There were caps and badges and tassels. Kinnock himself had a tassle when he became a prefect.

So, although he was now opposed, as a matter of policy, to grammar schools, obviously his father had not been? Mr Kinnock agreed: there had then seemed a rough meritocracy in passing an exam at 10. For himself, he did not object to the advantages grammar schools had conferred on a few but to the disadvantages to which they had subjected many.

At University College, Cardiff, he campaigned against South African oranges and for Nelson Mandela and failed his degree the first time round. When he married, his wife insisted that, having made a fuss about the oranges, they could not buy South African gold, and so her wedding ring is of Scandinavian silver.

At Cardiff he had been famous for singing hymns at 7 a.m. Did he still do this? He said he did. Not that he was a Christian, but Welsh hymns were sometimes more operatic than religious and suited his baritone voice. He demonstrated by singing a snatch in Welsh, and then translating into English.

'Treading evil, treading Satan, treading devil underfoot.'

Puccini, he said, couldn't do better than that.

And his devil was the Tory party? 'Its values.' Alec Douglas Home typified the Toryism they had beaten, Thatcherism the Toryism it remained for them to beat.

After some years teaching in the WEA, Mr Kinnock was in 1970 adopted for the very safe seat of Bedwelty. He appeared before the selection committee wearing his wedding suit, as his wife had insisted he should, and won the nomination by a majority of one. The man who, when he was a boy of only eight, had been taken to hear Nye Bevan speak, was himself in Parliament.

After Labour came to office, in 1964, he twice declined offers of undersecretaryships, partly because he disagreed with the line on Welsh devolution, but in 1979, in Opposition again, accepted the job of Shadow Secretary of State for Education. It was an offer he couldn't refuse, because it gave him a chance to influence party policy.

Before we got on to these policies I wanted to get one small thing out of the way. He is now forty-one, so he was ten at the time of the Coronation in 1953. They had street teas in Aberdare and it was a lovely day with sweets, pop, and jelly, and he watched the Coronation on television.

He says it was the pop that made him sick but agrees that even at the age he had a feeling against monarchy, not that he was embittered, but he didn't have a lot of time for such show.

It was consistent, then, that he declined an invitation to the Prince of Wales's wedding in 1981, but what I wanted to know was this: why, having declined, saying he had a previous engagement, had he, when asked what that engagement was, said he hadn't yet made up his mind? What was the point?

Now Mr Kinnock is very quick. You don't have to be with him five minutes to see that.

'*Two* things required my attention,' he said, 'and I hadn't made up my mind.'

Was that reply, I asked, an example of great tact, or of really rapid thinking? He laughed his baritone laugh, very good natured.

Mr Kinnock is also good on candour and repartee. Candour as when I asked if he didn't wish to use education as a means of social engineering and he came back, quick, 'It always is, by everyone.' Repartee as when I had suggested there might be natural differences in ability and proposed as an illustration that not every member of his class at Lewis grammar school had become Shadow Secretary of State; and he said, 'You could say the same of my contemporaries at Harrow.' You could say of Mr Kinnock, if he were a tennis player, that he takes his shots very early. It would make good television, but it is hazardous.

He wants to introduce peace studies into schools: what did that mean? Citizenship, he said – the tools of democracy, how to make a short speech, how to chair a meeting, how to understand what advertisers were really after, how to achieve a basic scientific literacy.

When I asked what this had to do with peace, he replied that there had been no objection to war studies, 'otherwise known as history.'

I objected that to many people history meant Europe in the nineteenth century and after 1815 there hadn't been many wars. At which he deplored the European focus of history, mentioned world citizenship, objected to the acceptance of war as a means of resolving human conflicts, and quoted Talleyrand.

And for my part, feeling that this was so much easy rot, I changed the subject to that of Labour's proposed abolition of fee-paying schools.

'*Fee-charging* schools,' he said. 'The process by which we will pursue the abolition is the eventual forbidding of fee charging for education. Right?'

But it had been suggested, hadn't it, that such an abolition would contravene the European Declaration of Human Rights? He said this stated that parents had the right to have their children educated according to their religious, moral and ethical persuasions. There was no way of proving that a desire to purchase education was in pursuit of such aims. He would enjoy his day in the European Court and he would win. And, he said, if you took the desire to purchase education to its logical conclusion, Labour did not propose to abolish private education anywhere else in the world. So, if it was exclusivity one wanted to purchase, one could.

Except, I suggested, that Labour would introduce exchange controls? He objected that this would apply only to large capital transfers.

Ah I wondered about the French Socialist government's recent rationing of foreign currency to £192 per man per year. Mr Kinnock thought this was a 'definition of the obligation of the citizen to society', a much more direct and honest obligation than, let him say, one to involuntary mass employment.

I tossed in a mention of freedom, he replied that freedom which depended on an ability to pay was no freedom but only privilege, to which I replied that there were privileges all over the place, and that MPs had a lot of them. He said he did not indulge his.

All this was most cordial. And Mr Kinnock agreed when I suggested that he was, of course, always ready to argue his case.

Well, in 1980 he had agreed to give a talk at Bradfield College but then withdrawn when he learned it was a public school? 'Yes.'

Why? It was very simple, he had no intention of going there as part of the entertainment.

But he was a good entertainer and he could have made his point, so why go back on his word? He said that he had at first believed he was going to speak at a current affairs forum or something; but his priority was the maintained school system.

So he would decline to talk at Eton? He said he already had. If the pupils of Eton wanted to hear him they could come to his meetings. Why, he asked, should he go to Eton rather than to Blogg Street Comprehensive?

This seemed perilously near what Mr Kinnock, in other circumstances, might condemn as discrimination. I said if he wouldn't go, Sir Keith Joseph might.

'Every man,' he said, 'to his own country.'

I said the first Cabinet minister I ever met had been R. A. Butler when he came to talk at my school, which was not a public school. If Mr Butler could do that, why couldn't Mr Kinnock go to Bradfield? 'The two things aren't the same. For those who are well indulged, let us say, with visits from the august, there is no reason to add my name to their visitors' list.'

Mr Kinnock also wants free and open access to all universities, without the previous inconvenience of A levels. I inquired if this might not dilute the excellence of those universities which had maintained any excellence.

'In order,' he said, 'to determine that which is excellent, it is necessary to have a breadth of access, real access, not Becher's Brook access . . . If you don't do that, all you get is a self-perpetuating group.'

Didn't he think the same thing might happen as in the United States, where anyone who got through high school could go to college, one result of which was great numbers of illiterate young people with master's degrees? He did not think so. The quality of British degrees was recognized all over the world.

For a change, we turned to the clean hack-and-thrust of Parliamentary infighting. I had once heard him say something off the record which I did not know whether he would like to say on the record. Put it on, he said; so I asked if he had described the Parliamentary Labour Party as a not very sophisticated housing estate.

'Yes,' he said. 'Because the PLP does follow whims.'

As simple as that? 'I would say it was as astonishing as that. But I still remember my astonishment at discovering the factors that can convince some, not all, far from all but *some* of my colleagues in Parliament about their intention of casting their votes.'

He was saying that some Labour members were more easily swayed than people in housing estates? 'Yes, yes.' When he had canvassed for Michael Foot in the Shadow Cabinet elections of 1970 the innocence of some reactions amazed him. 'The way in which you had to combat assumptions, moods in the PLP, in the same way as canvassing at 6.30 when people are getting the kids ready for bed . . .'

I said he had recently been talked of as a future deputy leader of the Party, with Mr Healey as leader: did this amaze him, when he had held no office at all? He thought it was surprising and might be something to do with the moodiness of politics. When people felt under pressure they looked round for alternatives and his name came up.

As a balance to Mr Healey – younger and further to the left? 'That's right. The first law of politics is the law of equilibrium.'

So he was a counterweight? 'I suppose so, yes. It was a fantasy. It wasn't going to happen.'

Was this something on which he couldn't be open with me, since he had after all canvassed for Mr Foot in the leadership election, and could not now say he would prefer someone else? 'No, it isn't just that. I mean, the person who would lose respect first if I was only supporting Michael Foot for reasons of sentiment, would be Michael Foot.'

What about loyalty? 'But loyalty might require the loyal person to go to the person to whom he is loyal and say, "Time to go". That might be the strongest evidence of real friendship.

But that certainly isn't the case as far as Michael is concerned. But loyalty, the loyalty that only says yes, is absolutely bloody worthless.'

Quick-wittedness, loyalty, and candour: these three. And the greatest of these . . .

16 April, 1983   **Terry Coleman**

Who would true valour see

'It's such a heavy agenda,' murmured a woman member, 'that I doubt whether that poor Mr Pattinson will ever find time for a bath.' It was an archetypal Anglican consideration. Church servants may not be expected to eat, sleep or even pray conspicuously during a session of the General Synod of the Church of England, but the Protestant virtue of cleanliness is still next to godliness.

The 550 members of the Synod moved into the University of York with light hearts. 'They like it up here, they can let their hair down,' said an official. It is in York, rather than the circular chamber of Church House, Westminster, where senior clergy rekindle passions for space invaders and where, during a previous session, a bishop was seen looped between the shoulders of brothers in Christ being escorted to bed overwhelmed by gin and tonic. And the York Synod is on the increase. For four summers out of every five, the university authorities will drape the pool tables and push the table football machines under the stairs before the visitors arrive.

The university is pebble dash rather than red brick; interlocking boxes of buildings relieved by clumps of trees and willow-bordered water courses. For a minimum outlay Synod members can buy a booklet explaining the mysteries of the coot, mallard, and common pochard who roost there, to the great delight of the Bishop of Bath and Wells, the Church's leading authority on waterfowl. Bridges link the various colleges across public roads. 'Chap died on this bridge one session,' said a cultivated young clergyman, 'only interesting thing that happened all week.'

On arrival each member receives a colour-coded badge denoting his particular accommodation, and an appeal from that poor Mr Derek Pattinson – the Synod's secretary-general, in fact – not to eat meals elsewhere. On previous occasions rumours of superior food had the ecclesiastical trenchermen moving to other than their allotted dining room, thus creating an imbalance of surplus and famine.

Social imbalance is revealed in the information that more than sixty per cent of the House of Laity had been university educated, half of them at Oxford or Cambridge. Dr George Moyser's recent analysis showed Synod to be less representative of church and society than it was ten years ago. Less than ten per cent are under forty; ninety-six per cent of members are labelled upper middle class by occupation.

But if class struggle was not high on the agenda at York, the heat was chastening. Reception committees at college entrances included a Synod employee in black jacket and pin-striped trousers, but once the session began, the temperatures dissolved dog collars, melted away jackets, and rolled up sleeves. Bare feet and sandals were not limited to the monastic representatives and shorts were in evidence. Most college doors, however, carried the notice: 'Please close this door to conserve the heat.'

The agenda was detailed, and a conscientious member would be awake early for mattins at 7.15 a.m. and still be tidying together his final order papers at 10 p.m. Once installed in his college he was under discipline. 'In particular it is expected that noise in residential blocks will stop at midnight,' said the notice on the back of wardrobe doors. 'Pets may not be kept in college without the explicit permission of the Provost.'

Synod is sometimes called the Church's Parliament, a gross slander, and one likely to be contested in the courts by a less self-confident body. In procedure, application, and debating style, the Houses of Bishops, Clergy, and Laity are a testament of refinement compared to the Westminster bear garden. Inflamed to a paroxysm of rage, usually after a verbal stiletto is tweaked into a reverend representative, members will murmur 'Shame, shame' quietly, about one session in four. One woman shouted pro-hanging protests as a bishop outlined the Church's case against it; but then, she was a member of the public, and a Roman Catholic.

What Synod does share with Parliament is an enthusiasm for paper. The assiduous Mr George Price, an expert in work study, weighed it. It came to five and a half pounds per member: a total of around 1¼ tons. There are the pink agenda and yellow notice papers; green reports from the Church Commissioners and a red report from the Central Board of Finance. Each day a group of radical clergy – the nearest the Church of England might assemble to a Militant Tendency – produces a fringe newssheet in a different colour, with cartoons.

There is also question time when Church leaders receive queries about their affairs. The valiant Rev. Eddie Stride, a vicar in the East End of London, tried to prise out of the Church Commissioners the size of their drinks bill. He failed. Another questioner wondered whether a statement in a Church publication that 'something of us goes on' after death was perhaps not doing full justice to the theology of redemption. 'I don't think it does full justice to the Greek,' said Bill Westwood, Area Bishop of Edmonton.

There's not a great deal of Greek in those confetti coloured papers, but there's a certain amount of gobbledygook. Take a matter of episcopal appointments for instance: 'leave out all words in (a) after "words" and insert "suche archebishop or metropolitane within this realme or in any the Kinges domynyons as shall please the Kynges Highness hys heires or successors" there shall be substituted the words "the senior bishop of the province in accordance with the Appointment of Bishops Measure 1983."'

Such is the small print of the Mother Church of world Anglicanism. The Archbishop of Canterbury tells a story, usually to non-Anglican audiences, of a Presbyterian who used to look at the gaitered doings of the Established Church and inquire: 'What has this to do with Jesus Christ?' Meanwhile, there is the knotty problem of historic resources, for which radical action might see changes by 1986, and that statement on relations with Rome to be drafted by 1988. And after that, there is always eternity.

16 July 1983   **Martyn Halsall**

What we deserve

I do not know what is the clinically acceptable period of convalescence from post-electoral melancholy, but I fear that in my case it will be some time. This alone excuses I hope a brief, and possibly final, retrospect after five days of adjusting to the inevitable, which is the acceptance of the fact that, as I see it, justice has not been done.

In these circumstances professionally one has to declare interest, though in my case it is only fair to say that I have never concealed it. I had wished for a fair deal for Michael Foot, at least from the trade we used to share and in which I operate today, and which explicitly he did not get.

The fact that one had for weeks foreseen the Labour catastrophe is of little help; Michael Foot is not blameless, and neither are we. But to see a very considerable career extinguished in ignominy says little for Labour, and less for loyalty.

I am not a member of the Labour Party, nor indeed any other. I could just possibly have been attracted by the Social Democratic Party, because I like the name and like them am tempted by compromise, but the Social Opportunist Party would have been more honest initials, and to share a bed with Roy Jenkins would be a hard price to pay.

I am on the side of Mr Foot for the following quite irrelevant reasons: because we were both journalists, because long ago we were founding fathers of CND, remaining loyal (which was perhaps Michael Foot's undoing, and may yet be mine), because throughout his doomed campaign he remained expressly faithful to his basic beliefs – give or take a few anguished equivocations after Denis Healey's sabotage operation – and because as far as I know he has never let a comrade down.

But when the debacle approached everyone simultaneously turned on him, with subtly different emphases. Michael Foot changed overnight from being the Marxist Menace, the Dangerous Disarmer, and became, with hypocritical compassion, the pitiful Lear of Labour, the ailing dotard of democracy, the senile socialist, the unhappy has-been, to be patted sympathetically on the back and sent back to the shadows.

This is a cruel and preposterous role for a sincere and vigorous man in his prime who in his time did more for the honest political Labour image than any of his generation, and if he fell at the last fence it was not because he was weary, though he clearly was, but because he was elbowed out by his fellow-runners, even though that ensured their own coming downfall. At least Neil Kinnock can in future look Michael Foot in the face.

That cannot be said for the Contemptible Comic, an obscure vaudevillian called Kenny Everett, who achieved surprising applause for an act that included spasms of gutter wit including: 'Let's bomb Russia!' and 'Kick Michael Foot's stick away!' I know nothing of this alleged comedian except that I hope he is disciplined by his union and ostracized by his trade. Or possibly employed as a columnist by the *Daily Mail*.

Mea culpa, too. I have exceeded my brief and my rights. You may have missed in the above the strict and stern objectivity in which this newspaper takes a proper pride, and which you will agree I follow scrupulously when not terminally depressed by what all around I see.

Which if I am watching the television, as who is not, is an endless succession of clips of Mrs Thatcher playing her Queen Aunty bit among her loyal clique and administering her semi-Papal blessing: 'Thank you so much . . . how kind . . . we are all right now.'

I begin to doubt that.

Some malign power ordained that we got our new television set last week. In protest at what it was obliged to show it at once went wrong. So it was not just eternal politics, but out of focus too. Often it is hard to know what to blame – there are politicians, like Mr Pym and Mr Jenkins, who would seem to spend their public existence just slightly out of focus, speaking earnest words of which one can detect the tune but not the meaning.

Our new TV is not very good but it has a mind of its own. It has the whim of suddenly changing channels of its own accord. Once that would have mattered; it mattered no longer. Everything was the same.

It was Mrs Thatcher being sweetly reasonable with daggered

eyes – 'but, Mr Day, what you do not appreciate is . . .' putting poor Sir Robin in a spot: should he start calling her Lady Thatcher? That is what I would have done, but I am nastier than Robin.

Or Michael Foot, reading the verities of life into words of one syllable – good and excellent and worthy words, but mostly the same ones: 'but' and 'yet'.

One jests for fear of weeping. There comes a moment when one must be serious. This *could* be the last General Election our generation will see. The combined battlewagon of Reagan and Thatcher could within that five-year period result in a climax neither will survive, not to speak of us. That is the stark simplicity that Michael Foot recognized and most of his colleagues shirked. I see it as the simple difference between professional politicians and racists – by which I mean those in favour of preserving the endangered race we call the human one. I wish us all a better half-decade than we deserve.

14 June 1983   **James Cameron**

The Party of the past?

The race for the Labour Party's leadership is in progress with scarcely a breath drawn since last Thursday's ignominious defeat. There are three-and-a-half months until the convening of the electoral college, time enough you might think to concentrate the party's mind on its predicament. The result is not a foregone conclusion, although Mr Neil Kinnock has been quickly installed as odds-on favourite. The speed at which some of the union leaders have plumped for a candidate suggests, however, that they are not much interested in yet another debate about the future of the Labour Party. If that is the case, it is to be wondered whether they have quite grasped the gravamen of the predicament they face, in spite of the somewhat desperate attempts of Mr Roy Hattersley and Mr Peter Shore to point it out.

Perhaps they would prefer to heed what Mr Michael Foot said to Mr Anthony Sampson a couple of years ago in an interview for his *The Changing Anatomy of Britain*. His warning today has added poignancy.

'If the Labour Party were to lose the next parliamentary election, it would be the most fateful loss since the party was founded in 1900. More peremptorily than ever before, if in a new form, R. H. Tawney's fundamental question is presented to us: who is to be master? If democratic socialists cannot secure the right answer at the next parliamentary opportunity, we may not be asked again, or rather this old famous socialist stream could perish in sectarian bogs and sands.'

The choice of futures presented by the candidates is essentially a simple one. Mr Hattersley and Mr Shore believe that the Labour Party must be brought back to the people, Mr Kinnock believes that the people can be brought back to the Labour Party. I seemed to remember that I had heard this argument before and reached to my shelves for dusty books. In 1959 Labour lost its fourth successive General Election and a bitter inquest took place. Hugh Gaitskell wanted to abolish Clause 4, Mr Douglas Jay suggested the Labour Party should change its name, and Anthony Crosland urged a 'direct confrontation' with the party conference in order to show that the party was 'dominated neither by the block votes of the trade unions nor by an unrepresentative minority of left-wing activists.'

The Bevanites took a different view. They attributed Labour's defeat to a failure of propaganda, not of policy. Aneurin Bevan himself said, 'The problem is one of education, not surrender.' Mrs Barbara Castle urged the party not to revise its socialism but to 'go out and make socialists'. She also said that in the 1959 campaign 'our ethical reach was beyond the mental grasp of the average person.'

These arguments, which raged for a couple of years, did so against a background of documentation which cast grave doubt upon Labour's long-term future unless it could revise its policies and modernize its appeal. The seminal text of that time, published as a Penguin Special, was *Must Labour Lose?*, which contained the results of an elaborate survey conducted by Mark Abrams, the leading opinion researcher of his day. The survey discovered that Labour suffered from what came to be called a 'cloth cap image' at a time when the old working class was busy acquiring television sets and cars and setting its sights on owner occupation.

Abrams also identified other changes in social attitude and opinion which have developed over the years since then and become increasingly relevant to Labour's appeal. These included the unpopularity of nationalization, the growing unpopularity of trade unions and the belief that they were 'too powerful', and the dislike of the Labour Party's internal power battles.

Moreover, in a prophetic passage Abrams wrote, 'It would be hard to overestimate the importance of housing as real personal political issue for the man in the street and its power to affect party support; apparently, in the recent past it has affected it in a direction favourable to the Conservative Party.' At that time thirty-eight per cent of his sample owned their own homes; today the proportion is estimated at sixty per cent.

The argument within the Labour Party about the meaning of these trends, and about the future of socialism, was never wholly resolved. Crosland, whose writings on the subject were the most elegant and incisive, urged that it should 'adapt itself, without in any way surrendering basic principles, to the realities of social change, and . . . present itself to the electorate in mid-twentieth century guise'.

'Guise' was perhaps the word for it when Mr (as he then was) Harold Wilson succeeded to the leadership upon the death of Gaitskell and proceeded to dress the Labour Party up in a technologist's white coat. The left-right issue was fudged and Sir Harold became fudge personified. Nevertheless, the party's posture at the 1964 General Election was essentially 'revisionist' and Croslandite; it proposed to de-negotiate the agreement with the Americans by which Britain had acquired a 'so-called independent nuclear deterrent' in the form of the Polaris but was otherwise staunchly pro-Nato and multilateralist; and the right was once more firmly in control of the National Executive Committee and the annual conference.

Crosland had also warned, however, that 'a party of the past' could always win a single election, as the result of a sudden crisis or because the governing party had been in power for too long; but he doubted both the wisdom and the dignity of relying upon this – 'especially since, if the underlying trends continue, they may well be reflected not in a Labour victory but in a stultifying swing towards the Liberals'.

In 1964, after thirteen years of Tory rule, the electorate decided that it was time for a change and returned a Labour government to power, although only just. In 1966, having proved himself in office, Wilson turned that into a decisive victory. In February 1974, in a sudden crisis, Labour was returned once more to form a minority government which in October it turned into the barest majority.

However, the underlying trends to which Crosland referred did continue and with them Labour's secular decline. Before we jump to conclusions about who might be the best Harold Wilson for 1988 some measure is needed of the Labour Party's predicament today compared with the future it faced in 1959.

In 1959 it polled 43.9 per cent of the popular vote; last week it polled 27.6 per cent. Over three general elections from 1951 to 1959 Labour's share of the vote dropped by 5 per cent; over three general elections since October 1974 it has fallen by more than 11.5 per cent. The swing required to win power in 1964 was a little less than 3 per cent; in 1988 it will be a Herculean 12 per cent.

In the 1959 General Election 62 per cent of the working class voted for the Labour Party. On Thursday only 38 per cent did. In 1959, 43 per cent of Gallup's respondents thought the trade unions 'too powerful'. Last year the proportion was 63 per cent. According to Gallup's post-election survey for the BBC, trade unionists voted 39 per cent Labour, 32 per cent Conservative, 28 per cent SDP-Liberal Alliance.

Professor Ivor Crewe, in his fascinating analysis of the Gallup survey and the election statistics in Monday's and Tuesday's *Guardian*, concludes: 'The old working class is now too small to give Labour electoral victory; the new working class too big to be ignored.' This 'new working class' is Mark Abrams's affluent working class come home to electoral roost – the home-owning, car-owning, working class, nearly half of it now living in the South, two-thirds of it employed in the private sector.

Mr Kinnock has an evangelist's fervour and a great deal of charm but he'll need every bit of it and more if he intends to take

28

Mrs Castle's 1959 advice and 'go out and make socialists' in the Britain of the 1980s. Mr Hattersley wears the mantle of Tony Crosland and knows what needs to be done if the Labour Party is to present itself to the electorate in late 20th-century guise; but the power structures and policy encumbrances of today make that infinitely more difficult than it was even for the Gaitskellites after 1959, and their success was only partial and temporary.

Nevertheless, the answer to the question, Must Labour Lose? remains the same. Labour need not lose, not if it becomes once more a modern and progressive party of the people.

15 June 1983   **Peter Jenkins**

Where the slump is good for business

Doors open at 9.30 a.m. in the pledge department, discreetly tucked away round the side of the shop. A queue has formed before opening time, since old hands at pawning know that only a limited number of loans are made a day. The shop front is a large modern jewellers, and a passer-by might not notice the three gold balls high up on the wall at one side.

Not all businesses suffer in times of depression. Some flourish and prosper; pawnbroking is on the increase. This particular shop was one of many branches of a firm in a poorer part of London. Several larger firms are opening new branches, and the National Pawnbrokers' Assocation reports expansion all round.

It isn't quite the business it used to be. Almost all firms now deal only in jewellery. You can't borrow money on Sunday suits, furniture, bedding, irons or fishing rods any more. And the jewellery has to be gold. But the brutal economics of the trade stay just the same – charging the highest interest rates to the poorest people.

I spoke to twenty or so customers that morning. Most were women, about half were young with small children, and half said they had taken to pawning their jewellery only in the last couple of years. Some said their mother used to pawn things, but many said their families would have died of the shame.

'I can tell you. I looked both ways carefully before I came here,' said one women in her thirties, with a baby in a pram. 'I looked in the window for a while, to make sure there was no one I knew around.' She laughed. 'It's silly, isn't it? There's no harm in borrowing a bit, but you just don't like people to know that you're broke, I suppose.'

She handed in a gold medallion on a chain. She was hoping for £40 as she got £35 on it a year ago, but was offered only £30. 'Can't be choosers, can we?' She gave her overdue gas bill as a means of identification – the very gas bill that was to be paid with the money.

A thin old lady in a shabby jacket, tattered leopard skin patterned slippers and long grey hair came into the office and approached the plate glass window at the counter. She was holding a grubby white plastic bag which she lifted up to hand over. The man behind the counter shook his head. 'Only jewellery,' he said, quite kindly, seeing the size of the object proferred.

'It's binoculars, my husband's' she said. 'We don't do that any more,' he answered. She looked crestfallen. 'You gave me a fiver for them a few years back,' she said, her voice cracking.

He explained that must have been over five years ago, when they still did brokerage. He suggested she tried selling them at a second-hand shop down the street. 'I don't think my husband would want that. I don't know,' she said. 'He's disabled now. Can't go out. Doesn't use them. It cost me 40p on the bus to get down here.'

She turned away from the counter. 'Don't know what to do,' she said. 'It's bills, and things I need. I always counted on these binoculars for pawning.' She took off her wedding ring. 'It's tin. The gold one went, oh, ages ago. Usually I manage, but things are so expensive now.' She just stood there for a while, not knowing what to do next, but finally left.

The manager explained that pawnbrokers had had to give up that trade since there was so little demand for second-hand goods. 'People don't buy second-hand suits like they used to. Electrical goods are so cheap they buy them new. Binoculars like those, well, you'd buy new Japanese as cheap wouldn't you? People can afford new now.'

A woman came in with her ten-year-old daughter. She handed over her engagement ring, for £10. 'She needs new shoes for school,' she explained. The girl was wearing battered trainers. After her came a young woman with a baby. 'My husband pawned my gold bracelet six months ago. He didn't tell me. I didn't find out till I went to the box to put it on and it was gone.' She didn't have the money to redeem it, but she renewed the ticket for another six months, clocking up another lot of interest charges, and paying the 'ticket money' over again. 'I didn't speak to him for a month. He won't do that again in a hurry. I've never pawned anything in my life.'

A young man came in with a bad hangover. He'd been at a party, stayed the night, and found his van had been towed away by the police. He needed the money to get his van out. 'I'll be back on Friday to get my ring out,' he said, folding the money for his signet ring and stuffing it into his back pocket.

One woman offered bags of 1p coins she had been saving to redeem a ring. She handed the coins over as a part payment, and hoped to redeem the ring next month. 'I lost a diamond solitaire here once,' she said sadly. 'I pawned it for £30, and it cost £200 new. But it was sold.'

The law demands that items must be kept in the shop for six months and one day. This shop usually keeps the jewellery for at least nine months. They reckon they make more money when people redeem their jewellery. They can then return to pawn it over and over again.

Pawnbrokers are not allowed to sell the unredeemed jewellery in the shop. First, the client must be informed by post that the item is to be sold, and then it has to be sent to public auction. The interest charges and auctioneer's fees are deducted from the money raised, and the rest of the money is supposedly returned to the client.

But the catch here is the clients probably don't know that they are entitled to that money. Once they have failed to redeem the article they probably assume that is the end of the matter. The manager refused to give any figures for the number of people who return after the auction to find out if any money is still owing to them. Clients would only know about it if they had bothered to read the exceedingly small print on the back of their original ticket. The letter they receive says nothing about it. If the client doesn't claim it, the pawnbroker keeps it.

At about 11 a.m. up went the sign on the door, 'Sorry! No More Loans Today!' The shop had lent £615 to twenty-seven people, and latecomers would have to search elsewhere for a pawnbroker who had not yet loaned his quota for the day. 'We could probably loan out twice that amount,' said the manager. 'The only thing that restricts us is cash flow. You can't borrow from banks to lend out again, otherwise our business would increase enormously.' They don't ever lend more than £50, though some of the items pawned may be worth well over £200.

Pawning is expensive. Even before interest is charged, a valuation fee is charged on every ticket – ticket money – and repeated if the ticket is renewed after six months. Ticket money varies, between 5p for £1 loaned, to £1.35 for £50. On top of that comes the interest charges, displayed by law at the counter – 39.47 per cent per annum.

What bank would dare offer such terms to its clients? But these people are not the kind of clients who interest the banks. They are too poor. Only one person I spoke to that day had a bank account. She was a widow who had run into financial trouble since her husband died four years ago. 'Loans, overdrafts, pawn tickets, you name it. I've got it,' she said. But the others looked amazed at the suggestion that they might ever enter the doors of a bank. No, said one after another, they had never considered a bank.

10 September, 1982   **Polly Toynbee**

Flexible friend of Jesus

A new ingredient has been thrown into the gentle games of one-upmanship played in Oxford senior commons rooms. Jesus is getting itself a flexible friend. The 401-year-old college, proud of its pioneering work on education and discreet new building, is computerizing its students from January. Their traditional system of living on tick while local authorities slowly process their grant cheques is changing from paper docket to plastic credit card.

Ox-cess? Jesuscard? The system has yet to be formally named. The college is still uncertain, too, whether to invite an appropriate old boy, Sir Harold Wilson, to bless the first peeps and whirrs of this latest bit of white-hot technology.

For the students and dons, the change will mean an end to the books of dockets used to buy meals and drinks against end-of-term payment of accounts. Instead, each of the 460-odd members of the college will be issued with an individual card with a magnetic stripe to be read by terminals in the bar and dining room. Occasional statements and warnings that the credit limit is approaching should prevent embarrassing scenes for absent-minded dons. A fail-safe sytem will operate long before the terminal has a chance to flash up 'limit exceeded', and confiscate the professor of theology's gin.

The NCR 9010 system was specially designed for Jesus, whose bursar, Dr Clark Brundin, took the view that nothing on the market met all the college's requirements. Apart from the credit system, which avoids the danger of large sums of money floating temptingly about, the computer will handle the college's records, stock control, and general accounts.

Other colleges will be invited to examine the system to see if it has any advantages on the Roman numerals which some of them are still thought to prefer. NCR, meanwhile, is hoping to sell the package under the name of 'Scolar' to take the waiting out of wanting at other universities, polytechnics, and schools.

26 October, 1982   **Martin Wainwright**

Nasty Right turn on the Left Bank

Forty Parisian students lay in hospital yesterday after the latest wave of street battles with the hardened French riot police. But on the fourth floor of the Law Faculty, in the Rue d'Assas, the centre of the right-wing student movement where the riots were planned, there was an air of victory and celebration.

It was a remarkable sight, a room that looked as if the Young Conservatives had joined forces with the Hell's Angels. The girls had a Sloane Ranger look, and half the men wore neat English tweeds and ties, while the rest were in macho leather, with crash helmets slung casually from their belts. This is the heartland of reactionary chic, or student revolt 1983 style. Their talk was of whether lemon juice or vaseline was a better protection against tear gas, and of the cleverness of someone called Jo-Jo in buying all those fire crackers in the Chinese quarter to hurl at the police.

On the window, a sign that reads GUD, which stands for Groupe Union Defense, and a large cross with a circle scrawled around its centre. The GUD describes it as a Celtic Cross, to symbolize the proud roots of the Gallic nation. More recently, it has been the symbol of the OAS, the secret army who tried to keep Algeria French, and of the Aryan sunwheel, symbol of the Nordic Neo-Fascist groups across Europe.

Downstairs, in the huge meeting hall of Assas, the most professionally printed of the posters strewn around are from the Young National Front, whose hatred of immigration and socialism makes them indistinguishable from Britain's own NF. Alongside them are posters for Action Française, the mystic Fascist group founded by Charles Maurras long before Adolf Hitler had been heard of.

These are the groupuscules of the right, tiny groups with less than three per cent of the votes in the last student elections. By contrast the Communist UNEF-SE got twenty-one per cent, and the Socialist-Trotskyist UNEF-ID got nineteen-and-a-half per cent. But the right-wing tactics of confrontation and riot have seized the initiative among the students in the street battles of the last ten days.

This is partly the fault of the left, whose student leaders have been torn between loyalty to the Socialist government and hostility to that government's planned reforms for university entrance and organization.

Ironically, the extreme right has recently been losing ground in the universities; and in faculty elections last week, they lost their places on the Paris-wide student co-ordinating committee to more moderate and non-political delegates.

It was these new delegates who tried to call off Thursday's march through Paris before it crossed the River Seine. But when the stewards who flanked the march announced a premature dispersion, the right-wing commandos (as they call themselves) turned upon the police with petrol bombs in a clearly planned manoeuvre.

34

Their tactic worked, partly because of an almost instinctive hatred of the riot police and partly because of the emotions of the moment, large numbers of hitherto peaceful marchers joined in the running battles with the police. Throughout the evening, violence flared in the Latin quarter, with cars overturned and flimsy barricades erected, and hit-and-run raids on police patrols.

In Paris, there is a great sense of tradition about such affairs, and certain streets on the Left Bank where barricades go up almost as matter of honour, in whatever cause. In 1968 it was the left, in the 1930s and this week, it was the right.

A night at the barricades is not necessarily a serious matter, when only students are involved. The events of May 1968 would have been just another demo, but for the decision of the trade unions to join in and call a general strike and thus challenge the very legitimacy of De Gaulle's government.

The great question over this week's events is whether the right can proceed from the nuisance of street battles to the kind of general mobilization that might seriously threaten the Government.

Perhaps the most significant event of this week was not the petrol bombs of the students, but the rather more staid struggle between police defending the Government's Price Control office and some 15,000 small businessmen. But the Government is meeting this challenge head on. Its immediate response was to order police throughout France to help enforce the Price Control Regulations, hitherto left to a handful of inspectors. With taxes, wages, and rates all rising the Price Controls have enraged the traditionally conservative small businessmen and shopkeepers who made up this week's demonstrators.

The two main parties of the Opposition are torn between taking advantage of these challenges to the Socialist Government and insisting that as the parties of law and order such street battles are beneath them. And without the full-blooded support of the Opposition parties, it seems unlikely that the events of May 1983 can begin to parallel the complete crisis that gripped France fifteen years ago. But the echoes of 1968 have seized the imagination of the politicians, the media and the students themselves and this is being deliberately exploited by the extreme right.

There is a great deal of vainglory about the right-wing students, a nasty blend of street fighting, macho and upper class snobbery. One of their leaders, Didier Roche, who is one of the leaders of the extreme right PFN (New Force Party) has announced: 'I have forty determined men behind me and that is enough to control 600 and more.'

Didier Roche leads the law students of Lyon University; but at Assas in Paris, the snobbery is more pronounced, as you might expect from its location by the Luxembourg Gardens. Imagine the law faculty of Oxford University being transplanted to the middle of Chelsea, and surrounded with elite schools like Eton and Winchester. Such is the happy position of the Paris university law school in the Rue d'Assas. It is fashionable and attracts wealthy students.

The wealth was plain to see in this week's demo, with groups of marchers being shepherded by new cars with expensive loudspeakers on the roofs, several of the stewards with walkie talkie radios, and others riding up and down on powerful motorbikes. It was a very high-tech demo.

And as far as the students were concerned, it was an intellectually respectable affair. The ideology has seeped into France very much more thoroughly than Britain.

The group of New *Philosophes* around Alain de Benoit who preach an elegant doctrine of Nation, Authority, Catholicism and the mystic destiny of European civilization exert the kind of influence that Sartre and the Marxist existentialists could claim thirty years ago. This group has its media outlet in the *Figaro* newspaper and magazine, and deploys political weight through the Club de l'Horloge, which is run by Giscard's former Minister of the Interior, Prince Poniatowski. And in the law faculties of Assas and Lyon this movement has found its militant student wing.

These various factions of France's new right will all meet up again on Sunday morning, to celebrate the Feast Day of their patron Saint, Joan of Arc. Since Sunday is also the anniversary of the defeat of Hitler's Germany in 1945, the Gaullists will be marching along with the National Front, the GUD, the Sloane Rangers and the leather boys of Assas.

As the Communist newspaper commented yesterday: 'These

are precisely the people who collaborated with Hitler under the Vichy regime. And now they celebrate his defeat while opposing those Communists and Socialists who fought Hitler. The right always tries to steal history even when it cannot change it.'

7 May, 1983   **Martin Walker**

Hunger in New York

On a Sunday morning, Zabar's is packed tight. At the fish counter, customers line up for smoked salmon, sturgeon and caviar. The meat counter is piled with sausages, chickens, exotic pies and sticky barbecues. In one corner, fresh biscuits come out of ovens, wave after wave, bubbling with chocolate, nuts and honey. Warm croissants are stacked on high shelves. Shining copper pots are strung across the ceiling.

Zabar's is both a bazaar and a feast; it is a celebration of smells and taste in a city of plenty. Outside crowds jostle on the sidewalk. Some are waiting to go in, other simply stand, heavy Zabar's bags by their side, wondering how they will get home with all these costly goodies. To be here, on Broadway, on a Sunday morning, is to be part of New York ritual.

Around the corner, by the side of Zabar's, another part of New York ritual is being enacted. Against the railing running between Zabar's and the church, a queue has been forming. It starts earlier these days than it used to. Some turn up at eight, most by eleven. Some tell jokes and call out to familiar faces. Others simply stand, eyes to the ground, lost in thought or merely trying to lose all thought.

Some are shabby, some smell rancid, but these days many more are well dressed and clean. Hunger unites them. By the time the church's soup kitchen opens at one, the lines will reach around the corner mingling with dreadful irony with those celebrants from Zabar's. Perhaps there are twenty soup kitchens scattered across the five boroughs of New York. No one dare even guess how many hungry people there are.

It is somehow assumed by those whose extra-strength, 30-gallon capacity, non-split Glad trashbags stand nightly outside the door, bulging with waste, that there is no such thing as hunger in New York. There are food stamps they say, as though food stamps were the needy's equivalent of all those ten cent off clip-out coupons in the Sunday papers and as easy to come by.

When there is talk of cutbacks and 'changes in eligibility', they do not know what it is to be without money and faced with the mega-bureaucracy of New York welfare departments. Weeks, even months, may go by between the moment that a woman first stands in an office and says, 'My children are hungry, we have no food,' and the news that her papers are being processed.

Because of cutbacks 138,000 people found they were no longer eligible for food stamps last year. About a million people still receive them – these magical, Federal handouts that are worth exactly forty cents per person, per meal.

There is an assumption, too, that hunger is equated with homelessness. Only the truly destitute suffer. The publicity given to the welfare system in this time of Reaganomics is almost all of rip-off and fraud. Its image is of a great plump cushion as if only those who wilfully turn away from it can escape its succour. When they talk of layoffs and redundancies and small businesses failing, they do not also think that it may be the person next door who has not eaten for three days.

How, in a way, could it be otherwise? This is a country of plenty and of surplus. Twenty per cent of all food produced for human consumption is lost annually in the United States, food that was perfectly edible yet somehow unsaleable or unavailable. Packing sheds alone spill over with fruit that is 'cosmetically unacceptable'. The debris discarded by supermarkets and restaurants could feed these lines winding past the soup kitchens and many, many thousands more who cannot even afford the bus fare to seek them out.

Soup kitchens and soup pantries of Manhattan do not advertise. They cannot afford to. They would be deluged by the response. On September 14, one new kitchen quietly opened on York Avenue on the east side, and served twenty-nine dinners that day. A month later it was serving 220 and turning people away. Soup pantries, handing out non-perishable goods for families to take home, regularly run out of food. Referral agencies, such as The Food and Hunger Hotline, have got

38

used to calling around to see whose cupboard is not yet bare.

The Food and Hunger Hotline is a private organization that was sponsored four years ago by the pop singer Harry Chapin. Few knew of it, let alone of Chapin's connection with it, until in the last few weeks hunger has become Hunger – a new York issue. The Hotline now needs to be better known; over the last year there has been a fifty per cent increase in calls from people without food. There is an urgency for more funding and without public glamour, there is no private need to give.

The Hotline operates out of two seedy offices in a rundown street at the far end of Manhattan. Its phones ring constantly. On one is a woman calling from a street: 'I have four children, no money – I have to get some food for them.' On another a man calls from a hospital. He is being released, his welfare cheques have not arrived, where can he go to eat?

There is no way to capture the desperation or the controlled fear in these voices that come through hour after hour. For each call received, maybe four or five must be made – to find food, to unravel welfare snarl-ups. Many of the callers are not on welfare; they have simply run out of money. Polite, educated voices asking where they can find a meal. The director, Donna Lawrence, a young Cornell University graduate, patiently fields query after query.

'There will be a phase, and it's probably starting now, when people will care,' she says at one point. 'And then a year from now, people will think it's all been taken care of and they'll go on to something else.'

6 November, 1982   **Linda Blandford**

A bigger bang for the buck

The vagaries of acquaintanceship in a shrunken world have thrown me in with a very rich man in Texas, who constructed a fortune out of a year's salary, and now controls a powerful company which internationally famous oil concerns have to keep an eye on.

There is no wild-cat 'Dallas' flash about him. He dresses conservatively, reads a lot, jogs assiduously, and pays substantial cheques to charity as well as to political candidates across the nation most devoted to his own iron belief in the divine right of capital. And he has his own view of the predicament of the great crippled cities I'd been visiting in the North and North-east.

'But Bishop, couldn't you give up nuclear weapons – just for Lent?"

17 February, 1983

'We can talk for two or three hours about what happened to those cities, but we're going to get down to one bottom-line statement. You know what that is? The politicians sold out, that's what happened. They bought votes, is what they did. What you had in the North-east is politicians who took tax-payers' money and, in different ways, passed it out to people. And what that did was weaken a lot of people in the East who would have been willing to work.'

That's the voice of Texas oil, or a sizeable pool of it, their first and final word on the plight of the cities, the predominantly black poor who increasingly inhabit them, and on welfare, politics and politicians generally.

40

My friend's view of American history seems to be that it took a wrong turn in preferring Jefferson's 'one man, one vote' to Alexander Hamilton's position. Hamilton believed, he says, 'that if you weren't a landowner you couldn't vote; and land-owners that owned more land should be given more votes.' Oh no, he agreed, it couldn't conceivably be reversed. 'But look what's going to happen now. The workers are going to line up on one side of the line, and the non-workers on the other side. You're getting very close to fifty-fifty now, of people that are getting some sort of cheque from the government – a huge number, eighty-five million, something like that. But I don't get a cheque from the government, and a lot of other guys don't. And at some point you're going to find, whether it's Democrat or Republican, it's going to line up as to who works and wants to work, and who doesn't want to work.'

As to the poor in the city ghettoes, 'These people are damn well tired of what you've given them – they're frustrated because they can't compete, and consequently they want what you have. And so they're coming out after it.'

The house we drove back to was a substantial but not overwhelmingly grand pile in a sort of Spanish-Texan baronial style. It was empty – the family was at one of their other establishments on the coast – but as we drove through the gates, banks of lights switched themselves on in the house and the courtyard. The phone was already ringing as we entered. My host answered briefly, then politely explained the call.

'See, our house here has cameras in it – that's why they called. They saw you in the car with me and they wanted to know if everything was all right. I have a particular word I use, it's very easy for me to use it, if you'd had a gun on me, you wouldn't have realized what I was doing – and I could have told them I was in some sort of danger.'

'They' were his security men, down town at the plant. 'They're watching on the screen there. Our manager of security is an ex-secret serviceman that used to work in Washington.'

Impressed, I tell him about the rather apocalyptic mood I'd picked up here and there on my travels: an un-American fear of the future. 'Well,' he said, putting logs on the dying fire, 'I don't know that I've heard that. But I have talked to secret servicemen

41

I've interviewed for our security over several years, and all of them independently said, "Oh yes, you're going to have some sort of uprising in this country. And there are going to be some people killed." '

It wouldn't be anything organized, he thought – there wasn't the money or the leadership for that – but a spreading series of riots and incidents. 'And I think you're already in it. I think that's why you have the crime rate going up the way it is – seventeen per cent in Houston. So I think there's a high degree of probability,' said this conspicuously astute and effective American businessman, amiably pouring more bourbon.

'For instance,' he went on, 'it wouldn't really shock me for us to be sitting here right now and see three guys come through that gate and start coming for the house. I wouldn't say that it would be a great shock to me. And at the same time – I'd hate to do it – but I could shoot all three of them. Could you do that, Bill? See, I could get to a gun in probably thirty seconds.'

He half rose from his chair, then sat down again.

'Start timing me, and see how quick I could get to a loaded gun. Just tell me when to go. I mean, let's say we've seen them come up to the gate and it's obvious they're up to no good and they have guns in their hands and all, and . . .'

And suddenly he was hopping energetically round my chair and into the den next door. In twelve seconds he was back with an extraordinary cannon of a pistol, half-smiling, this rather austere man, and flushed in a way that in other circumstances one might have called disarming. 'And it's loaded (spinning the chamber, shucking out some of the fat shells). A 367 magnum: that thing, it'd shoot the engine off a car!'

Or shoot a man's head off, I thought – and there came into my mind almost simultaneously the phrase: 'A bigger bang for the buck.'

Up in the vast plateau of the Texas Panhandle, far away from nearly everywhere except Amarillo and a little town called Goodnight, I drove next day down long dirt roads under immense gun-metal skies. I had come to look at the place where, day in day out for a quarter of a century – rocket and bomb and shell – they have been fitting together the tens of thousands of editions of the Big Bang that are felt necessary to preserve the American way of life. These include now, of course, the warheads for the cruise missiles intended for Greenham Common in infinitely remote Berkshire, and the Pershings ordered for Holland and Germany.

Final Assembly it's called, otherwise the Pantex plant, a sprawling range of barbed wire, sheds, pylons, watchtowers and the domes they call igloos, stretching across 10,000 acres of prairie. To this place, across half the highways and turnpikes of America, and finally by Amarillo on to Interstate and Defence Highway 40, roll, day and night, the unmarked armoured vans and trucks – with uranium 238 from Oak Ridge, California, neutron bombs from South Carolina, switch gear from Kansas City, plutonium triggers from Rocky Flats, Colorado, neutron generating devices from Florida.

Pantex is the end of the line of the Western half of the arms race, and it feels like the end of the world. For it is impossible, contemplating the unthinkable dark power contained in the banal structures of this anti-cathedral of our culture, not to respond emotionally and think symbolically.

A small and rapidly growing army of fat jack-rabbits, big as hares, has emerged from nowhere to conduct arcane manoeuvres in the grass between the inner and outer perimeter fences. As I end my contemplation and drive away from the gate, a car with blue-capped security men pulls out and follows me: zooms up to read my number plate, slows; and turns back.

Amarillo is about seventeen miles west of Pantex, and the history of the region round about is extraordinary enough. America has been there for not much more than a century, since the Indians started killing the men who were killing their buffalo, and the cavalry were sent in to kill the Indians, and eventually Colonel Goodnight rode in to establish the first of the Panhandle's mighty ranches. (Panhandle, because it's an arbitrary great stick of territory below Kansas and Oklahoma fitted on to the great 'pan' that opens out to Mexico and the Gulf; Pantex from Panhandle, Texas.)

Beef is still big in Amarillo: Free 72oz Steak, say the hoardings for the Big Texan Steak Ranch along Interstate 40 – and below in smaller letters: 'If you can finish it in under an hour.'

43

The Santa Fe railway sidings that split the untidy sprawl of the town socially still handle an awful lot of it, and the Texas Tech has 6,000 acres cheek by jowl with the Pantex plant, devoted to the experimental breeding of it. (Buried *below* those acres, I hear, is what's left of the bombs dropped accidentally off the Spanish coast at Palomares, and contaminated debris from the accident at the base in Greenland. With a curious kind of justice, nuclear weapons' mishaps come home to roost in Amarillo. Any more for 72oz steaks?)

Then, barely fifty years ago, there was oil, which turned some of the little German farming communities of the Panhandle into gold-rush boom-towns. By 1929 things had got so out of hand that the feds were called in to restore law 'n' order; one local history says that they flushed 2,300 prostitutes out of the formerly modest township of Borger, now a dormitory for the 2,600 men who do the job at Pantex, and their families.

There was a vast air base at Amarillo until 1968 (second longest runway in America), and during the war an equally big conventional explosives factory on the site now occupied by Pantex (which was run for the government first by the good people who make your soap, Proctor and Gamble, now by Mason and Hangar, who built the Lincoln Tunnel).

Despite the area's habituation to something like a wartime economy, there still seems something extraordinary about the great silence of the sixties and seventies. I found it hard, in this community where so many of the names are German still, not to think of the dialect prayer that people are supposed to have said in lower Bavaria in the Nazi Thirties:

> *Lieber Gott*
> *Mach' mich stumm*
> *Dass ich night*
> *Nach Dachau kumm.*

The Archbishop of Seattle, Raymond Hunthausen, in the days when the nuclear issue was just beginning to haunt the once famously conservative Roman Catholic Church in America, referred to the Trident submarine base being built in his archdiocese as 'the Auschwitz of Puget Sound'. Whether or not one is moved to see Pantex as anything like the concentration camp it resembles in physical outline, the people who live in its shadow were, and often still are, remarkably *stumm* about what is after all one of the biggest employers in the district.

That silence was broken briefly in 1977 when three workers were killed in part of the plant where conventional explosives are still manufactured for use in firing devices. But what ruptured it more enduringly was a series of moral or ethical detonations.

First, there was the statement made by the new Catholic Bishop of Amarillo, Bishop Leroy Matthiesen, following hearings about locating the MX missile in the western Panhandle, and the Reagan Administration's announcement that it was going ahead with the manufacture of the neutron bomb.

At the time it was the most direct challenge that had been uttered by a prince of the Church to the principalities and powers of his own nation, and concluded: 'We urge individuals involved in the production and stockpiling of nuclear bombs to consider what they are doing, to resign from such activities, and to seek employment in peaceful pursuits' – an injunction which, from the economic point of view at least, it has become less and less easy to follow.

In fact, some Catholics at the plant had already begun to worry. How can I reconcile working in this place with what I have been learning about the Just War theory? asked Robert Gutiernez, a layman studying for the diaconate. There was more uproar when $10,000 was donated by a Catholic lay missionary society to counsel workers who left Pantex for such reasons. And when Eloy Ramos, after fifteen years of servicing the nuclear freight-liners, took off his protective shoes and overalls, handed in his radiation film badge, and walked out in conscientious objection last summer. Amarillo was clearly established in the minds of the peace movement the world over, if still rather hazily located on their maps.

Only about ten per cent of the 150,000-odd population are Catholics in Amarillo, which has otherwise at least thirty-seven varieties of religious denomination including some fairly exotic fundamentalist sects. The Unity Church, for example, announced in the churches page of the Amarillo *Globe Times* the other day that 'the Rev David Drew, a Silva Mind Control lecturer and a graduate of Holistic Massage Training, will be offering "Superlove", the ultimate personal training program', beginning with 'tools and techniques for using Superlove to increase your prosperity'.

On the whole, as well as the other twelve Catholic bishops of Texas, it's the more conventional churches whose leaders have tended to support Bishop Matthiesen, among them the minister of the oldest congregation of blacks in the town, the Rev V. P. Perry, a number of whose flock work at Pantex, and who understand as well as anyone the social and economic pressures that keep them at a job that pays more than most in hard times, and gives blacks something approaching middle-class living standards. (One can see the alternative plainly enough in the dreary lots and crumbling houses around his church, and in the faces in the Chicken Shack Beer Lounge across the street, where an old man gives me the union handshake, thumbs up.)

It must pain President Reagan, busy preaching for the defence budget and against abortion to the Protestant 'moral majority', to learn that here, too, in Texas as elsewhere, a growing branch of the Catholic anti-abortion lobby find 'a strong relationship between the abortion mentality and the nuclear mentality', as a visiting lecturer put it recently. But the ol' Southern Baptists, whose great redbrick temples fairly blush with prosperity in Amarillo, are still solid – solidly anti-Matthiesen and solidly for the Bomb.

Indeed the South-West Baptist Church went so far as to hold a Pantex Appreciation Day to which 180 people turned up to be told by the Rev Alan Ford: 'This day is to say to the Pantex employees that you do not have to feel guilty working at Pantex' – a sentiment endorsed by Beau Boulter, City Commissioner ('Amarillo people should take pride in their Pantex plant'). But even old Beau and the Rev Ford may have felt that the Energy Secretary, James Edwards, overdid things a bit when, sent down by an anxious Washington to campaign for a local Republican, he told the voters: 'Amarillo should realize that Pantex is a labour of love.'

Bishop Matthiesen, it should be noted, is no trendy young in-comer schooled in Latin American liberation theology, but a plain-dealing rangy sixty-one-year-old Texan, son of a cotton farmer, who could ride and rope a steer with the best, and has spent all his ordained life in this diocese, as headmaster (and athletic coach) at the Alamo Catholic High School, editor of the diocesan newspaper, and even, for a time, as priest at the tiny parish church of St Francis of Assisi, right up against the Pantex fence.

It is an important part of his testimony that he was as slow to open his eyes as anyone else to what was being done in his name beyond that fence. For a long time, he says, 'I thought there was research and development for the *peaceful* uses of atomic energy,' and when I press him about it – for a quarter of a century? – he supposes that he too was subject to the 'psychic numbing' which he finds so widespread.

The strangest example he gives of its effects concerns his own family. His brother, he says, was in the army in Nevada at the time when above-ground nuclear tests were still going on. On one occasion, some time after a test had taken place, his brother was ordered with others to march towards ground zero to demonstrate that there was no harmful radiation left. Subsequently, 'two of my brother's children were born deformed and died at birth.' It was only last year that he brought the connection to consciousness and spoke about it publicly.

'The town is, I would say, about seventy-five per cent supportive of the plant,' says the bishop. 'They believe that it is necessary for the defence of our country, our free way of life, our Western civilization, I mean, name it: it's motherhood, apple pie – that's what they're doing out there at Pantex.

'What I think they're really saying is: we're scared of losing our two-car garages, our wall-to-wall carpeting, our cottage by the lake, our motor-boats and our campers, all that sort of stuff. But you talk to an American Indian: he says, no thanks, I don't want *this* way of life defended. Or you talk to the unemployed, or the blacks in the cities. Talk to the farmers – the farmers around here, who are having hard times, are beginning to say: Hey, there *is* a connection between the arms race and the fact that I'm going to lose my farm.'

Meanwhile, Bishop Matthiesen has been invited to speak at a debate on the arms race and Pantex at Amarillo College – 'that's new.' The Department of Energy is wondering whether, since it was so quiet here all those years, it might dump more high-level nuclear waste in the salt domes in Deaf Smith county, some miles south-west of Amarillo. And I hear, not from the bishop, that they're just about to get their first peace camp out there among the igloos and the jack-rabbits at Final Assembly.

5 April, 1983   **W. L. Webb**

How the President scares the Commies

Mr Reagan, perhaps keen to shrug off the image of the retired B-movie star, has turned instead to song and dance. Clad in a black and silver sombrero and draped in a scarlet serape he entertained more than 600 Washington journalists, politicians and businessmen to a private rendering of 'Manana' at an off-the-record six-hour Grid-iron Club dinner. A taste of his crooning:

> *My staff is always worried*
> *I might pop off and Misspeak*
> *and then I'll have to take it back*
> *And act so mild and meek*
> *But I can tell you this much*
> *I'll always know my facts*
> *Tho' I wish I'd kept my mouth shut on that corp'rate income tax.*

You want more? Very well:

> *Now I fight the mighty*
> *Battle of evil versus good*
> *Just like in my old movies*
> *Way back in Hollywood*
> *My words are fire and brimstone*
> *Yes, I often quote the Lord*
> *'Cause how'd I scare the Commies just quoting Jerry Ford?*

Funnily enough, his crooning was witnessed by the Soviet Ambassador, Anatoly Dobrynin. History does not relate whether seeing the US President perform in such a manner scared him or whether it scared him witless.

5 April, 1983   **Alan Rusbridger**

When the winds are perturbed

Ah yes, cancer, said Dr Trogawa Rinpoche. He was speaking in Tibetan through a Canadian interpreter, but this was his drift. Buddha had prophesied that such a disease would afflict mankind, and by the eighth century eighteen types of cancer and their cures had been identified. The success rate of Tibetan doctors with 'incurable' diseases was really quite encouraging.

The matter-of-factness of his reply illustrates the gap of understanding between Tibetan and Western medicine, which he has been attempting to rectify on a month's visit to London under the auspices of the Rigpa foundation of Buddhist meditation centres in Europe and America.

Dr Trogawa was born in Tibet in 1931 and is recognized among those who know these things as the incarnation of a famous Lama and physician. He completed a rigorous apprenticeship under a leading doctor in Lhasa, and before leaving Tibet in 1954 had practised medicine throughout the Himalayan region. He teaches occasionally at the Tibetan School of Medicine and Astrology, the repository of Buddhist medical knowledge at Dharamsala in India.

Interspersed with his London seminars, he gives interviews to students of Tibetan medicine. The People page arrived during one such session. 'How do you keep wind under control while fasting?' the student asked earnestly. 'There is no way,' he replied, 'only with massage.'

This was not a flatulent exchange. After 2500 years' experience, explained Dr Trogawa, Tibetan medicine had virtually rejected surgery in favour of herbology and meditation. All disease arose from desire, aggression and downright stupidity. Desire accelerated the bodily energies (or wind), aggression activated bile, and stupidity caused phlegm. 'The disfunction of these basic humours causes 101 diseases,' he said. 'Disease is only a characteristic. When the winds are perturbed they seek the path of least resistance.'

His doctor's bag contained numerous herbal sachets, needles beaten from unmelted gold ('We don't put them in very deep') and a long curved instrument for cauterization. The head of

49

this, which is heated and placed on the skin, must be made from the blade that has killed a man.

16 July 1983   **Stuart Wavell**

Dense pack and wide opportunities

On the other hand Mr Reagan could have said:

Mr Andropov has made some conciliatory remarks and some realistic ones. I have sent him a realistic and conciliatory letter. He says the Soviets have no intention of disarming unilaterally, because they are not naive, and he does not expect us to do so either. We are agreed on that. But there is no need for either of us to overarm, and that is what we accused the Soviets of doing under Brezhnev. Now we don't propose to follow that example, and what I have to tell you today is that we have shelved for the time being the MX missile system.

Fellow-Americans, this decision has two reasons. One is that we can't decide where to put the missiles. My predecessor wanted to build a larger version of the New York subway in Nevada. It would have 4600 stations but only 200 missiles, and the Soviets would never know which station to bomb. But this administration has a very deep concern for the environment. In any case we thought the scheme was crazy and it would have meant deep cuts in welfare programmes which, as you know, I am pledged to increase.

I therefore asked Secretary Weinberger, whose commitment to disarmament is beyond praise, to think of something else. He and his team at Defence invented a much better system which I will call 'dense pack'. By siting all the missiles close together we should ensure that if the Soviets launched a first strike their first missile would disable all the rest as they were homing in. We call this concept 'fratricide', but it is no different from some of the films I used to watch being made on set. Fifteen Keystone Kops in squad cars would all be chasing one getaway car. The squad cars all collided and the getaway car got away.

But while I was shaving the other morning, Nancy asked me: why do we need these missiles at all? Now you may have heard some politicians talk about a 'window of opportunity'. Their theory is that unless we can show the Soviets that our weapons system is invulnerable to their attack they will be tempted into a first strike. I may be getting old or I may have been too long in the job but this does not seem to me plausible any more. Even if they destroyed every one of our 1054 land-based ICBMs, and

they would need to be very good shots to take them all out at once, we would still have 656 missiles on board our submarines to hit them back. We've got 338 long-range bombers too. And, fellow-Americans, we are building eight more Ohio submarines, each with twenty-four Trident C–4 missiles. So I think you will agree with me tonight, as you relax in your log cabins and drive-in take-aways, that the country is very strongly protected.

And that goes for our European allies too. I hope they will not be dismayed by our decision not to go ahead with MX. The missiles that already defend us defend them also. Before I came on the air a few moments ago I had a telephone call from Mrs Margaret Thatcher, who shares all Secretary Weinberger's commitments. She asked me to tell the Soviets at the next meeting of our teams in Geneva, that as far as she is concerned the British will abandon their own independent nuclear deterrent if that will make the disarmament talks easier. She says she and her entire Cabinet recognize that the British deterrent must be added to ours for negotiating purposes.

I have invited Secretary-General Andropov to Washington or alternatively offered to meet him in Moscow. I think he has the same feeling as I have: that neither of us can disarm completely but that both of us have simply got far too many weapons for the good of mankind. Americans have been used to leading the way, not following. I believe that if we are realistic about the power of even one of these nuclear weapons we have in their thousands we shall realize that none of them can ever be used. For that reason I have decided against building any more. Thank you and goodnight.

But he didn't.
24 November 1982

Greenham Diary

You will be glad to hear that the MoD is much concerned for the wellbeing of at least part of the indigenous population of Greenham Common. A recent visit by the MoD's Conservation Group led to the spotting of White Admiral, Peacock, Speckled Wood, Comma and Tortoiseshell butterflies, and that was in just one patch of brambles. 'It is important,' says the group in its annual report, 'because of the great deal of development on site, that surveys are initiated soonest; this will enable conservation requirements to be considered in the planned development.'

8 March 1983   **Alan Rusbridger**

5 February, 1983

The fears of Bruno Kreisky

Bruno Kreisky has been Chancellor of Austria since 1970, and is thus the longest-surviving leader of a Western European country – because Austria, though neutral, and far to the east, can only properly be described as Western European. Partly because of his long tenure, his friend Willy Brandt calls him Kaiser Kreisky. As a young man, in the Anschluss of 1938, he saw his country disappear. In 1955, he was one of the delegation which negotiated the State Treaty by which Russia conceded to an occupied and astonished Austria its independence.

He is a Jew who has received Yasser Arafat of the PLO and who now says that Israel has, by its actions in Lebanon, destroyed the moral basis of its existence. He holds the same high office as Metternich once did, and though that prince was Chancellor of a very different Austria, there is a link.

It is this. The aged Metternich, having returned from the exile enforced on him by the revolutions of 1848, advised the new young emperor, Franz Joseph. That young emperor lived to reign even longer than Queen Victoria, and when he died in 1916, after sixty-eight years on the throne, the boy Kreisky saw his funeral in Vienna.

'I remember the funeral. I was five-and-a-half. I have a very clear – no, unclear – memory of a long, dark, and black procession.'

What had he seen? 'Horses. Black uniforms.'

What had he understood? 'I understood from the people round me, and because my father was in the army, that there were feelings of something more than the death of an emperor. A lot more.'

Two years later the First World War was over, the Austro-Hungarian empire had collapsed, the line of Hapsburgs stretching back 640 years was at an end, and the tiny Austrian republic, stripped of its power and territories, was established. It was a revolution, and yet the boy Kreisky knew it was no revolution. He saw that the same policemen who had previously watched the parks, and watched them playing football, still watched, and he told his friends, 'This is no revolution.' This he remembers clearly.

The Chancellor and I met at his villa on Majorca, where he was on holiday, and as he spoke of the end of the Hapsburgs he was looking out over the Mediterranean. I asked what he had meant when he said that his whole life had in a way been a bridge between the Hapsburgs and the years after. He said the collapse had been very real to his family. Some lived in Vienna, others in Moravia, which was after 1918 no longer in Austria. His uncles' textile factories were on a border which had not existed before. His mother was distressed when she went as usual to take her summer holiday on what had been the Austrian Riviera, which had become Italian.

'So,' he said, 'in all my life the empire has been present.' He had constantly asked himself whether the empire and the monarchy could not have been saved. If it had been, millions today would not be living under communism. Could the empire, he asked himself, have been changed into a kind of Swiss confederation, into a commonwealth of nations?

Even after the First World War? 'Not after. Not after. The first war had to be prevented. The monarchy did not prevent the war, because of the alliance with Germany.'

But we were talking about changing the history of Europe and therefore of the world? 'Maybe. If Austria had not been in the German alliance, things would have been totally different.' The whole experience of his life told him that nothing was inevitable. There was always a choice. The empire could have been preserved by reforms carried out in time; in 1934, their own, home-made Dollfuss dictatorship could have been avoided by a political coalition; the coming of Hitler in 1938 could have been avoided.

'We are responsible for our history. It was not others who destroyed Austria. We destroyed her. Our ancestors destroyed Austria.'

At the age of fourteen Kreisky took part in his first demonstration, against the Vienna school system after a pupil committed suicide. He says that, to be fair, many were not so much interested in school reform as in having a demonstration. By the

54

age of nineteen he was a militant socialist, and remained so throughout the thirties, when it was dangerous, in Europe, to be a socialist. He organized meetings of a banned youth movement in the Vienna Woods, and in 1935 was arrested and charged with no less than high treason. As he was to tell me later, as we were parting, he has always been grateful to the *Manchester Guardian* for reporting his trial so fully.* He was sentenced to one year.

The next arrest, after the Anschluss, was by the Gestapo, who released him on condition he left Europe. They said they did not want him around as a potential knife in the back. Could he, they inquired, go to South America? 'Bolivia?' he suggested. It was the first name that came into his head. He now says he might as well have named Mexico. In fact he went to Sweden, a country which profoundly affected him. Why?

Because, he says, for the first time in his life he saw a working democracy. In Austria there were only bloody demonstrations and near civil war. In Sweden in 1940 he met Brandt, who has remained his friend ever since. There was some longing for his native country, but on the whole he cannot say exile was a period of suffering for him. He returned to Austria after the war, but soon returned to Sweden as a diplomat, and in all spent ten years there.

When he returned to Austria for good it was as political adviser to the President and later as State Secretary to the Chancellor. In this capacity he went as one of the Austrian

---

* From the *Manchester Guardian*, March 17, 1936:

A young university student, Kreisky, gave his evidence courageously, and he was repeatedly rebuked by the judge. Kreisky was once a delegate of the Austrian Socialist Youth movement and went to represent this movement at the Brunn conference.

He denied having worked for an illegal organization. He had certainly met other Socialists, but this was not to be wondered at since the party had formerly 700,000 members in Vienna alone.

He discovered that a great demand existed for illegal Socialist literature among the masses, simply because the Austrian papers wrote nothing about the real state of affairs in Austria. He argued that the Socialists were not for forcible revolt: they wanted a peaceful change of regime. This however, depended on those who ruled the country.

delegation to Moscow to negotiate the State Treaty in 1955.

Now, Austria had been occupied by the four Powers since the end of the war. Three hundred meetings of the allied foreign ministers had failed to reach any agreement, and Austrian independence must have looked a remote prospect. So what did he expect from this summons to Moscow?

The Western Powers, said Kreisky, were pessimistic. The Austrian delegates were pessimistic. People said, 'They will put you up against a wall, and they will ask you to take Communists into the government, and, if not, the iron curtain will come down in the middle of Austria.'

Partition? Yes, said the Chancellor. But at Moscow airport they were met by the entire diplomatic corps, fifty people. The Austrian national anthem was played. Molotov, Malenkov, Mikoyan, Bulganin were all there.

And then? 'When we arrived at the Austrian embassy in Moscow there was great nervousness. I tell you this because I don't know how long I shall remember. Old men forget. There was great nervousness because they had invited the whole Politburo. They always did this; but they never came, only one minor official. But that evening they all accepted.'

All the Politburo? 'Bulganin, Molotov, Malenkov . . . only Khrushchev was not there because he was in Leningrad. There were not enough tables. So there we were and they made fantastic toasts, after every schnapps, every brandy. To friendship, and friendship, and friendship; we didn't understand. Finally the last speaker, about midnight, was the Prime Minister, Bulganin. And he started by saying, and I will never forget this, that they had come to the conclusion that there was no chance of a peace treaty with Germany for a long time, so they had decided to work out a State Treaty for Austria. 'We don't like to keep you waiting,' he said. 'This was for me – it still is – the biggest event of my life.'

Then, Kreisky, who felt a strong fellow sympathy with Mikoyan, asked him, 'What about Germany?'

'I will tell you something,' replied Mikoyan. 'I will tell you one thing. Austria's neutrality can be founded on a piece of paper. You will always respect it. But this cannot be done for a country of eighty millions. If the Germans accepted neutrality, one day they could change their minds. There would again be a tendency to have one hundred million Germans in an empire, and could we then go to war just because Germany gave up neutrality?'

The Russians, said Kreisky, understood that there would never be a strong communist party in a greater Germany, so they decided to keep a part of Germany and make it into a communist country, and to keep it as a cornerstone of the Soviet empire.

I supposed the Russians were very happy to have Germany in three bits – West, East, and Austria. 'They told me *four* pieces – Western Germany; what they call central Germany, which is the DDR; the Germany that belongs now to Poland; and Austria. I once told one of them, "But Austria doesn't belong to Germany," and he said, "For you, not; but for the Germans, always." '

Kreisky has been Austrian Chancellor since 1970. He will run again in the elections of next spring. I asked him if he would agree with Mr Heath that the leaders of the Western world nowadays lacked experience, and he said he would have to agree. Experience was almost all. There was always genius of course, but how to find it? President Ford had once told him Kissinger was a genius, and he certainly wrote big books. But experience was most important. Why, asked Kreisky, had *he* been among the first to see the real nature of the Middle East problem?

Then he answered his own question. 'I will give you the reason. Because I found out that the Palestinians are not only living in Israel; they are living all over the Arab world. They are nearly half the population in Kuwait. They have a decisive position in many other countries, in the Emirates for example. They have as decisive a position (in the Arab world) as the Jews did in Europe.'

Another diaspora? 'There *is* a Palestinian diaspora, which is more important, and more influential, than the Palestinians inside Israel. If we recognize the importance of the Arab world, we have to know who is important there – the Palestinians.'

That was why he had met Arafat? 'Yes. I am an old man. I am a Jew. I am anti-Zionist. I don't believe in this nationalism. I can do the job. If Ted Heath were to do the job, people would say he was at heart anti-semitic because he was a Christian, or something. A man like Mitterrand would be accused of being anti-semitic. The Jews are always finding anti-semites.

'But nobody can accuse me. I lost my closest relatives to Hitler. They were liquidated. I am not religious, but I have never converted. I am an agnostic. I accept Israel as a political solution, as a consequence of Hitler. But I tell you frankly, without Hitler and Mussolini and their anti-semitism, Israel today would be a little colony . . . It would never be a State. A feeling of guilt towards Jews created the State, and that is what I tell my Israeli friends.'

And was this European feeling of guilt as strong as it used to be? 'No. This is what I say to them: "You have destroyed the moral basis of the existence of Israel by your policy of war." '

What did the Chancellor think of the events of the last months in Lebanon? 'It's a castastrophe. The State of Israel has definitely, believe me definitely, lost its moral reputation. Why? How can a State built up by some of the finest men and women of Europe, and of the world, lose its moral prestige?'

Because of Menachem Begin? 'Begin, yes. How can a man like Begin be in power? I'll tell you why. The State of Israel of today is not the State of Israel of thirty years ago. It was a State founded by refugees from Russia, Poland, Germany, Italy, South Africa, Britain. Then because of the enmities between Israel and the Arab world, the Arab Jews were pressed to leave their countries. So today Israel has a majority of Moroccan Jews, Iraqi Jews, Tunisian Jews, Jews from the Arab world. That is the majority now.

'And these people never lived in a democracy. They are full of sympathy for the semi-fascist policies of Mr Begin and Mr Sharon. I am so pessimistic. You cannot change the nature of people. They will always think of war, and always elect men who are warriors.'

But surely if Israel continued to make war it would lose in the end because it was so very much outnumbered? 'Finally they will lose. No doubt about that. This is my conviction. . . . Once you are on a tightrope you have to continue, and they will continue. They made war against Lebanon. They can displace the Palestinian leadership. But somewhere the Palestinian leadership will be re-established. And then Israel will have to make war again, and again, and again.'

Then the Chancellor returned to Mr Begin. 'A semi-fascist is a man who believes in methods which are anti-democratic, in war, indeed in apartheid. The position of Palestinians in Israel is apartheid. They have nearly no rights, economically they are displaced, politically they are displaced, and they are dominated by the Israeli army. Now the Israelis are making war. They can only make war. They are not willing to sit down and negotiate with the Palestinians. This is fascist. I don't hesitate to use this expression. This is the real fascism; fascism is not only Hitler's being against the Jews; fascism is brutal force.'

At this point the Chancellor went in to answer a telephone call, and Mrs Kreisky offered drinks. When he returned I asked about this nickname of Kaiser Kreisky. He said it was the popular papers. First they had called him the Sun King: he didn't know why. Then, when he had run the country for so long, they had taken to calling him Kaiser. Brandt had borrowed the expression.

We were now chatting, and I asked if, working in the same rooms as Metternich once had, he felt in any way the spirit of the prince. He dismissed this. No more, he said, than Mrs Thatcher felt the spirit of Disraeli.

But then he went back to the time, in the middle of the nineteenth century, when the aged Metternich had been advising the new young emperor, and advising him never to make war. But the emperor had made war, and lost (forfeiting Lombardy and then Venice). Then, reflecting in his mind over many years, he said, 'And making war destroyed Austria, totally.'

He told me he was at present reading a history of Queen Victoria by a German journalist, who said she was a little bourgeoise. When he was in prison, in the 1930s, and been alone in his cell twenty-three hours a day, he read and read, studying the way in which great men had changed history – Napoleon, Disraeli, Kaiser Wilhelm. So, he said, he was probably, by accident, better educated than other politicians.

He had also, more recently, read a lot on the history of race. He had read a German philosopher whose conclusion was that to talk about an Aryan race was as silly as to talk about a blond language. Aryan referred to language, not race. He had found that the Jews were not a race. Jews did not come only from Palestine. Judaism as a religion had spread. Some Jews had come from the Caucasus, from Libya, from Ethiopia. There were big tribes of Negro Jews, tribes of 30 – 40,000 people.

'Why,' he asked, 'does the new Israel ignore this fact? Because the philosophy on which the State is built is that all Jews emigrated from Palestine. This is not true.'

So, not all descended from the tribes of Israel. 'That is not true.'

It's only fair to say that the Chancellor's views on Israel and on Jews will appear more emphatic in cold print than they did in conversation. And I report them at length because they are very apt at the moment. He spoke much more passionately on the subject of social democracy, and yet, though he spoke passionately, his views sounded very like those of the Labour Party in its previous 'rational' days. He hated the gap between rich and poor. Sons of working men should be able to become doctors. He wanted equality of opportunity. Social democracy should open the door. You had to give a man a chance. His views were such, it seemed to me, as could have been put forward by Gaitskell, or Olof Palme.

'I am *not*,' he said, 'saying that the best people are the proletariat. That is not true. But a man must have a chance.'

Thinking that the SDP in Britain these days certainly believe that the best people are the SDP, I asked the Chancellor's opinion of Mr Jenkins's party, but there he was reticent: he did not know enough about its policies, which has to be true since it is an answer that almost anyone could make with truth.

He returned to unemployment. He had already described what he had seen between the wars, and now he said: 'Unemployment in a capitalist society is the biggest human catastrophe after warfare. Everything that is insane in a society is multiplied by unemployment. Imagine people coming out of school and having no job for year after year. What will be the result? Criminality. Total moroseness. If it is only possible to create jobs by political measures, then take political measures. The economy is not an end in itself.'

He was suggesting something like Roosevelt's New Deal?

'The New Deal emanated from the same philosophy.'

We went back once more to the greatest event of his life, the Austrian State Treaty, and then on to the United States.

How much, I asked, had the 1956 rising in Hungary to do with the Austrian Treaty of 1955? 'It was a consequence. Seeing 50,000 Russian soldiers going home across Hungary, and the liberation. . . . Then it takes at least ten years for a new generation to arise which has not had the experience of defeat. Ten years after Hungary – Czechoslovakia. Ten years after Czechoslovakia – Poland. In the next ten or twelve years you will see it again.'

What about the theory, fashionable in America and on the face of it harmless, that Russia would fall apart from its own weakness? 'One of the reasons I am opposed to American policy is that if this policy – which is not one of containment, like Truman's – goes beyond containment and has consequences inside the Soviet Union, this will create restlessness, and this restlessness will create a military dictatorship of twelve marshals within the Soviet Union.

'This will mean war, definitely war. Because marshals are not going to wait until the United States is so strong that they have to do what the United States wants. Before that, they would start to destroy peace. Marshals always end their policies in war. The Argentine generals made war . . . Military dictatorships always end in war. They have to. The economy is bad, because the generals spend too much on the army. The political situation is a dictatorship, and they have to make war.

'In a time of détente there is a chance for liberalization. In a time of cold war there is a danger of hot war. We are now preparing the ground for a cold war. What does a cold war mean? Mr Weinberger (US Secretary of Defence) is talking today about a limited nuclear war. The Europeans are asking, "Where?" A limited nuclear war? Where, on the moon? It's the lack of experience of the new American administration that is so dangerous. I told you experience meant so much.'

After the war, said the Chancellor, the policies of Truman, Acheson, Marshall, and their contemporaries had succeeded in Greece, stopped the blockade of Berlin, hampered Russian interests in Yugoslavia, and concluded a peace treaty with Japan without the Russians. It was a policy of containment which had led to the Austrian State Treaty.

'But the present policy is weak. It's not based on a realistic analysis. It's based on a *feeling*. "We have to show the world the strength of the United States." I remember an American oil boss who told me over lunch in Houston, Texas, "You diplomats are all very bad. Every day, every morning, people all over the world should realize the strength of the United States." . . . Now Reagan is acting in this spirit. "Every day show them our strength." How? You may have an overkill capacity, but today you can never believe that the others will be so weak that they cannot destroy you. That is the problem.'

4 September, 1982   **Terry Coleman**

Final draft

The late Arthur Koestler was always a painstaking and fastidious writer. So it was endearingly typical that when his literary executor started going through his files he should have turned up no fewer than four drafts of his suicide note.

5 April, 1983   **Alan Rusbridger**

A diet grown unrelenting

Turn the pages of yesterday's *Daily Mirror*, lingering only for a moment over the page one splash ('Concern for Di's health', by James Whitaker), speeding past the account of Andrew's Falklands tribute on page three and the page seventeen piece about Anne's African tour, and you will come to a pertinent question. Across its centre spread, the Mirror asks: after her strange behaviour at the Albert Hall, IS IT ALL GETTING TOO MUCH FOR DIANA? Well, some say it is and some say it isn't. Yesterday's *Sun* had a front page story ('Charles's diet fears for Di') to prove that Mr Murdoch's men have been every bit as worried as their *Mirror* counterparts since the first news came from Midsomer Norton that the Princess of Wales had spurned a pork tenderloin cooked in cider and toyed indifferently with melon and mixed veg. The *Daily Star*, on the other hand, having pictured the Queen laying her Poppy Day wreath on page one, reported on page two that Diana had been 'radiant' on two occasions this weekend ('smiles ease worry over her health', it said). The *Express*, in one of five Royal Family stories in yesterday's edition, had an equally reassuring message ('Diana just smiles away those slimming fears') and also let the Princess in on a happy secret: Charles's Christmas present to her this year, it revealed, is likely to be 'something pretty from Asprey's or Collingwood, where the engagement ring came from . . . about £1,000 to spend here.' While the *Daily Mail*, in one of five Royal Family stories in yesterday's edition, reported that Diana was 'smiling again' after the Albert Hall mix-up and predicted that Charles, 'worried about his wife's apparent anorexic condition' would be wafting her away to the ski slopes before long.

The suggestion that Princess Diana is suffering from anorexia was hotly condemned by the Palace yesterday. Still, it is clearly a fashionable theme, especially since the Lena Zavaroni stories a week ago, and very much the kind of twist which any soap opera librettist would want to introduce into his story at this time. It certainly makes a change from the note of slavering adulation which has been sustained through the Royal Wedding and the Birth of the Royal Baby (whom Princess Diana does not wish to be addressed, according to one of ten Royal items in this week's *Sunday People*, as 'Wee Willie'). It comes, too, at a time when one of the best-loved themes of the past few years – Princess Anne as Royal Nasty – may have to be written out of the script following her recent tour of Africa.

The Royal soap opera differs from most other such entertainments, of course, in the fact that the characters portrayed therein are unequivocally based on real people. And the *Mirror*, at least, turns out, despite copious evidence to the contrary, still to have that consideration in mind. 'Princess Diana,' Mr Whitaker wrote kindly in yesterday's centrepiece 'is a strong lady with amazing will power and determination. It would be a disaster if we pushed her too hard, too soon.' Could that mean that the *Mirror*'s obsession with royalty will shortly be relenting? Has it accepted that, in its own words, it is 'all getting too much'? We shall see. Elsewhere, while it plays to its present

ratings and while so much of the real news remains disheartening-
ingly bleak, it seems much more, and sickeningly, likely that
this show will run and run.

16 November, 1982   **Leader**

Shreds of state

The Horseshoe crabs are of so old a family that their blood
actually is blue. A chastening reflection for Schleswig-Holstein-
Sonderburg-Glucksburg. I am quite partial to a drop of monarchy. That and old-time music hall. What a lark to be on such
intimate terms with queens as Sacheverell Sitwell who, as a
schoolboy, upset his lemonade down Queen Alexandra's ear
trumpet, or Noel Coward who wrote in his diary: 'Tomorrow I

'. . . an amusing little wine, but
not worth breaking into
Buckingham Palace for.'

24 September, 1982

64

go and dine with the Queen of Spain, who has been having trouble with her lower plate.'

The Men Who Would Be King (BBC-1), an amble round Europe's redundant royals, was a great disappointment. A toothless tour having trouble, you might say, with its lower plate. If I shut my eyes and try to remember it, I drop off. If I try again, all I seem to see is miles of moustaches.

When you meet the Queen she will say, 'You must have seen many changes,' but if you should ever meet a redundant royal be careful not to say this. It is, in the circumstances, tactless. Norman Field, who sometimes dines with ex-King Umberto, added a few more tips for the socially aware: 'You can't just breeze up and say, "What do you think about Jean Harlow's latest film?"' You must wait to be led up to him and then ask if he thinks Lindbergh will make it over the Atlantic.

Anthony Holden fawned around in a way even a self-respecting corgi would deplore. A fawn would have curled the lip at it. 'Your reign, Your Majesty, was an all too brief one,' he grovelled on, though the Italians, who were in a better position to judge, thought a month of Umberto ample.

Prince Louis Ferdinand Hohenzollern, grandson of the Kaiser, was 'a warm and welcoming host. He even answered his own doorbell.' Prince Louis has the most festive memories of the Kaiser, who one Christmas gave him a railway. The Berlin-Brussels express.

Prince Nicholas Romanoff (not to be confused with another Nicholas Romanoff, last heard of running a garage in Idaho) lives the life of Riley (heir apparent to the Irish throne of course) in Italy. When not collecting Romanoffs – thirty-three at the last count – he enjoys shooting wild boars. One day he heard a rustle in a tree 'and there was a wild boar peering at me, two feet over my head. I couldn't shoot the damn thing, it would probably have fallen on me.' In my view this was not a boar but a reporter. At a distance of two feet it is often difficult to tell.

Where, you may ask, can I get a good look at a redundant royal? Fortnum and Mason perhaps. David Williamson of Burke's, who has a disconcerting look of Ronnie Barker, was treating the jolly little ex-King of Tunisia to a knickerbocker glory there. It was in Fortnum's that Sir Thomas Beecham was hailed by an elderly lady he couldn't place. Feeling his way, he asked how her family was? Not bad, she said, though her brother was working too hard as usual. 'Still in the same job?' inquired Sir Thomas carefully. 'Yes, still king,' replied Princess Victoria cheerfully.

Royals surplus to requirements remind me of Miss Zelfredo, snake-charmer extraordinaire, who, when her snake upped and died, went on and performed her act without it. Denied their kingdoms, the redundant royals keep on reigning like true troupers.

27 January, 1983   **Nancy Banks-Smith**

The open sesame seed

The local historical society here in Des Plaines, Illinois, may have pulled off a totally unAmerican coup, stopping the juggernaut of change and progress in its tracks. If all goes well, a grotty little building on route forty-five – bang opposite the fire station and just before you get to the civic centre one-way system – will be handed down to posterity as a historic monument.

Perhaps it isn't Anne Hathaway's cottage or Dr Johnson's Gough Square home, but its cultural impact has probably been as great. In thirty different nations, 7,220 replica establishments bring a message that is meat and drink to people of all ages, creeds, colours and shapes. This was the world's first McDonald's.

A shock of disbelief transfixed Des Plaines' 50,000 citizens three months ago when the news broke that 400 Lee Street was to be razed. True, a big new alternative was going up across the road but that was hardly the point. This was where it all started, the birthplace of the 40,000 million and more all-American hamburgers that have laid waste to the palate of the world.

The curator of the Des Plaines Historical Society, Mr Paul Twardzik, says it began when the McDonald brothers from San Bernadino, California, wanted machines able to mix six milkshakes at a time in their fast-food joint. They found that the rights in the multimixer were owned by Ray Kroc, a middle-

66

aged entrepreneur who had dropped out of high school thirty-five years before and spent some years playing the piano in a Chicago bar. Having sold eight machines to the McDonalds and seen their operation, Kroc persuaded them to let him try selling franchises for similar operations throughout America.

On April 15, 1955, Kroc opened the first of these new hamburger bars at the Lee Street site. The place has, in fact, been enlarged since then, so it must have been minuscule twenty-seven years ago. Even today there is nowhere to sit down inside the building, just a chest-level ledge for customers who want to eat on the hoof. Round the edge of the car park are a few concrete Noddy-in-Toyland tables and benches.

Many of the now-familiar McDonald's characteristics are there in embryo, including a pubescent version of the big yellow arch, an integral part of the structure peeking above the flat roof. But the cash register is out of the ark – no trace of the micro-chip wonders now in vogue – and a general snax-at-jax air hangs over the place.

That, of course, is the problem. Unable to get enough vehicles into the car park or mouths into the restaurant, there is a conviction that an awful lot of business is going elsewhere. So the perfectly reasonable business decision was to buy out the Ground Round restaurant over the road, pull it down, and put up this brand new McDonald's on one of the main approach roads to the town.

The local council couldn't see anything wrong with the idea: the more business the place generates, the more it will pay in tax. The McDonald's Corporation didn't see any problem either, until it suddenly found itself under siege from the world's oddest band of conservationists. A nation that is only 207 years old has to grab its history where it can find it.

And McDonald's is unquestionably bang in the mainstream of the American tradition. Mr Kroc – who bought out the McDonald Brothers within six years for just under $3 million – is still president of the firm at the age of eighty. Its chairman and chief executive officer is Fred Turner, Mr Kroc's first employee and originally hired to mop the office floor.

In spite of the worldwide expansion, the Illinois connection endures. Not only is the first McDonald's in Des Plaines: the town also has the 1,000th in Oakton Street and the 2,000th in the market place shopping centre. The corporate headquarters is at Oak Park, a few miles down the road from the Lee Street point of origin.

Kroc and Turner may symbolize American free enterprise, but they run a pretty tight ship themselves. It isn't just any old Joe who can open a McDonald's. Would-be franchise holders are rigorously scrutinized and, once through that test, must undertake to invest $150,000 (half in cash) for a twenty-year licence. They must also enrol for a compulsory course at Hamburger University, just the other side of Chicago International Airport.

There they have a nine-day inculcation into the deeper aspects of minced beef, the preparation of milk shakes, chip frying and the production of that strange liquid which passes for coffee in every state but Louisiana (which mercifully clings to its French past). They also get a crash course in restaurant management.

The news of the threatened destruction of the original site galvanized not only the historical society but Americans from far beyond Des Plaines. Mr Jim Williams, the society's president, found himself getting letters and phone calls from far-flung citizens who do not share the national disdain for most of their own past.

Curiously, Lee Street is one of the very few sites not owned by the McDonald Corporation. It still belongs to Frank Martoccio, the local lawyer who originally put up the building and leased it to Ray Kroc. He says he is not in favour of pulling it down but he still wants to make money on it, having turned down Ray Kroc's offer of shares in the early days of the corporation.

Though no one will say it in so many words, it looks as if the preservationists have won. 'We have not yet decided exactly what we are going to do in terms of historical preservation,' said Steve Leroy at McDonald's headquarters, 'but we are looking at whether we preserve it on the spot, move it somewhere else, or restore it to its original state.' Everyone seems to have stopped talking about pulling it down.

10 March, 1983   **Harold Jackson**

68

A case of cut and run

Dr Johnson is the most lovable writer in the English language. Call a dog Johnson and I shall love him. He said something along those lines. He also said that a cucumber should be well sliced, dressed with pepper and vinegar, then thrown away. A man who said that should have a statue erected to him, preferably in the act of hurling a cucumber in the general direction of the BBC.

My God, he would have been wonderful on TV and so, up to a point, he was last night. *The Falklands Factor* by Don Shaw (or rather, as he wanted his name removed from the credits, not by Don Shaw) was based on Johnson's pamphlet, *Thoughts On The Late Transactions Respecting Falkland's Islands*. Not one of the world's snappier titles but not, like *The Falklands Factor*, a cliché either.

In 1770 the British, under a man called Hunt surprisingly enough, were bundled out of the Falklands by a Spanish force from Buenos Aires. There was a vociferous faction for war but the government settled the matter amicably and Johnson wrote a pamphlet supporting 'quiet negotiation'. Being Johnson, his broadside for peace would shiver your timbers at ten nautical miles, and Don Shaw used Johnson's big guns to pound the recent action – so manifestly not a quiet transaction – in the Falklands.

And rightly for, if a title is to mean anything at all, *The Falklands Factor* was a *Play for Today*.

Johnson's pamphlet, which has slumbered comfortably under its duvet of dust, came awake with a startling vigour and contemporary punch as if 200 years were only a refreshing nap: 'This was a colony which could never become independent, for it never could be able to maintain itself, where a garrison must be kept in a state that contemplates with envy the exiles of Siberia, of which the expense will be perpetual and the use only occasional.'

In the last minutes of the play Johnson, very finely played by Donald Pleasence, was superimposed like a prophet newly inspired on newsreel of the Falklands war. The great rolling waves of words broke over all too appropriate images of fervour and flags: 'It is wonderful with what coolness and indifference

*'These are your orders, chaps –
approach Port Stanley at 2,000
feet, swoop under radar cover and
drop £75 million on to the
runway.'*

14 September, 1982

the greater part of mankind see war commence . . . consider it little more than a splendid game, a proclamation, an army, a battle and a triumph.'

'The life of a modern soldier is ill represented by heroic fiction' – and young men on a troopship cheered. 'Men who, without virtue, labour or hazard, laugh from their desk while they are adding figure to figure, hoping for a new contract from new armament' – and lean missiles nosed out of their holes. 'As war is the extremity of evil, it is surely the duty of those whose station entrust them with the care of nations to avert it' – and Mrs Thatcher hurried from Number Ten to her car.

It seemed as if Pleasence's transparent face was filling up like a glass with images of cheers and ships, a stretcher party and a communal grave.

You did not need to be a prophet, inspired or otherwise, to see trouble coming. The preview, usually sparsely attended by a coven of critics, was crowded with reporters, trying to read *Thoughts On The Late Transactions Respecting Falkland's Islands* without licking their lips. The same day Brian Wenham, the BBC's director of programmes, ordered the newsreel footage to be filleted out of the last sequence, officially because it might cause offence or pain to the bereaved, and *The Falklands Factor* went out as a costume drama.

I did not myself much care for the use of newsreel. In his biography of Johnson, John Wain says, after some discussion of his political writing: 'These considerations will protect any twentieth-century person from trying to apply Johnson's solutions directly to problems of our time in any literal sense.' I wish I had had a small bet with Professor Wain on that one.

But if a writer, producer and director whom I respect, as I do Don Shaw, Louis Marks and Colin Bucksey, insist that a sequence is vital, I regard such scissoring of their work as an insult. They should take it as a compliment, a proof of power. Somebody is running scared. Or as Mrs Thatcher herself put it, 'Afraid, afraid, afraid, frightened, frit. Couldn't take it. Couldn't stand it.'

Johnson himself was censored. He had thrown some doubt in *Thoughts on the Falklands* on a prime minister's ability to count without using matches. It can happen to the best people. Indeed, if it is any comfort to Don Shaw, Louis Marks and Colin Bucksey, it only happens to the best people.

27 April, 1983   **Nancy Banks-Smith**

Falklands Diary

Until General Galtieri appeared and then disappeared from the scene, there was but one bobby on the Falklands Isles – PC Anton Livermore. Post-Galtieri Falklanders are now having the opportunity to experience more modern and sophisticated British police methods in the form of six coppers on secondment from the UK.

Consider the case of Mr Michael Bleaney, an employee of the Falklands Islands Company and his recent four-hour court hearing on a breach of the peace rap occasioned by driving the wrong way down a one-way street. According to Mr Bleaney, his encounter with PC Jenkins (as reported in the *Penguin News*) went as follows:

Jenkins: 'What's your —trouble, mate?
Bleaney: 'I haven't got any trouble – he has (pointing at PC Livermore).
Jenkins: 'I know you. You're a wise boy, Look at your —tie. (At this point PC Jenkins is said to have trod on Mr Bleaney's toes and said: 'Look at your — shoes'.)
Jenkins: 'Who the hell do you think you are, puffing your chest out? I spent twenty-seven years dealing with little ——like you. I didn't come 7,000 miles down here to deal with little ——like you, If you give me any more trouble on my patch you are in trouble.'

PC Jenkins, it must be said, denies this version of events.

Further evidence of the sensitive community policing approach being adopted came when my man on the spot encountered another of the new rozzers making discreet inquiries into the sexual activities of the Falklanders. 'Why are you doing that?' asked my man. 'Standard police work,' replied the faithful copper. 'Once you've found out who's laying whom you've got a pretty good idea who the troublemakers are.'

6 January, 1983   **Alan Rusbridger**

Hollow ring of steel

A bizarre version of Russian roulette is being forced by BSC on its five remaining steel-making plants. The bullets are not yet fatal, but the wounds constitute a progressive, self-inflicted maiming, as works close and men accept 'voluntary' redundancy. All the centres believe that Ian MacGregor might annihilate their emaciated productivity.

Scunthorpe cowes under this collective, consuming fear. As a measure of the demoralization of the place, a company town created by nationalization, a union official says in disgust,

72

'People are stealing milk from the doorsteps and cabbages from the allotments.' This activity, along with the muggings and the empty houses, were never part of the social landscape when steel absorbed all-comers: a workforce of 25,000 has shrunk to 8,000 in BSC.

Scunthorpe is a town of little nobodies wanting to be somebodies. (Before the town clerk starts to dictate a letter of complaint, that remark was mentioned to me, with approval, by another steel union official.) Maybe because steelworkers found the basic egalitarianism of the place boring, they had a reputation for being competitive. That ambition could be easily satisfied in the Fifties and Sixties by having the chromiest car on the night shift. The recession struck before the rivalry spread to videos. But now they're available, the redundancy money is running out.

With only one of three plants in operation, Scunthorpe has been allotted 2.7 million of the 14.4 million tonnes which BSC has said is the current national output. Even with this, Scunthorpe is working at only seventy per cent capacity, and more cuts are feared. It is a windy time and a desolate one for local union leadership – you are twice as likely to meet a former than a current trade unionist in a steel pub or club. And there is both bitterness and hostility towards the Iron and Steel Trades Confederation; though much less than towards the BSC.

Two facts that you might idly rub together in Steelville is that Scunthorpe's current output is almost the same as the amount of foreign steel imported to Britain. A couple of weeks ago, Bill Sirs and the executive of the ISTC decided to act on that connection. The port of Immingham is forty minutes from the town, and steel pickets were sent to stop a speculative cargo of unbought steel from leaving the dock.

Cynics observe that protectionism is the dying murmur of a supine union. There have been rumblings from car workers against the import of foreign-made vehicles; and from Yorkshire miners about coal imports. Steel imports have been on the confederation's agenda for several years, with little action taken. The Immingham picket says a great deal about the virtual paralysis of union protest in the teeth of the slump. Steel is, after all, the one nationalized industry to have a recent national strike

2 March, 1983

and the one most savagely cut. Its losses are high on the horror scale – currently £1 million a day.

The picket was well-intentioned, but faint-hearted. Of the handful who participated, Bob Haggerty says, 'We can't stop the steel, even with 1,000 pickets. The only way is with the agreement of the dockers.' Ted Hardacre, a divisional organizer with the ISTC, says that the picket was arranged at very short notice. He heard of the executive's decision by word of mouth.

The sudden calling-off of the port protest after a day has made some members sceptical about Bill Sirs' resolve. It was a token picket, just enough to get television coverage. But now comes the hard bit: sending members round to steel stockholders and users to persuade them to black imports.

'Naturally, we hope they're patriotic people who vote Conservative. It would be very embarrassing,' says Hardacre.

The question is whether the union will have the energy to do that; it seems to have lost the taste for a mass protest. There won't be any heroic gestures for future historians to record about the unions' role in the present slump; it will be quite unlike the Thirties and the hunger marches. It will be case-histories of individual survival rather than mass solidarity.

Scunthorpe is one of the centres in which the TUC – and the CBI – ought to be commissioning industrial psychologists to take readings on the future, because the recession is re-writing the role of the unions. The big ones will be smaller, chastened by the slump, distrusted by former members who have to find other jobs. Within the TUC, the balance of power will shift towards unions in new technology and communications; an alliance between compromised old giants may not count for much. And the unemployed could form the biggest union of all.

All this is speculative. But there is some recognition among steelmen in Scunthorpe that future battles are going to be in the political field; that marches and strikes are to be the back-up tactics, rather than the pivots on which governments swing their decisions. There are glimmerings of this among those who congregate in places like the Redbourne Social Club – old and young men questioning the value of the Confed.

Richard Hadfield is in his twenties; former charge attendant at Normanby Park steelworks, now closed. Retrained as a refrigeration mechanic. Still no job. He speculates on changed priorities. 'The union should ask for job guarantees rather than a rise, for three years.'

Ted Hardacre admits, 'We're not getting the response from our unions in the old sense. But the bigger the dole queue gets, the bigger the chance of aggression.' It is hard to accept this as valid: Scunthorpe has more than its fair share of the 3.3 million dole queue, and there has been no aggro, either against the Government, BSC, or the unions.

The will to fight among the rank and file, it seems to an outsider, is not there to tap. Hardacre knows that steel imports are on all the wharves of the Trent, from Goole to Gainsborough. The Confed is hedged in by the sour end to its national stoppage; by the lack of leadership from Len Murray ('the TUC never came up with anything during the thirteen-week strike,' says one of the Immingham pickets); and by the alacrity with which some accepted steel handshakes to quit.

If there is hostility towards the union, some is reciprocated to these former members. 'A Japanese car, knocking a slice off the mortgage, a month in Tenerife,' says Hardacre. 'They listened to all that crap and thought it was too good to lose.' One of his branch officials puts in, 'Many people were too near-sighted. They thought they'd be working again in six months. After two years, they're still out of work.'

Much of the labour force has been mobile; those who stayed in the last decade saw 3,500 jobs go with the rationalization of the new Anchor works in the town; nationally in 1979, the unions bowed to overmanning entreaties by the BSC and 30,000 jobs went. Haggerty says, 'We've got a parochial view. We've reacted to plant closures. We've concurred with everything MacGregor has ordered, and in the end it's been to no avail.' His fellow picket, Sid Sharkey adds, 'Irrespective of what Scunthorpe does, he will transfer orders.'

All blame the Government 'for being the lackey of the EEC, letting it take over our basic industries,' as one puts it, and there is a general admission that 'we've had to fall into line, in general, since the 1980 strike.' The other main initiative, apart from the Immingham picket, has been the local version of Scargill's triple alliance.

Isolation increases the impotence. Of council tenants forty per cent are in debt; 600 houses vacant. Gone are the days of part-time jobs (usually mid-week lorry and bus-driving for steelmen); the lucky ones have gone off, if they have the technical expertise, to South Africa and Saudi Arabia. The porter at the station has waved them goodbye. He should know – he used to make brickettes for the furnaces up to three years ago.

Other journeys have been less lucrative, but perhaps more radical. Richard Hadfield, who now helps in the family's fishing tackle shop, got out, too. To Bognor Regis and work in Butlin's and at an hotel. 'As a unionist I'd been used to certain rights. But there I was having to work all the hours God sent. And I'm still a unionist, even though there were no unions there.'

Maybe it is a solitary comfort to the ISTC men that Richard Hadfield still wants a union to belong to. But it is not enough to offset Ted Hardacre's anger that the only overtime being worked at the corporation is in the salaries office. There are jobs for seven more people there, he reckons.

'Overtime,' he spits, 'is absolutely bloody obscene.'

14 December, 1982   **John Cunningham**

Serving the distress

The day the bailiffs called on Mrs Webster (that of course is not her real name) there was trouble. She came to the door, a large tired-looking woman in her forties, to find Len, the senior bailiff, and two others, an ex-greengrocer and an ex-milkman, standing there with their van. They were demanding £178 the family owed in rent to Richmond Council. 'I can't pay that,' she said. 'I've no money at all.'

Len showed her the warrant. It said: 'Being in arrears with your rent, the council have issued a distress warrant against you and the above notice has been served. You must now pay the full amount shown including all costs to myself. Failure to do so will result in the removal and sale (by public auction) of the goods and chattels found in or about the premises you occupy, in accordance with the law.' This notice had been served on her six weeks before, and the bailiffs, a private firm hired by the council, could have acted on it within seven days.

Mrs Webster shook her head in disbelief. 'You can't do that. You have to take us to court first, don't you?' Len explained that the council could issue its own warrants without going to court. 'We've never owed anything in our lives,' said Mrs Webster. 'My husband has had all his overtime cut in the last few months. He earns half what he earned before. We just can't manage. The gas, electricity, telephone, we owe on all of them. They've cut the 'phone off now. . . .'

Her voice tailed away as she rubbed her hand across her face and sighed. She invited the bailiffs in – not that they needed the invitation. They were legally entitled to enter any way they wanted.

The Websters lived in a modern three-bedroomed council house in a quiet street. As the bailiffs came into the sitting room, they cast a quick professional eye around the goods and chattels. The two junior ones nodded to one another, noting the colour television, the video, and a radio cassette player. Len explained that unless she could pay, they would take away any goods to the value of the sum she owed.

'You could borrow the money?' Len suggested. 'Borrow? Who's going to lend us money?' Mrs Webster said. 'Friends, or the bank?' Len said. 'What friends with money like that? What bank would lend to us?' It didn't seem likely that a family of council tenants in debt who had never entered a bank in their lives would make attractive candidates for a bank loan. 'Then we'll have to take the goods,' Len said.

Mrs Webster began to look frantic. 'The video is my son's, and it's rented anyhow, from DER. That radio is my son's too. You can't take his things. He's got nothing to do with this.'

She began to run down everything in sight. 'This is all rubbish, rubbish. Old furniture, we got it second hand. Look, this chair's broken. My husband never mended it. The washing machine doesn't work, won't spin. The Hoover's broken too – I don't know why. Everything seems to go at once, doesn't it?' The two younger bailiffs were moving towards the video.

'You can't take it, you can't! My husband'll kill me. Wait till he comes, for God's sake. I should never have let you in, what a fool I am!' She shouted upstairs for her son. 'John, John, run down to the phone box and call your father at work, and tell him to come home at once. Tell him they're taking everything away. He'll stop them!' (John is not his real name either.)

An enormous nineteen-year-old skinhead in monkey boots, with tattoos all over his bare arms, came lumbering down the stairs. He had been lurking, listening on the landing with another large boy, his friend. He sulked and said: 'I gotta go out. I can't phone. I'm busy,' and made for the stairs. His mother begged and beseeched him, and he reluctantly agreed. While

78

she was fishing in her handbag for a 10p piece, the bailiffs began to peer upstairs. 'Don't you go near my room. Don't you touch my stuff, or I'll do you,' the great boy said, suddenly alerted to danger to his own property rather than that of his parents. His mother hustled him out of the front door, and he ran down the street, uttering oaths as he went.

He wasn't gone for long, but when he came back the three bailiffs were in his room, examining the array of equipment, including a huge stereo and a CB radio. Mrs Webster was saying: 'Don't touch it! It's my boy's, not ours!' and 'You've no right, no right at all!'

When the boy came back he bounded up the stairs, took one look at them in his room, and leaped back down again. He charged into the kitchen, where he grabbed a fierce carving knife, and ran back upstairs again. He thrust the knife at Len, six inches from his chest, turning it in his hand menacingly: 'Out, out of my room! Don't touch my stuff or I'll do you!'

The three men froze. Mrs Webster pleaded with her son. 'Don't, don't. You'll be in more trouble. . . .' She clutched at his arm, but he shook her off, and prodded the knife closer to Len's ribs. Len was small, slight, and no fighter. 'Come on lad. Don't be silly. Be a sensible lad now. Put the knife away John. . . .'

One of the bailiffs backed away into a room behind him, where a girl of about ten was cowering with John's friend. Len turned and glanced behind him. 'Look, you don't want trouble. You've got a young child here. . . .'

Mrs Webster tried again to hold John back, but was thrust aside. 'Go and phone the social services, John. Get them to come here. These men can't do this to us. Get the social services!' she said. Len kept talking. So did John's mother, and eventually the boy lowered his arm. He continued to finger the knife and to threaten but the danger was over.

Len sent one of the others for the police. Mrs Webster was keen on the idea, as she thought the police would not allow the bailiffs to take her possessions, John lurked and muttered and threatened. Three policemen in a panda car came soon afterwards, examined the bailiff's warrant, and Len's bailiff certificate. Mrs Webster sat in a corner and swallowed a handful of pills from two bottles in her handbag. She wept and wept, and kept saying: 'I wish my husband'd come! What'll he say when everything's gone? He'll say I should have stopped you!' She seemed as frightened of him as she was of everyone else in the house.

Under the eye of the police, the bailiffs took the stereo, the video, the television, and the radio. They explained she could redeem them in the next two days, but then they would go up for auction. 'What will DER say? It's their video,' she asked, her voice now slurred, either with crying or with pills. Len just said: 'That's between you and DER. We can take any property found on the premises, whoever it belongs to.' Mrs Webster cried harder, in utter despair: 'What can I do? We've got no money. And my daughter's mentally retarded . . .'

Mr Webster came home, just as the goods were being loaded into the van. He was a stocky man, and he shouted and protested too, as angry with the police as with the bailiffs. The police asked Len if he wanted to press charges against the boy for threatening him with the knife, but Len said he'd let the matter drop. The bailiffs drove away in the van as one of the policemen took Mr Webster aside to warn him about his son. Mrs Webster leaned against the doorstep and cried into her handkerchief.

Len drove off sucking hard on his Polo mint. He was feeling a bit jumpy. 'It's not nice work,' he said. 'I wouldn't advise anyone to be a bailiff.' He has been a bailiff for many years, and now works for a South London firm called Pete Wallis Today. (Today because, says Pete Wallis, they collect today and not tomorrow.) Most of the firm's work comes from the surrounding local authorities who use private bailiffs to collect rent and rates debts – small debtors like the Websters, or big firms, like one factory owing £27,000 rates.

Richmond's Conservative council is proud of its record on rent collection – its level of rent arrears is among the lowest in London. Only £105,000 is outstanding, just 0.9 per cent of the rent collectable.

One reason, they say, is that they use bailiffs and distraint of property. The 1,135 tenants in arrears owe an average of £92 each. They say they catch them early before debts mount too high, and claim tenants can clear their debts easily if they come to an arrangement as soon as they get into debt.

At the other end of the scale are the councils, mostly Labour, who do not use bailiffs and distraint of property to recover their rent. In Lambeth, one of the London boroughs with the highest rent arrears, council tenants owe £7,786,230 or 11.84 per cent of collectable rent. They use no distraint, and virtually no eviction (no eviction at all since Labour has been in power); 15,000 tenants owe an average of £512 each – a hefty burden on the borough's budget. Last year the district auditor suggested the borough should use distraint.

However, the economics of the problem look different when seen through the eyes of a distraught tenant who happens to have fallen on hard times. To her, this seemed like a punishment, a humiliation and a disgrace brought upon her by the council – not a simple means of collecting rent.

Mrs Webster (though not all rent defaulters) probably could have avoided such trouble. She had not known how to cope as her debts built up. Letters arrived, the bailiffs delivered a written warning when she was out, but no one came to sort out the worsening muddle of her finances.

'Maybe we'd be able to get something from the social security?' she asked herself. It had never occurred to her until then. 'My husband is earning so little now.' As the bills piled up, she had not known where to turn. She was not by nature a form-filler and letter-answerer. Ahead of her lay nothing but more trouble – first from DER for the video, then from the gas and electricity boards. Now her possessions from richer days had gone, there was nothing left to sell or pawn.

21 February, 1983 **Polly Toynbee**

The unthinkable men behind Mrs Thatcher

Almost ten years ago a young don of decidedly Conservative opinions called John Casey took over the editorship of the prestigious *Cambridge Review* and set in motion a kind of intellectual revolution, a long march through the periodicals to 'challenge the left-liberal orthodoxy with conservative values'.

Dr Casey was not alone. Another young don, Roger Scruton, who is now Reader in philosophy at Birkbeck College in London, took up the idea with rather more energy, and promoted it with passion in the *Cambridge Review*, and then in the *Spectator*, and currently as a columnist in *The Times*, and in a number of books. With the help of Sir Hugh Fraser, they started the Conservative Philosophy Group in 1975, a forum at which Tory MPs could meet the new breed of Tory dons and receive intellectual sustenance from them. Scruton also helped to found yet another Conservative intellectual forum, the Salisbury Group, which has now started to publish its own journal, the *Salisbury Review*. Its small circulation of about 1,000 understates its influence. One sees it in Ministers' waiting rooms, in Oxford and Cambridge colleges, in the odd Embassy.

In its first issue, Scruton frankly stated his political objective: 'It is necessary to establish a conservative dominance in intellectual life, not because this is the quickest or most certain way to political influence, but because in the long run, it is the only way to create a climate of opinion favourable to the conservative cause. The importance of regaining the commanding heights of the moral and intellectual economy has yet to be clearly perceived by the partisans of conservatism.'

There is nothing new about political entryism by academics. In the US, the process is vulgarly known as 'taking the K Train', after the career of Dr Kissinger. But Scruton and his associates are not bent on political office, nor on lucrative and influential jobs as consultants to Ministers. They see themselves as waging a battle of ideas, as fighting a war for the *Zeitgeist*.

There are four main reasons why this is not simply another flutter in the senior common rooms. First, there is a coherent plan to seize the commanding heights of intellectual life. Scruton himself has written on philosophy, on law, on aesthetics, on politics, on language. He is now working on a book on sexuality, and each of these themes he sees as crucial terrain to be clawed back from the liberal-left. Each issue of the *Salisbury Review* zeroes in to attack a different thinker of the Left. E. P. Thompson, Ronald Dworkin, Noam Chomsky.

Second, they have a receptive ear in the Prime Minister, who on occasion attends the meetings of the Conservative Philosophy Group, and takes part in the debates. Having come up through the state school system to Oxford, and then become a barrister, Mrs Thatcher is not at all intimidated by intellectuals, and believes that she has some respectable credentials of her own. Enough, at least, to slap down Mr Powell at CPG meetings with her catch-phrase: 'Please be serious, Enoch', and to dismiss the former Regius Professor of History, Lord Dacre, with a brisk: 'You're just being difficult, Hugh.'

Third, there are now some signs of this conservative intellectualism bursting through into the real world of public affairs. The resources of the CPG were mobilized to defeat the unilateralist threat in the Church of England Synod last month. Paul Johnson's paper on the morality of the deterrent, and the synod membership of John Selwyn Gummer MP. were aimed like Exocets at ensuring that the Synod would vote down the report, *The Church And The Bomb*.

And however half-baked the ideas in the leaked papers of Mrs Thatcher's Family Policy Group, they point to this Government's belief in a Conservative ideology, and to a Conservatism which is not simply dedicated to preserving existing institutions from Labour and SDP reforms, but to put into force a political vision of its own.

This is unusual for British Conservatism, which lays claim to no real politically engaged thinker since the days of Burke, almost two centuries ago. The most influential conservative thinker of recent years, Professor Michael Oakeshott, took the view that day-to-day politics were not very important, and the politicians thought much the same about the dons.

The fourth reason why this new trend is important is that in the work of Scruton and Casey and the school that is slowly building around them one can detect a coherent, assertive ideology of Conservatism. Significantly, it very nearly ignores economics, except that it mistrusts the free market as a doctrine of 19th-century Liberalism.

It is based on a reverence for order and for authority. It has a Hegelian reverence for the nation-state. Indeed, it drifts into mysticism when Scruton writes: 'National consciousness provides, therefore, one of the strongest experiences of the immanence of God . . . . Life which willingly sacrifices itself for the sake

83

of country inspires awe and admiration. It also represents the most vivid human example of the sacred, of the temporal order overcome by a transcendent meaning.'

That was written in the wake of the Falklands victory, and although Scruton himself is an atheist, he is a passionate believer in the political importance of a national Church.

The role of the Church is central to the new Conservatism, which is why this month's synod was such an important battle-ground. The Marquess of Salisbury, writing in the eponymous *Review*, dismisses the current Church of England as 'that self-appointed fifth-column of the Communist Party'.

It would be unfair to judge this new ideology by the excesses of the Marquess of Salisbury. But some of the extremes into which the new thinkers of the Right have ventured are danger-ous. Six years ago, John Casey wrote a provocative article on 'Anti-racialism' in the *Cambridge Review*, which roundly con-demned those who thought Britain could and should be a multi-racial country. His ears rang with the sound of cancelled subscriptions for some time thereafter.

Undismayed, he returned to the fray last autumn with a paper he delivered to the Conservative Philosophy Group in which he advocated, in an elliptical and even elegant way, the compulsory repatriation of coloured immigrants. 'This policy would have about it an air of inevitability once enacted, and of political control that might actually make it less damaging and less inhumane than a voluntary scheme,' he wrote, when his paper was then published in the *Salisbury Review*.

Now this, of course, is the policy of the National Front, and when you add that to a mystic reverence for the idea of the Nation, then you get a very dangerous mixture. How did Casey see his role as a Tory thinker?

'I see it as being able to think the unthinkable, to say the unsayable,' he said, during an interview in his rooms at Gonville and Caius College. 'Since 1945, this country has been domin-ated by the ideas of State Socialism, of *dirigisme*, a left-liberalism, and as faith in that started to collapse, it left an intellectual vacuum which conservative intellectuals may try to fill. But the effect of the long dominance of that old orthodoxy was to narrow the acceptable area of debate. It is our job to

84

re-open the argument by saying the unsayable.'

That is a response which seems tenable in the cloisters of Cambridge. In Brick Lane or Handsworth or Brixton, it would resonate rather differently; it would be an intellectual justification of racism red in tooth and claw. Roger Scruton, by contrast, rejects Casey's compulsory repatriation, and accepts that Casey's argument of 'saying the unsayable' logically leads to the prospect of civilized debate about anything at all, from bring back the birch to final solutions.

'There are three main things that I want to say,' Scruton said in an interview. 'The first is to convince the Left that the onus of proof about the need for political change must be on them. It is not for us as Conservatives to defend the current system, but for the Left to define their alternative. So far, they have got away with this by default. The second thing I want to do is to attack the influence of the Left upon modern thinking, because I do not accept the Marxist view of history, nor the concept of the class struggle, nor the suggestion that private property is a bad thing. And third, I want to understand the concepts in which we think politically, and to express concepts which have long been forbidden expression, like allegiance, legitimacy, the nation, authority.

'I do not want to influence the Tory Party as it now is, but the intellectual arena. I am not battling for the ear or the mind of Mrs Thatcher. She is a practical politician and has better things to think about.' He smiled. 'Anyway, a woman's emotions are what one battles for.'

Roger Scruton, like John Casey, is a clever grammar school boy who got to Cambridge on scholarships. He identifies with the grammar school background of Mrs Thatcher (if not that of Edward Heath) and sees the comprehensive school system as a result of 'the infiltration of *Guardian*-reader mentality into key intellectual positions.' ('*Guardian*-reader' is a common form of shorthand among the Scruton group for the post-1945 orthodoxy they condemn.)

Scruton is currently agonizing over how to reply to a letter from his father, accusing him of being a class traitor. His father is a working class man who has become a primary school teacher. The Salisbury Group also includes the traditional Tory

85

aristocrats like the Marquess of Salisbury and Lord Charles Cecil. Scruton is a firm believer in the hereditary principle and sees the House of Lords, like the Church of England, as one of the vital institutions which make up the nation.

It may well be the social background of Casey and Scruton that makes their philosophy and their ambition into something different for the Tories. After all, ambitious dons seeking a politician's ear are not new, and the Tory Party has long supported a large number of clubs and forums where intellectual can meet MP, from university political clubs to Burke groups to Political Economy circles. Hugh Trevor-Roper, Maurice Cowling, Shirley Letwin, Peter Bauer, Kenneth Minogue have been important (although remote) intellectual influences on the Party for a generation, and Cowling, indeed, can be seen as the immediate godfather to the Salisbury Group, and his Peterhouse College as its gestation chamber.

'If we are being more assertive, then it may simply reflect our age,' comments Scruton, who is 38. But other factors are involved. The decline of the country-house weekend, where Conservatives of another generation met their tame intellectuals, has led to the more tightly-focused political dinner and discussion, at the home of the well-heeled MPs like Sir Hugh Fraser and Jonathan Aitken.

Above all, when Mrs Thatcher won the Conservative leadership, she made it clear that she wanted ideas. She and Sir Keith Joseph established the Centre for Policy Studies, with the ex-Communist Alfred Sherman turning out position papers, and Professor Alan Walters as the Prime Minister's own free market economist with an office in Downing Street. The time could not have been more propitious for Scruton to make his assault on the commanding heights.

But others have had the same idea. The ranks of Tory thinkers are becoming dangerously overcrowded. One of the reasons why the Conservative intellectuals are now so much more visible and prominent is that those among them who are converts from Labour, like Paul Johnson and Lord Hugh Thomas, are skilled publicists and media professionals.

And it is, for many of them, a frustrating experience to be an intellectual courtier at Number Ten.

86

The most cautionary tale is that of Peter Bauer. Even some of the *Guardian*-reading orthodoxy might agree that his extended critiques of foreign aid, as destructive of the recipient nations and corrupting of the donors, have won the intellectual argument. And yet the foreign aid budget goes on, little curtailed by

'*This is a very interesting rose. No matter what you do to it, it always comes up smelling of Mrs Thatcher.*'

19 January, 1983

a Prime Minister who thinks so highly of Bauer that she has ennobled him. He may have won the ear, the heart and mind of Mrs Thatcher – but it does not seem to have made much difference. The Tory intellectuals may well be in for the long frustration which Labour's thinkers have suffered for fifty years. Indeed, the one British intellectual who saw his ideas converted into a fact of national life was Lord Beveridge – and he was a Liberal.

'Winning the argument and winning power are two different things,' says John Casey. 'And intellectuals are probably the wrong people to have much political influence. But what they can do, and what is being done, is to bring about a change in the political vocabulary, in what can be said, and thought. We may not yet occupy the commanding heights, but at least the liberal-left no longer occupies them by default.'

The danger, of course, is that while John Casey's eyes are fixed on the commanding heights, his argument for the compulsory repatriation of non-whites is being heard, and used to awful effect in the gutter. Intellectuals may ignore that; politicians and the rest of us live with the consequences.

1 March 1983   **Martin Walker**

Court and personal

It is worthwhile sometimes to collate the sayings and actions of the judges in whom we place so much trust. We will pass over Lord Dunboyne of naked ballet dancer fame and turn our attention today to Judge David Wild, who this week gaoled a young wife for three months for telling a lie about the length of time she had been separated to get a quick divorce. Only last year Judge Wild spared her ex-husband from prison for holding her hostage at gunpoint.

Judge Wild's sentencing policies are not always his strongest point. In 1977 he gave an absolute discharge to an Army officer who admitted causing the death of a motorcyclist by dangerous driving, allowing him 'due consideration because of his background and position.' He promptly gaoled an undergraduate for three years for dealing in cannabis.

In 1978 he told two Libyan students that 'People of your origin never admit anything – well, hardly anything, anyway,' and was warned by Lord Hailsham. Overturning another of his judgments in 1980 the late Mr Justice Wien described his attitude to a defendant as 'offensive'.

But perhaps Judge Wild's finest hour was his old chestnut last year about a woman who says No not always meaning No and reminding the jury of the phrase 'stop it – I like it'. His Honour Judge Wild is still only fifty-six.

16 June 1983   **Alan Rusbridger**

Chase Manhattan at play

The gale force winds wuthered across the Yorkshire moors, the trees bent perilously, the noise of the wild weather sounded like a squadron of fighters overhead. The guns stood their ground, green wellington boots planted firmly, barrels pointed sky-wards, eyes scanning the skyline. Tension mounted as the distant shouts, whistles and tramping of beaters' feet in the under-growth echoed through the wood like an army on the move.

'Forward!' went up the cry from down the line of guns, as a pheasant rose up over the tops of the conifers, hurtling through the air at sixty miles an hour with the great wind behind it. The nearest gun took aim well ahead of its flight path and fired. The bird jarred in the air, planed for a moment, then tumbled to the ground with a thud, sending up a flurry of feathers like a beaten pillow.

A black labrador bounded after it, sniffed it, sneezed a feather, picked it up gingerly in its soft mouth, and dropped it a few yards later as the bird still raised its sharp beak and struggled. The dog tried again, and this time brought it trium-phantly to its master's feet. The shooter's wife in plaid plus fours wrinkled her nose and cried: 'Oh God, it's still alive! I don't like that!' But the bird shortly expired.

This was no party of landowners, but the Chase Manhattan Bank at play, entertaining some of its more treasured clients. Four American men from the bank had hired a couple of days' shooting on Lord Bolton's estate. They had invited an English brewer, a ship owner, a BP oil man and an American oil executive and their wives for a few days in Yorkshire. The shooting alone cost the bank £2,500 a day. On top of that came the no doubt hefty bill for the party's stay in Constable Burton Hall, a Palladian private stately home where they were royally entertained.

89

This is, said the bankers, a very normal procedure, often followed by other companies to bind them closer to their important clients. 'You really get to know a man well on a shoot,' said one. 'You may talk business in the evening or over dinner. It's a comradely activity, you make real friends, and that's important. If a crisis blows up, you know something about the man, how he'll react, what he's like, and he needs to know and trust us.'

Colonel Christopher Egerton, a man in his late fifties, runs such occasions, with his own company, Shooting Field Services. Throughout the season – pheasants from October 1 to end of January, grouse August 12 to December 10, deer August 1 to October 20 – he organizes parties of all kinds to shoot on English and Scottish estates.

He owns no land of his own, but started out running all the shooting side of his uncle's estate. When his uncle died he ran the shooting on an estate owned in Yorkshire by Niarchos. When Niarchos gave up the estate Colonel Egerton found himself at fifty with no prospect of a job, so he set himself up in the agency business.

'At first I made the mistake of approaching landowners, and asking them if they wanted to let their shooting at all. I got some pretty dusty answers. Said they didn't want any damn foreigners wandering around their ground.' He smiles with a hint of glee as he adds: 'Then Mr Healey's screws began to squeeze. Some of the same owners rang me up and said "I say old boy, you think you could find anyone to take a couple of days' shooting?" '

'Damn foreigners' are now to be found on most of the shooting estates of England and Scotland for much of the season. At those prices, few landowners can resist. Colonel Egerton's success probably comes from the fact he actually likes them. In a recent article in the *Shooting Times* he warned those owners who fleece their visitors: 'It's a mistake to think that because a party doesn't speak English very well that they are bloody fools! So don't arrange drives which are obviously going to be unproductive. It will only irritate the visitors.'

The Colonel's wife looks after the wives. (The Colonel refers to them as animated hot-water bottles.) 'They're often bored with shooting, so I take them shopping. A lot of them come back time and again, and are great friends.' She marvels at the fortunes they spend on cashmere, tweeds, and antiques. She personally vets the private houses and local hotels where they stay.

'Some people just had no idea what first class means. It means things like private bathrooms, which a lot of big houses didn't have. It means fresh flowers in the rooms each day. It means warmth and excellent food. These people know when they get second-best smoked salmon.' A survey is currently being conducted to estimate the amount of money which is brought into the country not just for the shooting itself, but in accommodation and shops.

'And then there's the local employment,' the Colonel says. On the shoot that day there were three full-time game keepers, twenty beaters, hired by the day, and eight "pickers-up" who stand behind the guns with dogs to collect the fallen birds. The pheasants are sold to a game dealer at about £1 each. It costs approximately £12 to the shooter to shoot each bird and they only get two to keep at the end of the day. The beaters who drive the birds through the woods towards the guns are mainly retired or unemployed people.

'I get a lot of policemen and coal miners who take their days off to come beating,' the Colonel said. 'Coal miners, they behave like gentlemen's gentlemen on the shoot. I ask them why they voted for Scargill. They smile and say they had to vote for Uncle Arthur or the mines would be closed.'

It is an extremely dangerous sport. The Colonel gives every party a firm talking to, however experienced they are. No low shots, no swinging the guns round, they must see daylight under the bird before they fire. Anyone does anything dangerous, and he sends them home.

'Nearly every year someone gets pinged,' he says. 'Not killed, but nearly always shot in the head. One chap was shot through the ear lobe!'

Halfway through the morning, after three 'drives', the party stopped for silver tumblers of sloe gin. The man from BP had brought his own, labelled, 'Crude Oil from the North Sea'. Did BP organize such outings themselves? 'No, not shooting,' he said. 'Used to have three seats a week at Covent Garden, but no

91

one ever wanted to go. We have seats at the Barbican now, because we feel we ought to.'

Draining the dregs of our drinks the talk turned briefly to the question of cruelty. All agreed it would be much better to be a wild pheasant and risk getting shot, than to be a battery hen, calf or pig. It was the Colonel's wife, the night before, who quietly suggested: 'I do think pheasant shooting is a bit cruel. After all, they've been reared in the woods, and some of them are jolly nearly tame.'

However, the tame birds were the ones shot early in the season. By now the remaining ones were canny, having no doubt got the measure of beating. Many of them knew to fly low, and to fly back over beaters' heads, instead of ahead into the guns.

On went the shoot, another two drives before lunch in a ruined castle with a spectacular view across the countryside. The truck followed, bearing its cargo of bright plumed pheasants – about one hundred by the end of the day. Muddied plus fours, and spattered Barbours, they would return at dusk to the Hall for drinks, hot baths, a roaring fire, a certain amount of business talk, and then a wild game into the small hours, involving hitting billiard balls and running round the table. They would be up early next morning, clean trousers and jackets, ready for another day's shooting.

24 January, 1983   **Polly Toynbee**

Lost in the Twilight Hotel

'The only way out is when you're blanked,' says Andy. 'Things just get worse and worse.' Being young and homeless in central London used to be a staging post, maybe, to housing and a job of sorts. But the streets are dead ends these days. For a growing number of young people, homelessness is becoming a way of life. And they are finding out younger what that means.

How do you live if you're Andy, now twenty, who left local authority care in London with the promise of a place to live and no education at all in how to handle it, who after a spell in the army and a chance of employment blown, has now been around the streets for a year or more? Or if you're Garry, who first left home in Liverpool at fifteen and now, give or take the army and the ups and downs, reckons to have ten years of street-wisdom behind him? Official responses sound like a vicious game. There is no social security without an address to deliver it to and no possibility of an address without an income. It can take two days or more to get seen and there's abuse when you are. If you are Andy, there are days when you just can't take the hassle any more and opt to sleep out.

When the £7.60 the hassle produces for establishing an address can buy you, maybe, bed and breakfast which amounts to a dirty bed in a room shared with three others, a bit of bread left outside the door and the chance of catching nits, sleeping out begins to sound like not such a bad alternative. When Centre-point tells you that its night shelter must take new and very young arrivals to the West End, and that you are too old or too long on the scene; when you're barred from the Department of Health's own casual ward, or refuse to accept its regimentations; when you're young and like to keep yourself clean and wouldn't sink to a bed in a dosshouse, there doesn't sound to be an alternative at all.

So if you're Andy, or Garry, or another of the regulars that cluster by day in the New Horizon Centre in Covent Garden, you end up in Leicester Square when the pubs close and the cinemas finish, and you wait for the night to start.

You can tell the people who have a place to go from those who don't by the way they move. Not much point in hurrying, after all, if tonight's choice is between Cardboard City down at Charing Cross Station and the Twilight Hotel of St James's Park. Not much point, that is, until the police vans start their routine sweeps through the square. You scatter then. Who needs yet another CRO, that walkie-talkie computer read-out to see if you're wanted this time?

Midnight: Start with another cup of tea, laced strong with sugar against the hours ahead, at one of the all-night cafés. By now, Cardboard City is in the building, boxes dragged into service from the shops' throw-outs, black plastic sacks emptied for blankets, to stake a claim to the nooks of the subway, the places under the railway arches. If I were not here, Andy and Garry could be staking their own claims; the locks and patrols in the Embankment Gardens mean one option fewer. But their London is what they're showing me this night. So we keep walking, marking the boundaries of their patch from the Embankment up through Soho and down again. South of the river belongs to older men, the ones who still carry the stereotypes of the homeless. You go there in winter, maybe, because they have fires. But you only go when there are plenty of you, and not with a visitor.

2 a.m.: The lights are out in the Twilight Hotel of St James's Park, and you tread softly as you skirt the bandstand, because it's been taken over by the drinkers and their tempers are uncertain; these days you wouldn't go there to sleep on your own. But this is a large hotel, and away from the crowd you can build shelter with deckchairs and find peace on a summer night. Garry is persuaded as we sit on a bench by the lake to recite a poem that has just come into his head – a gentle hymn to the stars and a girl he wishes he was with. But the peace doesn't last.

They are alert to the police cars almost before they appear across the lake, these two. They see the torches almost before they flicker on the water. Five cars. That's trouble, maybe someone in the water. People do die in the night. Garry once found a man in a public lavatory with a syringe stuck in each eye. You get used to it. You'd be sorry if you knew them, but you can't afford to care.

The all-night café between the park and Charing Cross draws its regulars from both and neither – a motley of older men, of skins, of young men working the gay clubs. Friends pass in the street. One young Scot is on the run from his girl friend. She clapped him about the head with a saucepan when she heard he'd spent the Giro, £45-worth, on drink.

You buy what escape you can when you can from this life; otherwise, tomorrow might seem too like today. Another young man is on the run, too. But this time, it's from the police. He's been picked up four times in the last twenty-four hours and he doesn't want to make that five. There's research to show how this life and offending go together. Who's surprised?

They get younger all the time, says Garry. He wonders if anyone cares that kids are selling themselves for the prospect of a bed for the night, or less. A beautiful youth in the café works

94

around Piccadilly. Down from Liverpool, just seventeen, his dark eyes glazed with tonight's mixture of drugs, his hands shaking round the cigarette. They get younger all the time.

And no less desperate. In among the cardboard boxes in the Charing Cross subway, in among the scattering of young couples, not far from Scottish Dave, scrounging a cigarette through a haze of cider, in among the many more older men, is the young girl we last saw in Leicester Square. She's sixteen, says Garry, goes with men for £1 or less. He's given her 50p himself to try to dissuade her. But she's crazy. She should be in hospital, like quite a few others he knows.

Up in Mortimer Street, the north end of the territory, the cardboard houses make the queue for the casual work that might just be on offer when the Job Centre opens, and likely won't. That's not what Garry, qualified chef, is after. But how do you find a real job when someone has stolen your knives and your whites, when you've only got the clothes you stand up in to impress the interviewers with, when the Job Centre just doesn't want to know when you haven't got an address to apply from?

4.30 a.m.: The light is up. In St James's Park, the birds have shaken their feathers and the bandstand has emptied before the police start their morning clear-out. In the Charing Cross subway, they are stirring to beat the hoses which can soak you if you're not quick enough – though this morning seems to bring a dispensation from that, at least.

The night's bravado seeps away. It is very cold. The cafés are shut. There's breakfast at the Hare Krishna temple, but they want you to pray for it. The early workers have somewhere to go; that just underlines our aimlessness.

6.30 a.m.: Only now do we find a café open for breakfast. It's months since Garry and Andy had a cooked one; most usually, breakfast comes from the rolls and milk cartons stacked against café walls. But the anticipation of the day's coming hassles with social security, of working out where you sleep the next night, blunts the enjoyment. Garry is exhausted. He has a bad stomach ulcer. Two nights ago, he collapsed and friends took him to hospital, but he wouldn't stay, he hates the places. There's research to show that living rough over a period damages your health. Who's surprised?

95

7.30 a.m.: The day centre doesn't open until nine. Normally, this early morning would have been hours longer. Where do you go? The lavatories are already full of people getting what sleep they can; Andy has to pretend he's police to get in to one at all.

At least at the New Horizon day centre there will be the chance of a shower, a shave, and sleep undisturbed. But the place closes at 5 pm. The St Martin's youth club closes at 11 pm. That, says Garry, is when the loneliness really sets in. But who wants to know? They've got their cars, their families, their little house. Oh, yes, they've got a house.

11 August, 1982   **Ann Shearer**

The case of the exploding cheese

Let us turn our attention to the strange case of the senior tutor and the exploding cheese. It is all the buzz in Cambridge.

There have of late been a string of thefts from the undergraduates' fridges in Queen's College. Small things – butter, cheese, sausages, and the like – but disturbing all the same.

Especially disturbed was Dr John Green, the senior tutor and an expert in fluid mechanics and blood flow. Dr Green hit on the enterprising wheeze of booby-trapping certain items of food with a chemical possessed of the unusual property of turning urine an unfamiliar colour. Green, funnily enough.

It was not clear to the Junior Commons Room how helpful this would be in apprehending the villain. Why, they asked, do we not put locks on the fridge doors? But Dr Green was already working on another scheme – a red dye injected into Cheddar cheese which would vaporize when attacked by the thief and explode all over his hands.

Tactfully as they could, the JCR suggested they would rather think about locks.

The affair has been fully reported in the student newspaper, *Stop Press*, and, it is fair to say, has caused a certain amount of merriment. Which perhaps explains why Dr Green, tackled on the subject by telephone, replaces his receiver with a sharp 'No comment.'

2 February, 1983   **Alan Rusbridger**

Red light recession

Business was so bad on New York's Eighth Avenue on a recent snowy night that prostitutes grabbed passers by by the arm and wouldn't take 'No' for an answer. Often they pursued potential customers for blocks, attempting to caress their groin in the hope of changing their mind. Only when a police car was spotted did they give up and, if the police had nothing better to do and pursued them, there was a stampede of all the prostitutes on the Avenue into the nearby side streets.

It was a bizarre sight to see so many pretty, made-up women running in a squealing panic in search of somewhere to hide like birds getting out of the way of a cat. In boom times there wouldn't have been that many prostitutes on the Avenue without a customer, but the recession has hit this business like every other. In mid-week profits seem to be down as much as fifty per cent, though it is hard to get realistic figures because it is a business in which everyone exaggerates. The aggressive prostitutes on Eighth Avenue are in the same position as factory workers who try to boost production in the hope they won't be laid off.

At the same time as business has declined, the number of prostitutes has increased in cities like New York. Women suffering from the recession through losing jobs or through their husbands being laid off have turned to prostitution as a new source of income. Along that short stretch of Eighth Avenue, with the regulars who had been there for years, were a housewife from Long Island and a university student who was paying her way through college. Several pimps had tried to recruit them, and though it is as hard for a prostitute to remain independent as it is for a factory worker to be unrepresented by a union, so far they had succeeded in working for themselves – when they could find work.

Along Seventh Avenue near the big hotels were several of the new recession prostitutes – young women from towns upstate who had taken up the business only because no other jobs were available. With them, too, was a big increase in Spanish-speaking prostitutes, reflecting the vast number of illegal immigrants from South America. They had often worked as prostitutes in their own countries and so plied their trade in the

97

US as soon as they found nothing else bringing in the same money. Along with them were the usual young women from rural areas in the South who had come to New York to get away or to make it, sometimes with boy friends who acted as their pimps when they decided the only way to make it in the recession was on the street.

For a country that is so moralistic about prostitution, refusing to legalize it or even recognize its existence officially, the US takes a very ambivalent attitude, allowing a very well organized major business to flourish openly under the eyes of the police at the same time that politicians are condemning it and demanding reforms. Much of the business has now gone indoors and could only exist with police consent. Peep shows, massage parlours, dating services, model agencies – the covers are endless. But indoors as well as outdoors, the business mid-week is well down on what it was even a year ago.

It is sometimes hard to tell where prostitution ends and the drug trade begins because both are largely run by organized crime and one is used to further the other, but many of the customers whose demands are only sexual seem to have a greatly limited budget now that allows big business only from pay day on Fridays over the weekend. Monday to Thursday is 'dead', according to both veterans of the street and insiders.

New York salesmen who frequent most of the big cities regularly bring the same reports back from the West and the South. Business is bad all over. Prostitutes in Detroit, Chicago, Los Angeles and Atlanta, in fact, have been coming to New York in search of work only to find the same situation there drives them back home.

The recession has also affected some of the small-time pimps. One man from Mississippi, known in New York prostitution circles as 'Black Ice', used to find that his three women in New York provided enough for him to live in a comfortable hotel and rent a car when he felt like a drive. But over the last year takings have declined so much, court fines have been so frequent causing many days with no income, and his women have had several costly illnesses related to their work, that he accepted an invitation in December from a friend in organized crime to do the incredible – take a job. It was in a peepshow as cashier and bouncer. 'During the week business isn't much better inside than outside,' he said recently with great disappointment.

Like many pimps, he also acted as a male prostitute on the side unknown to his women, but that branch of the business – including supplying his women for other women – was bad, too, he said.

Another change has been in the racial make-up on the prostitution lines. In boom times, the majority on the street were black or Spanish-speaking and the few whites were usually Irish, Italian or East European women from large poor families whose homes were far from New York. Now in the recession, there are far more white prostitutes competing even on the street, and inside, where a woman is not as visible and therefore can protect her outside reputation more easily, there are sometimes more white women than black waiting for business in the booths or showing off their bodies in the small areas surrounded by peepholes.

The life of a prostitute is short in boom times, but under the much greater pressures of the recession, it is even shorter. The number of prostitutes in hospitals and psychiatric clinics has risen over the past year at roughly the same rate as business has declined. Prostitutes also share some of the fears of other workers – that technological developments may put them completely out of business. All the peepshows now sell substitutes – dolls to have sex with, vibrators, plastic vaginas and penises – and as one woman groused in New York, 'It won't be long before customers can buy a robot from the drug-store and they won't need us at all.'

It is easy to take an ambivalent attitude towards prostitution after hearing an experienced woman describe the kind of people she has to deal with. Every day they may include the unsatisfied husband or the husband who wishes to do far-out acts he can't with his wife, the incest-inclined father who wants to use the prostitute as a daughter-substitute, the machismo tough guy with closet fears he wishes to overcome, the bisexual woman who is happily married, the suppressed sadist, the would-be rapist, the hidden masochist. They are all people ready to explode if they don't get relief.

'We play psychiatrist and social worker and save the police

99

work,' said a veteran prostitute working in a leading New York hotel. 'If people can't afford to come to us, there's going to be much more violence in the home and crime in the streets.'

But when one witnesses the stampede of prostitutes down Eighth Avenue fleeing from the police, it is hard to see them that way – as a social benefit. They just look like people caught in a situation they can't escape, however much they try.

23 February, 1983   **W. J. Weatherby**

Panic in the Hamptons

Late fall out on Long Island is a very wistful time. Sea mists creep up from the ocean. Huge brown oak leaves cover deserted lawns. Row upon row of second homes stand empty, blinds drawn over the windows, garbage cans left upside down outside the back door. The only movement is that of the hungry gulls dipping over the beach and the odd sports car buzzing in and out of driveways engaged in the lucrative business of house-watching.

At weekends, though, the atmosphere changes. The predators arrive. It is hard to imagine where they come from, these young men in their late twenties, stalking about the houses for sale buttonholing bewildered owners with the news that it's okay – they have 'green'.

This reference is usually lost on the gentlefolk of Quogue, given as they are to believing that life in the raw means gardening in a Pendleton flannel shirt. One such Quogite was horrified to learn that at the closing for the sale of his $345,000 marble and stucco 'cottage', he was expected to collect almost half in dollar bills. He duly turned up at his lawyer's office with a moonlighting policeman in tow. He walked through the New York streets, knees trembling, heart pounding, one hand on his brown bag of money, the other against the comforting gun inside his companion's jacket. 'How can this be happening to me?' he wailed all the way to the bank.

How quickly things happen. It was only a year ago that realtors apologized for bringing around anything less than a society gynaecologist with offices on Fifth Avenue or some

Waspy type with hornrims and topsiders. Now they produce to the desperate home-owners of the Hamptons this endless stream of jumpy young men with their talk of doing deals in green. Panic has run through the Hamptons like quicksilver. Those who insisted last summer that they wouldn't consider selling for less than $350,000 now jump at the chance to get half of that. And yet very few of these sales have any reason behind them. The owners are not moving away, their need for money is no greater than it has ever been. There is a fever to sell as once there was a fever to buy.

The Argentinian leather tycoon whose cedar and glass split-level is currently being hawked about by officers for the bankruptcy court is the exception. Rumour has it that everyone is selling and therefore everyone wants to sell. Except, of course, that they can't. Word has gone out that the Hamptons have gone bad. All that has changed is the word but it changes everything.

Houses are not homes but showbusiness – one moment they're hot, the next moment they're out. Three years ago, it was the fashion to build large 'woodsy' boxes: natural cedar with dark trim. Now those are has-beens: the new look is glamorous, Palm Beach white. Two years ago the all-electric house with heat pump was the star, even among those with no idea what a heat pump was. Now oil is back in favour and a heat-pump is a selling liability. There is no thought of what might be in five years or even next summer. The moment is all.

All of this, of course, makes of the realtors a very sad bunch indeed. They, too, are subject to fashion. Just before the market died, there was a sudden burst of competitive decorating among the various real estate offices. Neil Rego in Quogue started it. He decided to refurbish his cosy, cluttered office to be more in keeping with the elegant jogging outfit in which he works. Out went the rickety old chairs and desks until then thought to be the epitome of shabby Hamptons chic. In came wall-to-wall carpeting, glass, pine and a muted colour scheme of cream and white.

Hampton Properties responded with a flurry of building and even more imposing modern classics at which to sit their salary-less sales' agents. Not to be outdone, Rick Kelling of Resort Properties moved his whole show over to a stunning new suite on the corner of Sunset Avenue, where a gleaming Mercedes outside announced his presence. Last summer, the builders even moved into the familiar old shop in which Norma Reynolds, the doyenne of Westhampton Beach, had long held court.

There they sit now, amid their expensive decorating, talking of 'steals' and 'Bargains' and what it is to 'bleed'. In hard times here, it seems, bleeding is what business people do a lot of. Their offices are emptier now, of course. All those divorced ladies in their forties and fifties who saw real estate as modern-day Tupperware have had to steal away. They have had to find other means with which to pay the mortgage taken out on some over-sized house they were seduced by in the palmy days when they thought commissions would go on forever.

Some people, though, cannot accept that the rules have changed. Their dreams sprang from the time of plenty. They do not know how to let them go. All over what remains of the Quogue woodlands, great paths have been cut through the trees revealing yet another subdivision of one-acre plots. Twenty-three acres here, fifteen there, five here. The pine barrens are laid bare right back to the railroad tracks and even beyond.

Out on Route 104 near the highway, Al the Plumber has at last put up the house he dreamed of building while installing all those jacuzzis and one-piece fibreglass shower units on which others made the profit. The house stands empty, of course. Freddie Junior, the 23-year-old son of Freddie Senior from Quogue's grocery store, has just broken ground for his own spec-house in Bayberry in partnership with Bill the Policeman. Ken Tedaldi, the Schoolteacher, beavers away in Boxtree putting up one house after another with tennis court and pool.

And at the latest meeting of Westhampton Beach village there was concern expressed at the cost of piping village water to the last streets without it. The private wells all show signs of contamination. Some people say that the fresh water supply will run out here in thirty years, some say twenty. At a rough guess, a thousand new bathrooms are going up for sale in Quogue.

8 December, 1982   **Linda Blandford**

Follies as the Fleet heads south

The small wars in Central America are swiftly developing into a conflagration of major proportions – and the United States Administration, by its every action, seems intent on heaping more fuel on the flames. This week's decision to send a battle fleet down the Pacific coast from California to patrol the waters off Guatemala, El Salvador, Honduras and Nicaragua, coupled with an earlier scheme to establish a large American military base at Puerto Castilla on the Atlantic shores of Honduras, is a further frightening indication that the United States is still toying with apocalyptic military solutions. Next month thousands of American troops will arrive in Honduras for exercises, perversely described as 'routine'.

Yet in some sense these manoeuvres are routine, the deadly routine of a superpower – with all the vast panoply of weapons and the infinite availability of information and analysis at its command – gearing itself up for a superbungle. Not the routine of Vietnam, with the tragic inbuilt belief that one more heave would finish the job; more the routine of Cuba in the years from 1960 to 1962, when the United States did little to cloak its ambition to overthrow Fidel Castro. From that bruising encounter the Cuban revolution emerged fortified, albeit driven into a lasting Soviet embrace. The American participants in that hopeless scheme are for the most part dead, their memoirs remaindered. But nearly a quarter of a century later, Castro survives – an enduring symbol of defiance, lasting proof of the vincibility of American power.

Now the American Administration seems set to make the same fateful error. It has been decreed in Washington that the Sandinista regime in Nicaragua shall not survive. To that end mercenary armies have been assembled and funded, global priorities have been distorted, friends and allies have been ignored, the Mexicans and Venezuelans have been intimidated, the Socialist International forced into acquiescence. Efforts are now being made to bring a reluctant US opinion into line. Henry Kissinger has been dragged into the fray, allowing the tarnished lustre of his name to be used in support of Administration policy.

The aim of this frenetic activity is to change the government in Managua, though there is a dwindling band in the State Department which still hopes that cauterization of the Nicaraguan wound, rather than outright amputation, may prove sufficient. The hope of President Reagan and of his two most forthright advisers, Jeane Kirkpatrick and William Clark, is that those engaged in the continuing struggles in El Salvador and Guatemala (and the incipient unrest in Honduras) will – with Managua neutralized – be cut off from the tap root of their material support.

It is an intriguing illusion, one almost totally at variance with the facts. Obviously the Sandinista revolution has had a huge impact on opinion in Central America (and elsewhere), encouraging the belief once current in the early years after the Cuban revolution that radical change is actually possible in a region so long dominated by the United States. Crushing the Sandinistas, if that were possible, would clearly put a dampener on revolutionary aspirations elsewhere. But rebellions on the scale of El Salvador and Guatemala do not rise or fall according to such a simple barometer. There is a deep-rooted internal dynamic driving these countries to revolt, regardless of verbal (or even material) encouragement from outside.

America's almost wilful ignorance of these dynamics has been one of the chief characteristics of recent policy. It is well illustrated by its handling of Honduras, now its most important ally. Honduras is being prepared by the Americans to do battle with Nicaragua, yet its traditional enemy (with which it is still technically at war) is El Salvador. It is one of the poorest countries in the hemisphere – in the same league as Bolivia and Haiti – yet the bulk of its American aid now comes in the form of weapons.

All over Latin America, from Colombia to Chile, the same dreadful conditions that drive people to rebellion in El Salvador or Guatemala can be found in less or greater measure. The challenge to the United States, the challenge that should (but will not) be examined by the Kissinger commission on Central America, is not one posed by Cuban or Soviet subversion. It is a question asked of the United States itself. How can it learn to live in peace in its own hemisphere with people who are waking up to the fact that their condition of oppression – for which the United States bears some historic and present responsibility – is not forever immutable? The United States can adapt to change, or seek to resist it. It cannot – even with the Marines – prevent it.

21 July 1983   **Leader**

Smile on the face of the tiger

Watch out for it this afternoon. Even at the very height of the feverish mayhem at Twickenham, you will certainly catch a glimpse once or twice of the most engaging smile in bigtime sport.

No Willis-type, trance-like cocoon of concentration for England's rugby union captain. Steve Smith is all perky awareness, a bustling busybody at the heels of his pack; darting eyes and feet as he snaffles and tidies, observes and encourages, rabitting all the while as he calls the shots for more creativity, commitment, or caution. And at any time, suddenly illuminating a television nation's sitting-room, might come that marvellous schoolboy grin. 'Jolly good fun, innit?'

Actually, talking of Bob Willis, it is not ludicrously beyond the bounds of reason to reckon that Steve Smith might even have been England's cricket captain in Australia this winter. He has a passion for that game, too. Ten years ago he was going in first wicket down for Loughborough Colleges' most famous cricket team: batting order – A. Borrington (Derbyshire), J. Tolchard (Leices.), S. S. A. Hampshire (Jack's brother), G. Barlow (Middlesex). . . . In the summer of 1972, Smith was in the runs and there were interminable rumours about a trial with Gloucestershire. Then the England rugby side called him to join the tour to South Africa – since when it has been rugby tours most summers and club cricket for Brookwood in the Lancashire and Cheshire League.

'So I haven't had a real "holiday-type holiday" since 1971; Greece with three mates; the old rucksack on the back; those were the days; penniless; queuing on the steps of the old blood donor's bank; wine two bob a bottle; give a litre of blood and you could get smashed for three weeks.' And the memory of it ignites again the magnificent melon smile.

Persistence has made him England's most capped scrum-half in history. Through the Lillywhites' dank and dotty days of the last decade – in forty-one matches between 1970 and 1977 England chose twenty-one different half-backs – Smith, from 1972, alternated on the scrum-half carousel with Webster, Page, Kingston, Lampkowski and Young, till he made the position his own sixteen matches ago when the selectors determined on a more consistent policy. In last season's enterprising win over Wales he overtook Jeeps's scrum-half record of twenty-five times being called to the colours.

Sometimes, when he was dropped, he admits he might not have been quite fit enough. He puts on weight easily. He has to train harder than most – every evening when he gets home from his job as a marketing manager for a sports clothing firm. 'I'm a poor man's Lester Piggott. The knack is to weigh in every day. I can put on four or five pounds just like that: a couple of nights on the piss and it's all got to come off again. The hardest part of training is putting on your tracksuit. Luckily I've no wife to greet me from work by plonking down a whacking great tea in front of the fire and switching on *Nationwide*.'

'Lucky, then, that you don't fancy the lovely Sue Lawley.' 'Ah, do you, too? I think about her all the time I'm out there running, don't I?' That grin again. Not that he has ever been greased lightning. 'Lack of speed was always my weakness. But now it doesn't seem to matter much. I think I compensate now I'm older by being able to stand back and read the game better, consider all the options. Suddenly it's not all instinct, it's observation and know-how.'

The captaincy of England came, of a sudden, when Bill Beaumont retired so dramatically. Over the years Smith had been given a good schooling. His first international captain was John Pullin – 'big JV, strong and silent: "We forwards are going to get the ball for you, then it's up to you".'

Then Fran Cotton, dear friend and Sale clubmate – 'he could have been the most complete captain of all; a great motivator, but very tactically aware; people think "great big thick props", but it's an art and a science as well as strength; but he was hard

106

was Frannie: I was best man at his wedding but he still managed to inflict' (and he pulls up a trouser leg) 'these seventeen stitches when he trod on me in a Lancs v Cheshire game. Not on purpose, mind.'

Suddenly you realize how the red rose has served English captaincy so well, for next came Tony Neary – 'smashing bloke, but a loner; never a rant or a rave; he'd just do his own thing and you'd want to follow.' Same with Roger Uttley – 'big man with the soft voice and that great big, lovely ugly face; and what strength! You could see the muscles in his eyelashes.' Then Beaumont – 'a big cuddly bear who became, quite simply a very great captain; everyone loved him; at first he wouldn't say boo to a goose, but in the end old Bill became a bit of a tub thumper.'

Smith chuckles as he admits to the glorious bog he made of his first dressing-room exhortation as captain – against Ireland last year. 'Even a drama critic guy like you wouldn't have believed it. My eyes blazed passion; my fists were hammering the table; I was completely gone; I was ranting on about history and our English heritage and all that, even the IRA got a mention! So what happens? We all ran out and played the hurly-burly like bloody headless chickens didn't we? We were awful. It was all my fault. And I deserved all the stick I got, too.'

By the time France were ready to be well beaten in Paris a fortnight later, Smith had got his act together. 'I realized the job was not to hype up the team, but to calm them all down. You must realize that international matches are so manic and pressurized that, for us players, they seem nearly over before they've begun. Everything goes at a 1,000 miles an hour, and my job is to cool it, to get the guys to stay calm and aware and keep concentrating on what we've planned and worked out in training sessions.'

So he wouldn't be reminding his men of Hastings or Agincourt soon after lunch today. 'No I will not. The IRA indeed!' and he laughs fit to bust at the memory of his first speech.

'What you must understand is that in that little room at twenty past two there are fifteen glazed eyed, quivering lads with involuntary muscles in their backsides going at a rate of knots. We're used to playing in front of 500, not 70,000.

'Tony (Swift, the new England cap) won't know what's hit

him when he runs out. Then it'll all go so fast. I'll tell him what I told Tony Bond when he got his first cap: "keep your eye on that clock; it'll go round so fast that you won't remember a thing, but when there's ten minutes to go just pick up that ball and charge like hell; anyway you won't know how you've played till you read John Reason next day – and then it's bound to have been badly!" '

Smith sees the scrum-half as simply the fourth man in the back row. Offensive and defensive. He anticipates a battle royal this afternoon. 'Whenever anyone asks me who my most difficult marker has been I just say "the French pack of 1976".' England were beaten 30–9. 'It could have been double that. We were annihilated. Frannie had terrible troubles against that giant, Paparemborde, who has these sloping shoulders so there's nothing to scrummage against. At the singsong after the match, poor Frannie was so upset he refused to join in. "I'm not man enough to sing with those Frenchies," he said.

'Four years later in Paris, at every scrum, Frannie packed down with his head spearing into Paparemborde's breastbone. It was an astonishing feat of strength and technique. We destroyed them.' At the final whistle Smith embraced Cotton and whispered: 'We can drink with the men tonight, Fran.' Together, they fashioned two of the most glorious hangovers since the night they invented champagne. By the by, one of Smith's little jobs this week was to give England's current prop, Colin Smart, Cotton's phone number – 'for a bit of revision on Paparemborde's breastbone!'

Smith's advice to us all is to 'watch the first three scrums this afternoon: they could even decide the whole Championship; the front row battle will hold the key; the French could have the best front three in the world; if we match them for the first twenty mins we should be O.K. Mind you, six of their seven backs can do the one hundred metres in eleven seconds – which is about ten minutes faster than me!'

But then he looks around his dressing-room and thinks, 'Hey, we've got a fair old team, too: what the key men do affects all us others: old Dusty at the back, all calm and dreamy; Swifty and JC on the wings, all nerve ends and one hundred mph; Les at standoff, who hates losing and will always pull out something with his Yorkshire cunning; Scottie the hard man, the complex man, extrovert and insecure at one and the same time, but what a great player; Maurice, knowing he's now in Billy's shirt with all that entails; and Peter Wheeler, well what can you say? He's the world's number one, but still just gets better and better, like good wine.'

They'll all do for him. He looks around at his men and nods to himself, well satisfied. Not a bad turn-up for a soccer man. Not bad for that little long-ago Stretford Ender who was passionate about Man. United as well as cricket, till he got his eleven-plus and went to grammar school where they did this rugby lark.

He's still dedicated to United, but doesn't go much now. Well, when it's not rugger or running, there's squash at the Sale clubhouse. Soon he'd like to immerse himself in water sports, sailing and surfing and so on. Meanwhile, England's loss of the cricket Ashes niggles away at England's rugby union captain. He stayed up, of course, to watch the last rites on TV.

'Hey, and do you know that Tavare? Well, next time you see him, ask how he can possibly expect to get the ball off the square when his hands are so far apart on the handle? It's a blithering impossibility. I'm telling you.' And he gets up to play a sweet and imaginary coverdrive, and he simulates the sound of leather on willow with a satisfying click of his tongue. And this charming young sportsman holds the pose in his follow-through – and then a great big grin of pleasure lights up his face.

15 January, 1983   **Frank Keating**

A Day at the Zoo

Sonia, one must say, has improved out of all recognition. She first appeared in *A Day At The Zoo* (BBC-1) as a newly-hatched Andean Condor chick, looking in two minds whether to be a petrodactyl. On Friday there she was on page three (of, admittedly, the *Guardian*) wearing an off the shoulder powder puff. The eyes peering out of this explosion of iridescent fluff were undeniably beady. Someday, one saw with sorrow, Sonia would be just an old buzzard but on Friday she looked like Esther

Rantzen at the BAFTA awards or Barbara Cartland at breakfast.

Ron Wood, her keeper, was gazing at her with the pride of a man who has raised a prize-winning marrow. Sonia's expression was harder to decipher. She may think he is mother. She may think he is dinner. You can't say with a condor.

The affection of the keepers for their charges was one of the most attractive things to emerge from *A Day At The Zoo*. Through it there ran the case of a kudu, an antelope with spiral horns, which had fractured her skull on a bar in her cage and, despite surgery, lingered four days then died. 'What's she worth?' asked Esther Rantzen, never afraid to put the awful-child question. 'She's worth a lot to us,' said her keeper, Jack.

Suka's keeper, elbowed by Esther into the admission, agreed almost irritably: 'All *right*, I love that orang-utan.' Suka, a big girl in a rather disconcerting shade of orange, lowered her pale eyelids. Her manner was strikingly modest. When Sebastian, a male giraffe ('male giraffes are two a penny'), was being shipped off to Dublin, it was his keeper, Ron, who briefed the driver anxiously: 'There's three low bridges on the M1.' 'You really prefer sea lions to people?' asked Esther at the pool. 'Good God yes!' barked Charlie. 'I want to come back as a sea lion.'

Charlie, you feel, would not have to come back far. Nor Peter, who has virtually adopted an orphaned chimp, Benjie, feeds him, burps him, changes his nappy and takes him to bed when he cries. I am not saying Peter looks like Benjie but Benjie looks remarkably like Peter.

It was a pale gold day in – judging by Sonia's age – May. Elephants and camels moved across the sky-line like hills out for an amble. ('It's a great, big creeping rock!' cried a blind child, feeling a giant tortoise.) London Zoo may well be disappointed at the time of transmission of *A Day At The Zoo*, just as the schools are going back. With a million-pound loss each year, they need the publicity. Esther Rantzen's attitude was ambivalent. Anybody's must be. On the one hand: 'Soon there may be no more wild places left in the world.' On the other the kudu's cage, she said bluntly, looked like a prison.

The camera touched with delight on a real, wild squirrel.

Sonia, who should float on ten foot wings 23,000ft over Chimborazo, will never fly at all.

1 September, 1982 **Nancy Banks-Smith**

The rubber Chancellor in Moscow

No one could accuse Helmut Kohl of being anything but amiable, and as he beamed his way through a series of frosty encounters in the Kremlin this week his bouncy geniality only seemed to grow. At his press conference on the third day he cheerfully told one angry Eastern European questioner after another that he was 'immune from Marxism'. An almost equally angry West German reporter asked whether Pravda's one-sided coverage of the talks was accurate. A grinning Chancellor Kohl replied that he who paid the piper called the tune.

By the time he and his entourage of 200 journalists reached the Ukrainian capital, Kiev, for a day's sightseeing Mr Kohl was euphoric. While his aides visibly wilted with the jaw-tightening effort to stifle their yawns as the Ukrainian Prime Minister rattled off the statistics of his republic's success (three opera houses, twenty-two million pigs, etc), the rubber Chancellor listened attentively. When his turn came to speak, he proudly described his eighteen years in charge of one of West Germany's smallest states, the Rhineland-Palatinate, which included dealing with the problems of water-sprinklers.

At the more political level, the Chancellor repeatedly used his encounters with his Russian hosts to draw attention to his hopes for eventual German re-unification. Konrad Adenauer, the last Christian Democrat to visit Moscow in 1955, was constantly mentioned by Mr Kohl as though he came to Moscow in his direct line of descent.

For the Russians this strange mixture of provincial politician and 1950s throwback was a confusing combination. Clearly they did not like it. Before he even entered the Kremlin, strolling in on foot, they signalled their discomfort. His programme was kept uncertain until a few days before he left Bonn. President Andropov did not see him on the first day. While he was still in the country, Pravda printed an attack on his first 100 days in office, put out in Bonn by the opposition SPD.

To the Russians it seemed that Mr Kohl was behaving as though a decade of Ostpolitik had not happened, and that between Adenauer's visit and his own there had been a vacuum in Soviet-West German relations. It is true, of course, that the Chancellor referred to the various treaties between West Germany and its Eastern neighbours, and pledged to respect them. But there was a ritualistic tone to his remarks, and with his continual harping on German unity he seemed to be going against the spirit of the treaties. No longer were the Russians dealing with an architect of Ostpolitik or a defender of détente. They now faced an ungrateful heir of an unloved policy bequeathed by others.

Having weighed Kohl in the balance and found him wanting, as they expected, what will the Russians do now? The special relationship with Bonn is over. In the SPD days they never expected to be able to drive a wedge between West Germany and Washington. The only time they succeeded with that in Western Europe was when they enticed the respectably conservative President Giscard of France to meet President Brezhnev in Warsaw in May 1980 at the height of the West's anger over Afghanistan.

But what they did gain from Mr Schmidt was a channel of communication with the West and a man who was capable of understanding, though not always agreeing with, their perception of events. Mr Kohl, by contrast, has managed to make West Germany as politically uninteresting to Moscow as Mr Mitterrand's France or Mrs Thatcher's Britain. It no longer carries weight.

From now on the Kremlin's choices are reduced to three. They can make another effort to persuade Mr Kohl to put life into détente. They can be nasty and create difficulties on the issue of West Germany's relations with the East. Or they can ignore him, as they ignore Mrs Thatcher and President Mitterrand. If the West German election has deprived them of their last West European 'interpreter', they might as well speak direct to Washington itself.

Being nice to West Germany is the least likely option of the three. The insensitivity which the Russians believe that Mr

Kohl showed on his trip this week was not an aberration of the moment. It is part of a provincial, small-town, anti-Sovietism which he has had since his water-sprinting days in Mainz.

Being horrid to West Germany by being disruptive on the German-German frontier is not a probable option, either. Mr Kohl's advisers cleverly organized a massive credit package 'without strings' for East Germany only days before he left for Moscow. The loan was so soft that many of Mr Kohl's allies in the Christian Social Union have accused him of betraying his pledge not to give any economic concessions to East Germany without a compensating political return.

The Chancellor's plan is more far-sighted. He hopes to mortgage East Germany's freedom to put pressure on the border question in terms of restricting family visits and the like. More than that, he hopes to strengthen East Germany's willingness to resist possible pressure from Moscow for a harder line with Bonn.

This leaves Moscow with Option Three – to ignore Bonn. From now on, under this option, the Kremlin will deal with the West by going to Washington direct. If the three major Western European states are determined to present a united front behind President Reagan's hard-line approach to the Soviet Union, then the Kremlin will find itself forced to deal with the White House alone. This does not mean it will not continue to maintain and develop its trade with West Germany, its major Western partner. It has continued to trade happily with Japan, even though Soviet-Japanese political relations are almost nil. There is no automatic connection between political and economical relations.

So Moscow's eyes will increasingly be on Washington, as the summer progresses. Its attitude to the medium-range missile talks in Geneva will be decided less by the reaction of West European electorates and governments than it was in the past two years, and more by its perception of how serious the United States is prepared to be in abandoning its confrontation with Moscow.

Moscow saw the Carter Administration shuffle between co-operation and confrontation in its first two years in power, then sign the Strategic Arms Limitation Treaty (SALT Two) in Vienna in 1979, and finally lose faith in it a few months later as the US election campaign hotted up. It is not beyond the bounds of possibility, therefore, that the Reagan Administration after its hard-line start might shuffle back towards cooperation with Moscow as the election draws near.

The Kremlin is unlikely to put much hope in this possibility. It sees the Reagan Administration as a group of ignorant, unscrupulous, and ideologically-motivated men. If they start talking about détente and summit meetings and East-West accords then it is probably nothing but an electoral ploy. When Mr Andropov talks of a summit meeting having to be well-prepared, he means it. If it comes at the end of a road which is paved with solid evidence of a fundamental change in US strategy, he will agree to attend. He will not come if it seems to be merely the beginning of the road to Mr Reagan's reelection.

Mr Reagan may be as bouncy and amiable to Mr Kohl, but this will not be enough to open the Kremlin's door. Mr Andropov was willing – just – to receive Mr Kohl for a single day. Barring a miracle, he will probably not meet Mr Reagan at all.

9 July 1983   **Jonathan Steele**

Moscow revisited

Almost exactly half a century ago, there appeared in the *Manchester Guardian* (as it then was) three articles I had written describing a visit to the Ukraine and the Caucasus, then suffering from a severe famine brought on as a direct result of Stalin's ruthless enforcement of the collectivization of agriculture and liquidation of the so-called kulaks, or better-off peasants.

For some months previously I had been acting as the *Guardian*'s Moscow correspondent, and hearing much talk of acute food shortages. So I decided to go and have a look at the state of affairs for myself. I knew that if I asked for official permission to undertake such a trip, either it would be refused out-of-hand, or I should be provided with a guide who would ensure that I only saw what the authorities wanted me to see, backed up by fraudulent statistics. Such were the conditions under which foreign journalists had to work, and I doubt if they are much different now.

'And now in our series for
minority audiences, a programme
especially for spies.'

11 November, 1982

I therefore got the Russian secretary of a fellow-
correspondent, A. T. Cholerton, to buy me the requisite railway
tickets, and set forth, making first for Rostov, and breaking my
journey from time to time to look round. What I saw was
unforgettably horrifying – empty villages, desperately hungry
faces everywhere, neglected fields, peasants being loaded into
goods-trains as alleged kulaks on their way to the labour camps
in Siberia, Solzhenitsyn's Gulag Archipelago. What I was
seeing, I realized, was not just a famine, but amounted to a state
of war with the peasants, and the consequent total breakdown of
agriculture in some of the most fertile land in Europe.

When I got back to Moscow I wrote it all down, and sent off
my three articles by diplomatic bag, obligingly made available,
to ensure their safe arrival in Manchester. As I well knew, once
they were published my situation in Moscow would become

untenable. From being the correspondent of a paper well disposed towards the Soviet regime, and with credentials from Sidney and Beatrice Webb, my wife Kitty's uncle and aunt, who were among the most abject and uncritical of the regime's admirers – as Beatrice put it, they were ikons in the USSR – I should be seen as a class enemy and anathema, and have my visa withdrawn. How many truths have been suppressed to save a visa! How many falsehoods propagated!

By the time the articles were published I had left Moscow, and no longer had any connection with the *Guardian*. The response was very much what I had expected – much criticism, and numerous accusations of my being a liar. It was not until Khrushchev's famous speech at the twentieth Party Congress denouncing Stalin that I was exonerated. Khrushchev put the deaths in the famine at five million – and he surely, as an important member of the Ukranian *Apparat*, ought to have known – and altogether gave a more drastic account than mine of the consequences of the collectivization of agriculture. No one, in the light of his revelations, apologized for accusing me of unfair and distorted reporting; the golden descriptions by Walter Duranty, Moscow correspondent of the *New York Times*, of granaries overflowing with grain, apple-cheeked dairymaids and plump contented cows, still stood. Indeed, he received several Pulitzer Awards for his reporting from Moscow.

In spite of a certain professional malaise resulting from my sojourn in the USSR, I had every reason to be thankful for it. From my point of view, it had been infinitely worthwhile, enabling me to understand as nothing else would what the Soviet regime was about, how it functioned and what was its impact on neighbouring countries and the world in general.

The dream of the early Socialists, myself among them, that the Russian Revolution would in due course bring about a brotherly, peaceful society which had shed the lure of war and conquest, and the exploitation of the poor by the rich, of the weak by the powerful, was lost for ever. The Soviet regime itself, I came to see, was about power, and little else; the disparity between the apparatchiks and the workers and peasants was, if anything, greater than between the skilled and the unskilled, the employers and the employed in the rest of the world.

As for bellicosity – the first priority soon became building up the defence forces, especially the Red Army, and getting rid of the Old Bolsheviks, the true begetters of the Russian Revolution, by the simple expedient of inducing them by one means or another to confess that they had been working for foreign intelligence services and sabotaging the fulfilment of the Five-Year Plan, and then shooting them. As a good number of them happen to have been Jews, liquidating them touched off a reversion to traditional Russian anti-semitism.

Among the articles I wrote after leaving the USSR, I thought for ever, was one that no newspaper or magazine would publish – not even the old ultra-conservative *Morning Post*, long since defunct. It was entitled 'Red Imperialism', and pointed out that delivering the toiling masses from their economic servitude would prove as good a pretext for Russian Imperialism as had, in Tsarist times, restoring the church of San Sofia in Constantinople to the Christians. In the post-1914–18 war years, however, with Litvinov, in his capacity of Commissar for Foreign Affairs, proposing total disarmament all round on all possible occasions, and pacifist organizations everywhere receiving support from Moscow, Red Imperialism seemed too far-fetched to be worth serious consideration.

Now things are very different, with the Kremlin building a worldwide empire that may soon take in Western Europe and Latin America, leaving only North America to comprise what we go on calling the Free World. Traces of some such development were found among the documents of the German Foreign Office during the Nazi regime. For instance, the record of a conversation between Molotov and Ribbentrop in November, 1940, which took place in a Berlin bunker because an air raid was on at the time, in the course of which Molotov stated the terms on which the Soviet Union would agree to form a military alliance with Hitler's Germany.

The terms were, the immediate withdrawal of German troops from Finland, the recognition of Soviet interests in the Balkans and the Straits through virtual control of Bulgaria, and the establishment of bases in the Bosphorus and the Dardanelles. If this is not Red Imperialism, I should like to know what is.

The conundrum that continued to occupy my mind – still

does for that matter – was how it came about that some of the most famous and highly esteemed intellectuals of our time, in observing and assessing the Soviet Regime, should have displayed a credulity and fatuity that would be surprising in any half-wit or bemused Marxist. Thus, for instance, Bernard Shaw expressing satisfaction that the Soviet Government balanced its budgets, and that the people of the Baltic States had voted freely and overwhelmingly for incorporation into the USSR.

Or the venerable Dean of Canterbury, Dr Hewlett Johnson, in spite of the anti-God museums and propaganda, and the persecution of Christian believers, going on proclaiming in the pulpit that Stalin was building the Kingdom of Christ. Or Beatrice Webb, somewhat troubled by my *Guardian* articles, going to Mr Maisky, the Soviet Ambassador in London, to be put right. It was Mr Maisky, too, Beatrice Webb told me, with great satisfaction, who had been kind enough to go through the galleys of the book – *Soviet Communism: A New Civilization?* – she and Sidney had written about the Soviet regime to ensure that they had made no mistakes.

Surely some future Gibbon will derive great pleasure and satisfaction from describing how the fine flower of the intelligentsia of the twentieth century were prepared to believe anything however outrageous, admire anything however cruel, excuse anything however barbarous, in order to keep intact their conviction that under the auspices of the great Stalin a new, more just, more equitable society was coming to pass. There an office-holder in some local branch of the League of Nations Union, there a godly Quaker who once had tea with Gandhi, there scarred and worthy veterans of a hundred battles for truth and freedom, all singing the praises of the most ruthless, comprehensive and murderous dictatorship the world has yet seen.

I assumed that after the appearance of my articles on the Stalin-made famine, I should always be refused a visa to enter the USSR. On the one or two occasions that I applied, this proved to be the case. Being thus barred, to my surprise, rather saddened me; there still remains something rather wonderful about the country itself and its people. There is in them, a superb stoicism, a wry, underground humour, a brotherliness in their endurance of the appalling hardships and oppression to which they are subjected. Behind the dreary, cruel proposition of Marx, one seemed to hear the ancient greeting: 'Christ is risen!'

As it happens, despite being on the black-list, I did manage to visit the USSR four times. The first occasion was accidental; I happened to be in Peking, and on an impulse applied at the Soviet Embassy for a transit visa to return to London via Moscow. This was stamped into my passport without any questions being asked, and I spent several days wandering about the streets of Moscow finding them just as before, with the same nondescript crowd drifting along them. Maybe, I reflected, the only way of ensuring that no changes take place is to have a revolution. Those who bring about the revolution then know how easy it is to make one, and so stick furiously to their new status quo, like a man in a cold bath who keeps quite still to avoid feeling how cold the water is.

The second occasion was accompanying Harold Macmillan on his visit to the USSR when he was Prime Minister; a guarantee had been given that no accredited journalists should be barred, and this included even me. As it turned out, it was a somewhat ribald outing, and included a visit to a collective farm near Kiev, when the Prime Minister in his speech referred to how long ago a Ukrainian princess married into the English royal family, and went on to express the hope that this amicable relationship might be renewed. The crowds that turn out for distinguished foreign visitors in the USSR always have a top layer of Lubianka men with bulges under their arms – then the GPU, now the KGB, but the same essential personnel. I took a look at their grey, stony faces as the Prime Minister made his point about the Ukrainian princess, and observed in them, not a smile, but a tiny twitch at the corners of the mouth.

While the Macmillan visit was on, I had an interesting talk with the editorial staff of the Soviet satirical magazine, *Krokodil*, on the subject of satirical humour, which, I contended, has by its nature to be directed against those set in authority over us. The others were inclined to agree, but sadly admitted that such an attitude was not permissible in the present stage of Soviet society. After all, I said, they had in Mr Khrushchev a head-man with a funny face – a great rarity, as I remembered from my time as editor of *Punch*. Yet they made no use of him. Subsequently, my attention was drawn to the fact that *Krokodil* published a caricature by Low of Mikoyan, a member of the Politbureau; a unique occurrence, permissible, perhaps, because Mikoyan was an Armenian and Low an Australian. Anyway, it is the one and only appearance in a Soviet publication of a satirical drawing of a Politbureau face.

The last occasion that I visited the USSR was in connection with a series of TV programmes called *A Third Testament*, jointly commissioned by *Time* magazine and the Canadian Broadcasting Commission. I did the commentary, and two of the programmes – on Tolstoy and Dostoievsky – were filmed in the USSR. No difficulty was made about my visa, doubtless because it was applied for in Ottawa, not London.

To describe all the complications and humorous situations that arose in presenting these two great and prophetic writers in the setting of the Soviet regime would require much more space than is available here. Suffice it to say that, quoting them, thinking about them, as it were living with them, gave me very strongly the feeling that out of the suffering, the moral, spiritual and intellectual vandalism that has befallen Russia since the Revolution, will come some great new fulfilment of the genius of the Russian people. As Solzhenitsyn has said, there are no Marxists in the Gulag Archipelago, and in losing freedom there, it is found.

12 April, 1983   **Malcolm Muggeridge**

Yuri and Titania

Is all well with the marriage of Yuri and Titania Andropov? It is a good question, but one we shall not be dealing with this week. Inappropriate to ask, one was made to feel somehow. I didn't know he had a wife, another common reaction.

No, the USSR is not the land of the gossip writer, and yet there is so much gossip about. Rumour, rather. No shortage of ex-Minister's wives who have shot themselves in the past week. A positive epidemic of diseases that have prostrated Mr

Andropov in the past month. And as for Mrs A. Well, she didn't
turn up for the Women's Day Parade last month. Nor did he.
Where's he been for the past three weeks, anyway?

His people had better get used to it. Mr Andropov does not
believe in keeping a high profile at the best of times. It is the
exception to find his picture in Government offices. And, beat
this, there are only two Andropov jokes. Joke number one goes
like this. Lackey to Andropov: 'Comrade Andropov, how do
you know your people will follow you?' Mr A.: 'If they don't
follow me they'll follow Brezhnev.' Pick your self up and dust
yourself down for the second one. You'll love this: There is a
knock on Mr Andropov's door. He does not say *voditye* (come
in); he says *veditye* (bring him in). Of course, it's the way you
tell 'em. Or perhaps the way you translate 'em.

11 April, 1983   **Alan Rusbridger**

On being Russian

To ask official Russians for introductions to unofficial Russians
– ordinary men and women with ordinary hopes, thoughts and
fears – is to ask for the moon. The officials say 'of course' and 'no
problem' and wait, hoping you will soon lose heart and go back
where you came from. If you do not, eventually they dredge up
an official unofficial Russian who, through official translators,
tells you what officialdom wants you to hear.

So you must manage on your own. With an unofficial English-
speaking Russian, met through friends of friends of friends, I
travelled east, west, north, south on the Metro to the last
stations on the lines and took buses and trolleys through waste-
lands of melting snow to the vast housing estates that ring
Moscow, there to meet those mythical creatures – ordinary
Russians.

The concrete blocks they inhabit are daunting, so huge and
set so far apart that curtained windows are unnecessary, neighbours are no more than rectangles of light across a sea of mud. In
contrast, each flat is dauntingly small and shoddy but very warm
and very cheap. One family pays just over £13 a month and £1

per month for heating, another family, buying a flat for £8,000, pays £24 monthly as repayment on loans.

Igor and Ludmilla have a boy and a girl. The children sleep in the only bedroom, while their parents use a sofa bed in the sitting room. The atmosphere in the tiny flat is of love and concern as if, the outside world being hostile, the family is drawn together. The children, six and eight, are quite unique by our standards: quiet, poised, intelligent and radiating delight at the simplest games and in the simplest toys. Their faces light up with joy and amusement, they turn like sunflowers to any source of warmth, they are the children we have lost to luxury and television and go-getting Western life. Their parents, in contrast, are care-worn and look older than their late thirties, but they, too, are innocents, moving in their candour and their pleasure in tiny things.

They bring out for me their treasured collection of postcards that show the beauties of museums and galleries and buildings in countries they will never see. I do not question them directly. Their feelings merge in small explosions of words that hang in the air for a moment before the subject is changed. Ludmilla's dream is to educate her children at home. She is startled to hear that parents in England are sometimes allowed to do this. She clasps her hands in ecstasy at the thought. Schools, she says, are too disciplinarian, the text-books are old and 'say wrong things'. At this Igor flushes, argues with her in Russian, tells her to be quiet. She is irrepressible. She envies villagers their roots, she longs to live in the country with a cow and a pig and grow her own vegetables. She sees the ugliness of her surroundings, mourns the distance between neighbours.

Carried away by the glories on her postcards – some of pre-revolutionary Russia – she says at least the Czars created beauty, brought colour into life. She pores over golden cupolas and the rich glow of icons. 'But the suffering, remember the suffering,' Igor says anxiously. She shrugs and says defiantly she envies Sakharov. 'He is lucky, they sent him to Novgorod.' It is *beautiful*, Novgorod.' Quickly, Igor passes over the dissidents – they are brave, yes, but perfectly irrelevant. In a moment of silence he says heavily, 'Our Government, they have absolute power, there is nothing we can do. Nothing.' Both of

122

them look embarrassed. I am asked if I would like more coffee.

We talk of travel and Ludmilla is stirred, waving her hands 'When they lift restrictions, then Europe would see a real invasion of Russians! But to think we would not come back! Of course we would. This is our home.' It is evident that both of them share most of the household chores and both juggle their working hours to be with the children. Ludmilla does the cooking, her staples beetroot, potatoes, and carrots, bread and milk, other ingredients variable. She serves a fish pie, mackerel, carrots, onions, covered in bottled mayonnaise. The only house-wife's aids she has are photostated pages from a Leningrad cookbook dated 1887. It instructs her to tenderize tough chick-en by boiling it with quartz and she has the quartz, picked up in the Urals on a camping trip. 'What is Cream of Tartar?' she asks me, raising her head from the book, 'I cannot get it here.'

Over coffee, without warning, Igor says in English, 'Small is beautiful.' 'Schumacher,' I say, and he nods, pleased. 'I would like,' he says, 'Russia to be Russia again. Everything is too big now. It is a drain on us, we don't need it.' Then they both tell jokes against the leaders and Igor sighs. The one good thing about Andropov, he says, is so far he keeps quiet and there are no pictures of him everywhere. 'You know, we believed Stalin was our father, till they told us what he did. Then we believed Khrushchev, then they told us *he* was wrong. Now we do not believe our leaders, our faith has gone.'

'But still,' Ludmilla bursts out, 'Russia needs a father.'

'No,' Igor says, 'no father.'

'It was better when we had a father,' she says hopelessly.

'No,' says Igor.

As I go, I say inadequately, 'You have beautiful children.' They smile politely. They think it merely a compliment. As so often, they can make no comparisons; they know what they lack, they do not know their blessings.

Later I visit a newly-married couple, proud possessors of a newly-built flat. Already the skirting boards are warped, the veneer of parquet peels, the kitchen cupboards hang askew. Icy winds whistle between the blocks, bundled women push prams through oceans of red mud, a canyon of mud yawns, one day to be a car park.

The bride has just come home from work, picking up on her way three cartons of sour milk, milk and cream, two cucumbers, three small loaves of brown and white bread, a mackerel, two tins of Bulgarian apple juice. The groom, a student, comes in minutes later.

He has been to query his chances of avoiding national service. Come again later, they said.

We get on to the subject of civil defence. 'Yes,' says the girl, 'we are told about nuclear war, we see pictures of Hiroshima on television. Children are taken to see shelters, they crawl about in gasmasks, protection against chemical weapons and radioactive dust. So they say,' and she smiles. I show her a CND badge. She tells me that is what hippies wear. It stands for pacifism. She does not know what the letters mean but she knows about the Greenham Common women: 'They are brave, your women.' She has, I gathered, a vague impression that they are European workers striving for revolution.

Neither husband nor wife shows any particular belief in their leaders. They trust them in one thing only – they *know* they say, that no one wants war. This trust, perhaps, is one reason why individual peace movements do not flourish in Russia. The people recognize that their leaders suffered in the war as they suffered. Here, the leaders' age, so often joked about in other contexts, works for them. They *knew* war.

I ask what both of them think are the real priorities for ordinary Russians. It depends, they say, who they are. Young marrieds want a flat, then they want furniture, perhaps a car. Students worry about what kind of work they will get and where. The man, a student himself, says he tries not to think about leaving university. He does not look forward to a working life, though he evades reasons. The woman says work is boring, boredom overwhelms you, the women in her office spend all their time in front of the mirror in the lavatories, gossiping, arranging their hair. She reads to pass the time. One book goes round five people in five days, you stay up all night to read it.

She talks of the 'black economy'. If there is no meat, you ask the butcher. He says come round at five o'clock. At the back of the shop, chunks of meat reach the ceiling. You pay four times the official price. If you do not want to wait all day at the doctor or the dentist or at the garage, you take a present the day before. You must give presents to everyone. 'I wanted to give my boss a present for his birthday. He is a nice man. My mother-in-law said you *must* give him a present, then I didn't want to. All relationships are spoiled this way.'

I question the husband on what being Russian means to him. He thinks a while, then says, 'We used to be a family. We looked after each other, an orphaned child was passed from house to house. Now, in the towns, this is disappearing, but such traditions are still there, in the villages.' He adds that he cannot understand Western fairy stories. 'Ours are about the search for happiness and goodness. Yours are cruel, children are mistreated and deserted. We would not tolerate that.'

As to the Russian character – 'We are nationalistic,' he says and tells of a trip he took in a bus to the Crimea, with Russian officials among the passengers. 'They talked of how we had done everything for others, pulled the Uzbeks out of the dirt, were helping the Afghanistanis. One man was there with his Moldavian wife – he was told "Divorce her, she is no use."'

Does he feel the same? 'Not really,' he says, looking doubtful, 'but that is why we criticize our Government. We aren't going ahead fast enough because we help others too much. We think the Poles are lazy. They hoard food. We know the Hungarians are better off than us and that is because we pay for their defence, so they can afford other things. No, people do not feel guilt. We feel they ought to be grateful.' There is a silence, then he says: 'Perhaps this is the way people get resentment out of themselves, by criticizing others.'

In response to another question he says no, he does not worship Lenin, that propaganda comes from the top. 'You believe it at school, maybe; later, you do not.' But he says yes, there is serious and spontaneous discussion about Communism and he thinks, on the whole, things in Russia are going the right way. For himself, he would choose Communism now but some might think differently, if they could compare. 'The West is criticized all the time as a terrible place, yet if you do well, you are sent there as a reward.' He smiles. 'World revolution' – he makes a circle with his hands – 'Communism everywehre, that would be fine. But we must keep one small place with capitalism, where we can go to have fun.' He laughs.

We get on to the Stalin years. Both know about the purges and the labour camps. 'My grandmother, though,' says the man, 'she does not believe and many who went for years to camps did not believe, either. They thought Stalin did not know they were there, they thought it was a bureaucratic muddle or someone had betrayed them for gain. It is a question of your generation. And I don't believe the mud-slinging about Sakharov and Bukovsky, I think they are brave.' Does he feel he lives in a police state? A short pause.

'No,' says the young man, that is bourgeois propaganda. We see peace marches in Europe and the police break them up. They are police states.'

Another day I stop twelve Russians of different ages in a little Moscow park. All are pleased to talk, though some are shy. Of the twelve, eight lost close relatives in the last war (grandparents, parents, aunts, uncles, brothers, sisters, depending on age). A young mother pushing a pram says yes, she thinks about war every day, of course. Another says her grandfather died in Poland. Her mother has visited his grave three times.

'Do people in England think Russia is a threat?' asks a middle-aged woman. 'Well, that is nonsense, why should we wish to attack anyone?' Her companion, a man of seventy-odd, says suddenly: 'Can't you do something about Mrs Thatcher? You have unemployed people and she wastes money on military expenditure. War is terrible, terrible to think about, but we must.' A young man, whose grandfather was killed in Byelorussia, says he is confident the forces of peace are stronger than the forces of war in any country. 'Your women are strong,' he says.

Asked why Russian brides go on their wedding day to the Tomb of the Unknown Warrior, a woman explains that they feel a duty to the memory of the people who fell. 'When you are happy, you must thank those who made that happiness possible.' An old woman in black confides that she lost a nephew and a brother-in-law. Does she fear the West? 'No,' she says, 'the men who killed my relatives were not Westerners. They were *Germans*.' A woman of forty-odd tells me her mother died in the seige of Leningrad. 'You must remember,' she adds, 'we were undefended when the Germans came. We cannot risk being undefended again.'

I pass these conversations on as I would pass on pieces in a jig-saw puzzle. Fit them where you think best.

12 April, 1983   **Jill Tweedie**

Buy GUM? No fear

Deprivation leads to obsession. It is true of food, warmth, sleep, love, freedom and, indeed, frocks. In the Soviet Union there is very little in the way of clothing which is stylish, well made or flattering. There is even less which is amusing, youthful or fashionable, so the search for what little there is becomes a time-consuming passion amongst young women.

Almost everywhere in the world young people use clothing not only to identify with the rest of their generation but to distance it from the previous one. An awareness of fashion in clothes indicates an awareness of fashion in everything else and thus imparts status which leads to acceptance by one's peer group. In all cases, however, a *soupçon* of individuality is also desirable. If it is all easy to achieve, then it is a source of pleasure and occupies a small part of one's attention. If it is difficult, it becomes dysfunctional – a life-dominating obsession.

Young women in Moscow, an English student working on her thesis at Moscow university reports, talk compulsively of clothes and make-up; a months-old copy of *Vogue* brought into the country by a foreign student or tourist is passed tenderly from hand to hand; its soft-focus artistic photographs are analysed, the positions of the seams guessed at, a copy, in infinitely less suitable fabric, attempted.

Courtauld's second largest customer for synthetic yarns and fabrics, after Marks & Spencer, is the Soviet state. The fabric department of Moscow's second largest department store appeared at first glance to be crammed with merchandise yet empty of people. A closer inspection revealed that the material was totally uncovetable: hideous of pattern and coloration, unpleasant to touch. And the people were just around the

127

corner, hundreds of them in a serpentine queue at the head of which three toiling sales assistants were cutting lengths (at least a dozen per customer) of printed cotton which had obviously just been delivered.

Muscovites discriminate when they shop – a fact which is giving headaches to both the Ministry of Light Industry which oversees the production of consumer goods, and to the store managers. In the warehouses of GUM boxes and boxes of harsh-coloured knitted polyester frocks, alleged one informant, rub shoulders with torn and bulging parcels of lurid woven polyester skirts which no one can bring themselves to buy at any price. The utilitarian approach to dress can only go as far as need and decency compel. Beyond that, the customer wants more.

And somehow, whether by skill, ingenuity or privilege, the customer in Moscow gets more. The young women on the metro average a higher smartness rating than the young women on the London Underground who are, literally, spoiled for choice, confused and intimidated by the variety of merchandise available to them. Absence of choice concentrates the mind.

It is quickly apparent, when the rush hour crushes you up against them in the metro, that their clothes are mostly of poor quality cloth with cheap trimmings, but Russian women know that, from a couple of paces, they look good. They study for hours before a mirror how best to drape the precious shawl or muffler they queued for hours to buy. Your tourist may clump around the Moscow streets in her heavy, flat rubber-soled boots; the Muscovite teeters on her lovingly polished high-heeled Italian boots, trophy of yet another interminable queue and the envy of her friends who must make do with the cruder Russian copies till they too happen across the right patient throng in GUM.

There is, too, a black market for Western clothes which is supplied not only by tourists and citizens returning from abroad but by cabbage from the many Soviet bloc countries which now manufacture clothing for export or under licence to American and European companies who find it cheaper to make their clothes in Hungary or East Germany than in the Far East. Cabbage, for the uninitiated, is what is left when enough fabric for, say, one hundred coats is delivered by state or licenser to the

128

factory which, by dint of clever cutting, manages to make 110 coats. When these garments filter on to the black market they are often for sale only for hard currency – which accounts for the bright young things who sidle up to Westerners on the street offering four or five the official exchange rate for pounds or dollars.

For some, of course, getting more is a little easier. For the privileged there are special up-market shops, discreetly resembling office blocks. And there is, as there is in Paris, Rome and London, couture.

Moscow's top couturier is Slava Zaitzev. Born in a small town, Ivanov, he went to Moscow to study textile design and went to work for the All Union Fashion House as a fashion designer. In the All Union Fashion House, which is part of the Ministry of Light Industry, several designers work together producing designs which will be bought by factory managers from all over the Soviet Union to be put into mass production. Each is also allowed to run a couture business making clothes for private customers.

The All Union Fashion House is an old, high-ceilinged building with large display windows framing attractive clothes little more than a season laggard of London and Paris. If this is where the toiles come from, one muses, why are the clothes in the stores so dreadful? Because these fabrics are specially imported from Italy and France and are unthinkable for mass production. And because factory managers in the Soviet Union tend to care more about productivity norms than product quality. Many managers of clothing factories, I was told, are unaware that there is such a thing as fashion. It is expensive and surely unnecessary, goes their thinking, to buy new designs more often than once every five years. The consequence, of course, is GUM's cluttered warehouses.

Slava Zaitzev outgrew the All Union Fashion House and this year opened on his own in a smart modern building across town. The Fashion House, as this new venture is called, is, of course, state-owned and Slava is its Chief Art Director. That doesn't stop it being a little bit of a family business. Slava has two adopted sons, Yegor Vlasenkov who is also a designer in the house, and Dima Vlasenkov, a successful photographer who usually takes the pictures of the collection.

Slava's fashion shows are held in an auditorium for which his British colleagues would probably be willing to trade a healthy limb. Its centre is a long, wide beige-carpeted runway decorated where the models enter with large potted plants. The luxurious seating, upholstered in a rich brown tweed, is comfortably spaced and the rest of the decor is all cream marble and smart blinds. The lighting is the work of a professional and the music is *Zarathustra* or the theme from *2001*.

The second title was probably the one Slava, now clutching a microphone and getting the capacity paying audience to giggle and applaud, had in mind. Among his impeccable camel coats, stunning rainwear, pretty grey flannel dresses, bright Chanel-style suits and pretty, satin evening dresses (where do Musco-vites wear them?), there was also a set of fantastic sci-fi outfits.

Apart from this play to the gallery, Zaitzev's styling is completely in step with mainstream European fashion. True, he tends towards the occasional superfluous flourish – a redundant bow here, one frill too many there – but it is only occasionally and it is only on his womenswear. His menswear, a new development, is superb and even has its admirers among the dapper young men at the British Embassy.

Zaitzev's critics call him a fast and brilliant copyist. Too fast to be true – unless a goodly number of the alleged spies François Mitterrand has just sent packing were engaged in subverting the staff at Chloe and Montana for microdots of the designer's doodles.

By means of an introduction, Christiane Arnaud, wife of the French Ambassador (who firmly intends to buy a Zaitzev evening coat, and what better testimonial could a non-French designer dream of?), gave me a copy of *Economie* to pass on to Zaitzev. It carried a picture (by Dima Vlasenkov) of Slava and Pierre Cardin in a warm embrace. The story was about Cardin's recent trip to Moscow to discuss his plan to open a Maxim's restaurant (he now owns Maxim's), a bar to be called Minim's and two shops – a boutique to sell Cardin's ready-to-wear collection and a food shop to sell Maxim's exotic own-brand gourmet goodies. All for hard currencies, of course.

Quipped the man who has licensed more than 600 manufacturers and retailers in ninety-three countries to use his name and designs: 'Why shouldn't Cardin be written in Cyrillic?' He was, reported *Economie*, given a serious hearing from which he emerged in optimistic mood.

The hard currency catch means that few Muscovites will get to buy Maxim's Dijon mustard or Cardin's frocks. But those determined young women with sewing machines will be able to press their noses up against the windows and get the positions of the seams right.

14 April, 1983   **Brenda Polan**

The house in Znamenka Lane

Of all the houses in all of old Moscow the one I most wish had been left untouched by the Revolution was the one which stood at eight Znamenka Lane. And the room in the house that I would most love to be able to visit now is the dining room. For it was here, against a baroque backcloth of stucco and gilt, lit by flickering chandeliers, that Sergey Ivanovich Shchukin hung his sixteen Gauguins.

He arranged them in tiers like the blazing wall of icons in the iconostasis designed by Theophanes the Greek for the nearby Cathedral of the Annunciation in the Kremlin. Shchukin's room saturated the senses of his diners with hot Tahitian yellows, the glistening, sweaty bronze of immature Polynesian girls, the sultry, syphilitic moods of the dying Gauguin. To surround yourself with such concentrated atmospheres while you were eating required a voracious imagination. To do so in Moscow at the very beginning of the twentieth century required courage as well as prescience.

Sergey Shchukin's collecting spirit was a variety of greed. Apart from the sixteen Gauguins he owned thirty-seven Matisses, sixteen Derains, nine Marquets, eight Cezannes, five Degas, four Van Goghs, and fifty, yes fifty, Picassos. He was probably the only man who could ever boast that he owned more Picassos than Picasso. And yet this greedy man at his dinner table, surrounded by his Gauguins, was a frugal eater, a vegetarian. Like most of the fascinating characters who emerge in Beverly Whitney Kean's book,* Sergey Shchukin was a complicated man.

The author calls them Merchant Princes, the plutocrats of late nineteenth-century Russia who, in their absurdly brief reign of power, built up some of the most staggering art collections ever assembled – staggering in bulk as well as quality. The book is called *All the Empty Palaces*, for it was into the palaces vacated by the impoverished Russian aristocracy that the *arrivistes* moved themselves, their families and their collections.

Sometimes the crowded lives of the great plutocratic dynasties, the Morozovs, the Shchukins, could indeed pass for episodes from *Dynasty*. The book is littered with their suicides and depressions, with the disappointments of fathers whose sons are fey or mad or deaf or simply not interested in continuing the family business. Surprisingly enough, the best collectors were also the best businessmen. But even as level-headed a textile tycoon as Sergey Shchukin had a seam of self-destructive moroseness running through him which you can only put down to his being Russian.

I enjoyed the comment of the guest who praised the room filled with Shchukin's best Matisses – twenty-one of them, in a display designed by the artist himself: that it was impossible to feel depressed in such a room, because 'One cannot fall into a Chekhovian mood'. As the Revolution approached, it becomes clear from Beverly Kean's book, the manic, compulsive collecting was another way of fiddling while the Rome around you burns.

This is a hard-working historical account. When a particular character comes to life, as Sergey Shchukin certainly does, it is through the accumulation of rich details rather than any sleight of the pen. Others are not so lucky because, unlike Shchukin, they have not had half the book devoted to them. Diaghilev flits briefly onto the stage. Tatlin and Malevich are unglued from the pages of an art history book just long enough to share a cathartic

* All the Empty Palaces: The Merchant Patrons of Modern Art in Pre-Revolutionary Russia, *by Beverly Whitney Kean.*

experience in the extraordinary room where Shchukin kept his Picassos.

Thorough, informative, the author relies on others for her best quotes. Prince Shcherbatov joined the crowds visiting Shchukin's house when it was finally and inevitably opened to the public – it seems as if everyone in this book wanted one day to open their house to the public – and he describes the Moscow youths who 'stood with their mouths agape before the canvasses like Eskimos listening to a gramophone.' Confronted by fifty Picassos, thirty-seven Matisses and sixteen Gauguins I suspect that most of us would still behave like Eskimos.

21 April, 1983   **Waldemar Januszczak**

The Devil has all the best goods

There is a kind of theatre we never see in Britain: all-out director's theatre. We place the writer and actor at the top of the theatrical pyramid. In France, Germany and the Soviet Union, however, the director is often regarded as a creative figure in his own right.

With a second-rate talent, the results can be chilling. But given the cascading imagination of Moscow's Yuri Lyubimov, director of the famous Taganka Theatre, for whom the text is no more than the raw material supplied to the 'author of the production', the upshot is to make one realize how much of the theatre's rich physical vocabulary generally goes unused.

I have reported from Paris and East Berlin on Lyubimov's celebrated Taganka *Hamlet* (starring the late cult hero, Vladimir Vyssotski) with its onrushing, mobile, black-wool curtain symbolizing Elsinore and his incredibly jaunty, full-blooded version of Brecht's *The Good Woman of Sezuan*. But even these are eclipsed by seeing in Moscow his production of Mikhail Bulgakov's *The Master and Margarita*, which attacks the senses and the soul with equal ferocity and which, after six years in the repertory, looks as fresh as paint.

Bulgakov's novel, fiinished in 1938 but not published in Moscow till the late 1960s, is a complex, multi-layered masterpiece. It describes the devil, complete with naked girl, black cat and two demons, arriving in Moscow and breeding disruptive anarchy. At the same time, it shows the power of redemptive love through the eponymous hero's Faustian passion for Margarita and the capacity of Christ's ideas to reverberate down the ages. Indeed the novel raises questions which, even today, one is surprised to find aired on the Moscow stage. Is all power, for instance, a form of violence? And if there is no God, then who rules the life of man and keeps the world in order?

Lyubimov's sensational production, using vaudeville, jazz, symbolism and dialectic in a great Meyerholdian mix, suggests that man is constantly caught between the polarities of good and evil, Yeshua (Christ) and Wolend (the Devil). Once again he employs the vast, black, mobile Hamlet curtain to evoke the wild, frenzied, anarchic disorder of devil-plagued Moscow. And at the front of the stage there is an omni-present clock-face which can become a swing sailing out over the heads of the audience, a tram decapitating one of the characters, a symbol of the time out of joint.

At the climax, the two vital elements of the set come together with Yeshua Wolend spotlit at either side of the black curtain and the clock-face swinging between them in eternal pendulum motion.

I grant that, watching a play in an alien tongue, one can easily be swayed by visual effects. Even so, I was still astonished by Lyubimov's ability to use all the ingredients of theatre to make good and evil tangible. Squatting on a coffin, the devil and his acolytes turn Moscow into a crazy, phantasmagoric Hellzappopin.

Bodies cling frantically to the whirling curtain like sailors clutching a mast in a storm, a contortionist appears atop a piano with female upper half and male legs, trunkless chorines dance to 'Yessir, that's my baby', the devil's cat picks a live mouse off someone's head and we, the audience, are included in the condemnation of a corrupt, decaying society. But, offsetting this, is the steely sobriety of the scenes in Jerusalem: a gaunt, tattered, bruised Yeshua stands before Pontius Pilate, encased behind a miniature proscenium-arch, while the back wall of the stage looms with stark images of crucifixion.

Quite how the authorities square this production with current

134

political orthodoxy, I don't know: perhaps it's by seeing Jesus as the first great revolutionary and the Devil as the outward manifestation of a gross, debased materialism. But what makes *The Master and Margarita* such a stunning piece of theatre is that it conjures up the potency of evil in all its frightening seductiveness: the devil's ball becomes a nightmare dance with puppet humans hurtling round the black curtain to thunderously amplified music from Tchaikovsky's *Romeo And Juliet*.

Perhaps the final irony is that this sense-battering piece of director's theatre ends with the actors turning to applaud blown-up photographs of Bulgakov, sardonic and cheroot-smoking, who spent much of his life fighting the Soviet establishment.

One thing the Taganka production also does is to demolish the myth that Moscow theatre is riddled with physical puritanism. And that notion was further dispelled by a visit to the youth-oriented Lenin Komsomol Theatre (where Tarkovsky once staged *Hamlet*) to see Mark Zakharov's highly fashionable production of a rock opera roughly translated as *Juno Perchance*.

This is Moscow's answer to *Cats*. Based on a poem by Andrei Voznesensky, it concerns the true story of a Russian captain who sailed to America in 1806, fell in love with a Hispano-Californian girl called Conchita, sailed home to get permission to marry a Catholic, died in a storm and left the hapless Conchita waiting a fruitless thirty-five years for his return.

Zakharov told me later that he was a great admirer of American film musicals like *West Side Story* and *Oklahoma*; and that one of his aims was to bring Soviet musical theatre – bogged down in the world of Viennese operetta – up to date. He has certainly succeeded since his production is a busy, clangorous compound of Russian choral music, live rock, laser beams, miked songs, communal festivity and bare-chested sailors who might have stepped out of *South Pacific*.

Most surprising of all was a highly erotic *pas de deux* between hero and heroine that left little to the imagination and that set the ship's overhanging prow rocking in sympathy. The moral of the show appeared to be that there was room for rapprochement between opposing cultures and ideologies; and Zakharov's exuberant production was living proof of the fact that an essentially Russian narrative can miscegenate with Western showbiz.

135

But just as a week in Moscow demolished the myth that their stage abounds in propagandist tributes to tractor drivers, so it also dented my notion that they play the great Russian classics with abundant Slav volatility. At the Satire Theatre, I caught a tired-looking, ten-year-old production of Gogol's *The Government Inspector* that was largely an excuse for a star turn by a popular favourite.

And at the Sovremennik (Contemporary) Theatre I saw a production of *The Cherry Orchard* by Galina Voechek that was light, clean, picturesque (the setting consisted of white furniture silhouetted in space with a few stripped branches evoking the orchard itself) but that left one's withers unwrung. Moscow abounds in Chekhov: there are no fewer than four production of *Three Sisters* currently occupying main stages. But I had the feeling that too much of the great man, like us with Shakespeare, leaves directors desperately searching for novelty.

The best Chekhovian acting I saw was (where else?) at the Moscow Art Theatre in a decade-old play by Mikhail Roshchin called *Old New Year*, directed by Oleg Efremov. Like a cross between Eduardo de Filippo and Ayckbourn, this was a satire on the collapsing aspirations of two neighbouring patriarchs: one who greedily filled his house with consumer goods, the other who loftily condemned material necessities. Both saw the folly of their ways and came together in an Art Deco bath-house.

But I was as much struck with the acting as the play. It proved the truth of Stanislavsky's dictum that there are no small parts, only small actors. And one figure, Evgeny Evstegneev, had the whiff of greatness. Playing a drunken chorus pottering between the two households misquoting Ecclesiastes, he had, even when getting his coat impaled on a stepladder, the righteous dignity of the permanently stoned; and yet, in all his pocky baldness, suggested he contained a wisdom denied the hectoring patriarchs.

One can, of course, get too starry-eyed about Soviet theatre: it was good to be reminded that *The Mousetrap* is very popular around the Republics. All the same a week in Moscow persuaded me that their theatre is popular, diverse and abundant. Their greatest flaw is artificially preserving the life of particular productions and companies: ours is a built-in obsolescence that

136

scraps productions before they have exhausted themselves or their audience. If one could combine their continuity with our flexibility, one would have a Utopian theatre.

15 April, 1983   **Michael Billington**

Two voices straining to be heard

In a minuscule modern church, some thirty miles outside Warsaw, a small man – balding, dark-bearded and in dark slacks, an open brown shirt and a black leather jacket – is addressing the congregation after Sunday mass. 'Our first priority is to learn grass roots democracy. Parties only breed rivalries. What we need in this country today is to learn how democracy works at the base and to create national understanding. If we Poles have learned to forgive the Germans,' he goes on, 'then it should be simple enough to maintain friendly coexistence with our neighbour, the Soviet Union, which is there to stay. We don't want our neighbours to be our enemies.'

The speaker is Stefan Bratkowski, President of the Polish Union of Journalists. The union was dissolved by General Jaruzelski soon after martial law was declared. Expelled from the Communist Party in 1981, Bratkowski escaped internment, and emerged from hiding about three months after martial law. Although he has published a handful of articles since then, yesterday was the first time he has emerged, briefly, into public view. He was speaking at Podkowa Lesna, in the church, which has become known as the 'Solidarity Church'. It is a small haven whose outspoken priest welcomes 'internal émigrés' and encourages them, as he declared yesterday with great passion, 'to speak the truth'.

For a full hour yesterday Stefan Bratkowski spoke inside the church, while loudspeakers carried his message outside to the forecourt where many more had gathered under a wan blue sky. Then, for a second hour, he answered questions in a small church hall next door. Behind him was a crucifix, a Christmas tree, a huge photograph of the Pope. In front, on hard, wooden benches, sat young and old, prosperous and not so prosperous.

137

A militia car was parked nearby. No doubt members of the security forces were listening to every word.

Bratkowski, relaxed and oblivious to the consequence of inviting official displeasure, compared the gathering to the Anglo-Saxon tradition of town meetings. 'We should discuss soberly, realistically.' His other model was Mahatma Gandhi. Scathingly critical of Poland's present regime, and what he described as its dead-end policies and secondary leaders, Bratkowski also argued against active resistance, let alone terrorism – and even against underground activities. Polish society, he said, should find its unity of purpose by the same methods that Gandhi used.

Had Bratkowski left it at that, his message might not have seemed all that many worlds removed from another scene, two days earlier, when three British journalists had sat in a television studio in Warsaw with the Deputy Prime Minister, Mieczslaw Rakowski, and questioned him about the regime's policies. Rakowski, who had no advance notice of the questions for *Face The Press* (shown on Channel 4 yesterday), not surprisingly defended the decision to suspend, rather than lift, martial law.

It would serve as 'an umbrella', he said, while the situation in Poland 'is still unstable' and the economic crisis unresolved. Yet Rakowski also insisted that 'a fundamental process of reconstructing our system' is under way. Like Bratkowski, he too did not seem to think that the creation of new parties and institutions is necessarily the best way to secure national understanding. Rakowski too appears to assume that it is possible to heal the deep divisions in the Polish nation by discussion. He actually thinks that the division between government and people can be resolved. It should be possible, he argues, for all except the absolutely irreconcilable to accept that 'there is a place for them' in General Jaruzelski's system.

Mr Rakowski has one example that must gratify him greatly. His eldest son, whose defection to the West in 1981 was widely publicized, has apparently decided to return for good and is due back in Poland this week. But there are many others who have not left Poland and have no desire to leave Poland; but also cannot see their way to cooperating or even tolerating the

138

present regime. These internal émigrés regard any intellectual, or former Solidarity leader, who does opt to cooperate with the regime, as akin to a quisling. That indeed is where Mr Bratkowski and Mr Rakowski part company. Mr Bratkowski may yesterday have been preaching unity, democracy and mutual understanding. Yet he reserves his deepest contempt for former friends, for ex-journalists like Rakowski, former editor of the once-reformist weekly *Polytika*, or for Mr Jerzy Urban, now the official government spokesman, who also once worked for *Polityka*.

He spoke of their arrogance and argued that the regime was pursuing a deliberate vendetta against the intellectuals. The military regime and its supporters, Bratkowski argues, is seeking the Polish people's capitulation. Yet like Hannibal's armies, the Polish military – by concentrating on the occupation and enslavement of the Polish nation – will become bogged down and destroy themselves.

Rakowski, on the other hand, argued that the participation of the military in Poland's present government acted as a safeguard against the abuse of power. He recognized that it had to be temporary and envisaged that martial law would end this year. But neither he, nor Bratkowski, nor anyone else, appeared to see any prospect of a solution whereby men and women locked in highly personalized antagonisms can again find a way of listening to each other, let alone working together. They may both speak of democracy, or reform, of self-governing trade unions, of responsive and responsible government. But they are absolutely unprepared to respect each other's position.

Poland, with martial law under suspension, has plainly entered a 'hold phase' in which a whole society is virtually paralysed. The regime continues to speak of national reconciliation. Yet it admits that it is far from finding a way to the hearts and minds of the workers and that the new trade union movement exists, so far mainly on paper.

Rakowski believes that time is the great healer. The economic crisis, he argues, remains Poland's greatest immediate problem. Mr Bratkowski, from his pulpit yesterday, might say amen to that – but not without adding that the economic crisis will never be resolved by what he sees as 'slavery', but only with the support and understanding of the Polish people.

10 January, 1983   **Hella Pick**

Beirut stunned by barbarism

Bereaved women from the two main Palestinian camps on the outskirts of Beirut began drifting back to their ruined homes yesterday, weeping loudly as they sought relatives amid the blackened and bloated corpses of men, women, and children.

Little effort had been made to remove the several hundred Palestinian and Lebanese dead who lay where they had fallen on Friday at the hands of Christian militiamen.

The speed of the assault, carried out while Israeli troops encircled the two adjoining camps with tanks, was such that some women were gunned down while cooking in the kitchens. Others had obviously been caught while frantically thrusting clothes into a suitcase to flee the sudden carnage.

In small courtyards of the ramshackle single-storey buildings that make up the Chatilla camp old men could be seen slumped in hiding-places behind chairs or beneath tables.

Many of the houses had been dynamited or bulldozed, so that all that remained to be seen of their inhabitants were crushed limbs, hair matted with blood, or a hand sticking out of the rubble.

But elsewhere in the warren of little lanes that lead off the main street through Chatilla it was obvious that the militiamen had hunted down their victims. Entering the tiny dwellings yesterday proved a traumatic experience, since the outer rooms would prove empty and silent except for the flapping of curtains in the breeze, while in the inner room chosen as a final refuge whole families would be found.

In one instance a mother and father had been shot repeatedly while trying to shelter three children who lay in their arms, their faces frozen in death masks of terror.

Where the Christian militiamen did not strike immediately, they rounded up the men in a family and bundled them against a

140

nearby wall for execution. In one such case, the bodies of twenty-one Palestinian men lay heaped against a wall that was plastered with their blood and bone fragments.

Estimates of the overall number who died are hard to make, but in a one-hour period searching a quarter-square-mile of the Chatilla camp on Saturday morning I counted fifty-one bodies, and that is a small section of a large camp which was not itself the exclusive target of the militia's blood lust. Neighbouring Sabra camp was also the subject of similar massacres on Friday.

The accounts of the survivors of the carnage are understandably incoherent, but the pattern emerging is one of deliberate slaughter by Christian extremists acting out of the barbaric impulses which have fuelled Lebanon's savage blood feuds for centuries.

From eyewitness accounts it appears that the Phalangist militia, based in East Beirut, was responsible. At least a battalion of this force was seen mustering outside the camps under Israeli supervision on Friday morning.

The Israelis have admitted that the Phalangists went into Sabra and Chatilla on Friday to flush out guerrillas who were sheltering in and shooting from the camp. But the critical element in the Israeli explanation of the massacre is that it was not until two hours after the Phalangist deployment that the Israeli colonel realized that something was going wrong with the operation.

Those who have visited the site of the killings and have seen the location of Israeli forward positions as they were on Friday, not a quarter of a mile away, cannot believe that the massacre went on unheard or unseen by the Israelis. Apart from anything else, the Israelis have established command posts on top of two high-rise buildings overlooking the camps.

The clear inference is that not only could the Israelis see the Phalangist operation, which was carried out at least partly in daylight, but they must also have heard the screams of the dying.

Although Israeli complicity at that level is quite apparent to camp residents, such is their terror of the Phalangists that Israeli foot patrols were welcomed yesterday when they appeared for the first time inside Sabra.

141

A patrol led by a paratroop colonel, an unusually senior officer for such a task, was begged not to leave the area by Palestinian and Lebanese women. With a few of their menfolk, these women dropped Russian AK47 assault rifles abandoned by guerrillas and bandoliers of ammunition at the feet of the patrol, urging them to remain and protect the camp. Through interpreters, the women explained that Christian militiamen had continued to penetrate the camp even after the first massacres were revealed on Saturday morning.

The colonel, speaking Arabic and using a loudhailer, tried to reassure the residents, and said that the Lebanese Army would be deploying that morning throughout the camp, as indeed it did.

This news brought a ragged cheer from people who seemed almost too shocked to understand the final act of barbarism which has befallen them after the separate disasters of invasion, siege and occupation.

20 September, 1982   **James MacManus**

Mistress of the high ground

Later, she was to write of it as her two-year honeymoon in Italy, though that is like calling a Parkhurst stretch an Isle of Wight holiday. Still, it was the two years after she, aged sixteen, married the exiled son of a great Venezuelan family, a man of thirty-five, as enigmatic, as alluring, and finally as remote as the Andes foothills where the Terans had lived in great wealth since the time of the Conquistadors.

It was two years moving constantly around and into and out of Italy, with anything up to four exiled and wanted Venezuelans, a group that dispersed and re-formed as whim or the urgent fear of arrest or assassination dictated. Years when her new husband did little but sleep and complain and pretend to a life-style he could no longer bankroll, the days of whine and poses.

Not, she says, the kind of honeymoon she would wish for her daughter, but out of it Lisa St Aubin de Teran has made her second autobiographical novel, *The Slow Train To Milan*.

It is an intimate group portrait of people who belonged to that permanent sub-strata of European life, the political exiles who have turned to terrorism, or crime, or simply petty self-deception as a way of life.

The Slow Train To Milan ends where her first, highly praised novel *Keepers Of The House* began, at the point in the early seventies where the exiled husband is able to return to the family estate with his girl-wife, to what must have seemed to her in prospect as a home at last.

The first thing she realized was that she had made an appalling mistake. 'I just was not accepted. The whole family, all the way back, had always intermarried. There were not just the people who thought my husband should have married in the family, there were the women who thought he should have married them. Nobody spoke to me, except wonderful old Benito, who was always too drunk to take any notice of what anyone else was doing. I was in Coventry. There was a campaign to get me to go away, and I would have given anything to get out. But I couldn't drive. It was 600 kilometres from Caracas, there were road blocks along the way, and my husband's family was so powerful that police would have told him at once if I had tried to leave. I just had to stay and hope that somebody would come by. But nobody ever came by there. We were six kilometres from the nearest village, ten from the nearest town.'

The culture shock was formidable. Her mother is from Jersey and is head of a remand home in England. Her father is from Guyana, the novelist and journalist Jan Carew, now Professor of African-American Studies at Northwestern University in the US. She was brought up in England and educated at James Allen's girls' school, and was heading for anthropology at Cambridge when she met the fateful Venezuelan.

She learnt the history of her husband's family from the hundreds of stories she was told by the nonagenarian Benito and by others, all of them, she says, with an element of drunken fantasy, but pieced together some of them to provide the long, central, most Marquesian section of *Keepers Of The House*.

To be accounted anyone, she knew, she had to have the whole family tree off by heart, and after two years, when her first child was born, she ceased to be a non-person, she was accepted, and came to love the place, with its huge sugar plantations and its avocado farm, and its remoteness.

By now her husband was ill, and she was running the estate and all its workers and servants. 'Women just have an abominable time in Venezuela, but after a certain point, and I just don't know how, they become able to be more powerful than most women in this country. I wasn't the first woman to run our estate, there was a woman who did it around the turn of the century.' But that woman was not nineteen?

'No, and she was not a foreigner. But it really was sub-feudal. Nobody would do anything without asking permission. They would ask my permission to marry, to have an affair with somebody, whether they could have their child back in the house with them, where to bury their aunt. I was just horrified that people should still live like that.'

She was horrified by many things. By the way all the workers assembled outside the house every morning, so that she could pick out the twenty to fifty she needed to work on the estate that day. She knew they were all very poor, and in what she thought a helpful gesture, started hiring all of them every day, to dig ditches she did not need, or plant trees she did not want.

After a while, they sent a deputation to her, to ask her if she would please only hire so many each day, for daily work was disrupting their whole life pattern. They had no time to cultivate their own allotments, and no time to sit and wait for mañana.

When they were eight, the daughters of the peasants would go to work as *cargaduras*, baby carriers, for no woman of family or substance would carry her own child, or do anything else for it. And the sons aged eight would start work in the plantation, clearing up the cane fields.

She sent all the children to the free schools, only to find the teachers got rid of them by sending the parents long lists of equipment the kids supposedly needed, and that none of the families could afford. She brought more girls into the house as servants, and let them bring their younger sisters too, until the whole place was filled with them, and they took their pay home as sacks of badly needed food.

The estate workers were Catholics who had never heard of the

Pope, who knew no higher ecclesiastical authority than the village priests, to whom they went only for christening, marriage and death. There were three scales of funeral, and for the minimum fees the peasant could afford, they got only the minimal service. 'Those priests could get through it in forty-five seconds,' she says, and gives a gabbling imitation of that brief dispatch.

Life was as cheap as death. 'No one will ever stop to pick up an injured person, because the law says if he dies on you on the way to hospital, you are responsible. Once when we had a child who was badly gashed by a machete, and bleeding very badly, I couldn't get any car to stop, I had to catch one. I stretched a rope across the road, so the next car had to stop. Then I held the driver at gunpoint and made him drive us to the hospital.'

This is the society she describes in *Keepers Of The House*. It is the unseen background to her new novel, and to the one she is still writing. It is what Otto warns her against on the Slow Train: 'It will destroy you . . . It's feudal, and it's evil, and they'll never accept you.'

She is deeply influenced in her thinking and in the writing of her first book by South America, and by writers like Gabriel Garcia Marques. It shows, for instance, in the way crisis and disaster and violence simply blend into the weaves of everyday events, narrated in the same cool even tone.

She came back to the relative peace of England five years ago to see her family, never meaning to settle here. She now lives in a vast Victorian rectory in deepest Norfolk with her second husband, the poet George MacBeth, their four-month-old son and her nine-year-old daughter.

She received us in the library, where she sat by a huge coal fire, within reach of the bell pull which she cranked once, to have the baby taken away by the help, and a second time, to have the coffee brought. Except for the fire, you felt she still might be commanding her hacienda. She is thirty this year, but she still looks the eighteen she was when she went to South America and sent her sugar and avocados to Caracas, listened to all those stories, and gave permission to marry lovers and bury aunts.

3 March 1983 **Hugh Hebert**

Wriggles feels the wrath of Willie

In the wake of the Government's defeat by the combined forces of moral and ethnic darkness the Prime Minister made a statement from the Dispatch Box yesterday about her relationship with the Home Secretary. She denied that it was a marriage of convenience to allow Mr Whitelaw to go on living here.

This was good news because it tallied exactly with the version Willie had given out the previous evening. There are plenty of people who would like to see the relationship break down before the general election so that Willie could be sent packing. It would stop the wagging tongues to know that they are very happy together – despite everything.

The Home Secretary's own contribution yesterday was of a different order. He was determined to show that he is still a man to be reckoned with when roused. He did this by bullying Mr Ian Wrigglesworth.

This is the political equivalent of catching flies and pulling their wings off. It may make one feel better, but is it right? Mr Wrigglesworth is not to blame for Mr Whitelaw's humiliation. Mr Roy Jenkins is the Brains behind the SDP, just as Dr Owen is its Brawn. Mr Wrigglesworth is only the Bottom behind the party, the man with front bench responsibility for keeping Mr Jenkins' seat warm while the leader is still at lunch.

But Mr Whitelaw picked on him all the same, not once but twice. In fairness he was unable to pick on Mr Jenkins in person because Mr Jenkins was absent when Home Office question time began yesterday. Doubtless his sedan chair had been held up by cheering crowds outside the Reform Club, Le Gavroche, or the Connaught Hotel. Touched by cries of 'Bless you, Guv, for upholding the European Convention' and 'Let's tar and feather Whitelaw, lads', Mr Jenkins had probably stepped down to pacify the mob.

In any case Mr Whitelaw had tried to pick on Mr Jenkins in person during the fateful debate. It had not been a great success. So now Willie got at Mr Jenkins through young Wriggles.

It had been a typical Home Office day: plastic bullets, 'phone tapping, video porn, glue sniffing. But there really was a holiday atmosphere to the deliberations. Christmas had finally arrived.

Then Mr Wrigglesworth, who also keeps Mr Jenkins' Home Office policies warm, rose on a question about the crime wave. When was Mr Whitelaw going to fulfil this manifesto commitment? he boldly inquired. Willie suddenly went ape. He roared; he poked his finger at poor Wriggles; he bellowed. It was the kind of behaviour that gets motorists run in at this time of year. 'Who says he's finished?' cried Dennis Skinner in mock alarm. 'I didn't,' said Mr Speaker quickly.

As far as one could tell in the hubbub, the drift of Mr Whitelaw's reply was that Mr Jenkins had once been Home Secretary and was thus partly responsible for the crime wave, the fiancé wave and the rape wave before becoming responsible for various Euro-waves.

This was confirmed a few minutes later when Mr Wrigglesworth dared to try again. In doing so he let slip a fateful reference to 'the welcome increase in bobbies on the beat'. Mr Whitelaw roared again. 'The Hon Gentleman is a great tiger for punishment,' he said flatteringly. 'I have given him one go and I am going to give him another.'

This time the drift appeared to be that Mr Wrigglesworth's party was undeniably led by the man who had taken policemen off the beat and put them into panda cars – another mess which he, Willie, was having to put right. So that was Mr Jenkins responsible for the panda wave.

We were getting the general idea. Sure enough, Mr Whitelaw went on to tell the SDP's Edward Lyons about Mr Jenkins' responsibility for the disgraceful state of the nation's prisons – the porridge wave! – as well. It was becoming plain that Mr Jenkins would be well advised not to fall into the hands of the constabulary over the festive season (Got a licence for that sedan chair, sir? I see. Would you mind blowing into this bag? Born in this country were you, sir?')

17 December, 1982   **Michael White**

A country diary: Keswick

These unusually windy months have brought rain and snow but only occasional sun. However, one morning lately when there were still blue shadows under Helvellyn the sky was clear and the light of the unrisen sun was turning from silver to gold in the gap of Dunmail Raise. Thirlmere was in shadow, too, but there was sunlight on the frosty tops of the Armboth fells as I went up through the dense juniper thickets towards Harrop tarn, ignoring an older trod that curves up from behind the ruins of West Head farm. West Head, in its day, used to be one of the best farms in the valley and famous for its sheep. I used to think that the dairy there must have been built round the immense stone slab which stood at its centre – how else could it have got there? Now there are only fallen walls and one empty cow-house, sunk in nettles in summer and the haunt of owls. The junipers here are a mixture of high and low level types and their mounds, columns and spires create a world of their own – dens for red deer and shelters for sheep. It is not only the animals who have valued them: savin (juniper) charcoal was once most highly-prized in the Westmorland and Furness bloomeries. Then, too, savins are more benign to the soil than other conifers: their prickly leaves, fallen, add valuable humus to the ground so that violets, wood sorrel and even primroses thrive at their roots. Today the green-bloomed savin berries were as cold as ice in my hands – but they will warm many winter stews.

31 January, 1983   **Enid J. Wilson**

Winter migrants

La Guardia airport is a rough place: busy, overcrowded, packed with impatient men waving heavy carry-on bags and brisk women nipping stray ankles with their overnighters-on-wheels. It is an airport from which travellers must expect to emerge with bruised body-parts and seething tempers.

For the last week or so, the system at La Guardia, such as it is, has been sabotaged by the yearly emigration of New York's white-haired population to the balmy climes of Florida. The kerb-side skycaps now find hanging from both arms a cluster of old ladies worrying that their yellow plastic suitcases with identifying scarlet pom-poms will not make it to the plane.

148

Seat selection clerks whose conversation normally ranges no further than 'smoking or non-smoking?' suddenly find themselves engaged in long, intricate discussions about emergency exits and the whereabouts of favoured window seats. The corridors are a forest of walking canes while those leaning on them flutter and panic in search of the right gate.

The blue-hairs, well-to-do, attired in Bergdorf Goodman, turn off by the boards marked Miami and Palm Beach. Those others, the apologetic white-hairs, dressed by Sears or J. C. Penney, flock towards the signs announcing Tampa. For some reason the west coast of Florida, overlooking the Gulf of Mexico, has never had much social cachet. The villages, developments and residential hotels around Tampa Bay are still affordable to those on careful pensions.

St Petersburg, the quietest seaside town around Tampa, is the favoured wintering spot of those who never saw themselves of much importance even when they were young. Something of 'St Pete's' character can be suggested by reference to the much-loved public art collection – a vast number of concrete nymphs and cherubs donated to the city in the 1920s by a developer who found himself with two spare shiploads of the stuff.

On the choice run to Palm Beach, the air hostesses know to be careful. Into each seat on the crowded plane settles seventy years of snapping and pushing – woe betide the youngster who is less than respectful. On the flights to Tampa, the meek and mild quiver before those in charge. 'Miss, I'm very cold.' 'I'm sweating like a pregnant pig and she says she's cold,' announces the airways' finest to the cabin at large. 'Miss, could I please have a cushion, I'm so uncomfortable.' 'You lose four inches before you fly next and then you'll be comfortable,' comes the answer.

Thus is the crowd tamed – as they were always tamed, those who asked for no more in life than the chance to be left alone. In New York city they are merely old. In Florida they will be surrounded by advertisements (usually for real estate firms) inviting them to enter 'the best years of their lives'. Just over 600,000 people actually live in Tampa. Every year, nearly five million come to visit – many of them these gentle, threadbare couples and widows carrying their paperback copies of Billy Graham out into the sunshine at Tampa Airport.

149

It does not cost much to come here: the airline war that can be relied upon to break out after Christmas has, this year, brought down the fare from New York to $99 – or $79 for the really crafty shopper. A three-month lease on a tiny flat, as undistinguished as its tenants, is at most $1,500 or so. The winter folk have learned to eat carefully and the only highpoint of the social week is the Saturday night concert of the Florida Gulf Coast Symphony at the Bay Front Theatre – invariably sold out.

The presence of all these winter migrants has its effect mostly on the roads. All along, the huge signboards point down tracks into virgin marsh: 'Don't dream about this lifestyle . . . Live it.' Not a puddle of palm trees that does not have its adult community condo project underway within it. And past these signs, trundling carefully along at half the speed of those around them, the winter rental cars swerve from lane to lane in an endeavour to see some way out back to safety from the mysterious experience of highway driving.

Hero of the week must surely be Detective Jay Rogers of Miami, who noticed an old Chevrolet circling round and round a deserted building site. Inside it he found eighty-three-year-old Gustave Buckel who had, it seems, set off on a leisurely Sunday afternoon spin from his home on the Gulf Coast 250 miles away. 'I just took a wrong turn,' he told the policeman. 'I just usually take short trips around my home. I don't go on no long trips.'

Detective Rogers spent several hours trying to find help for Mr Buckel. Obviously he could not drive back again alone since he had already been defeated once that day by the endless majesty of Interstate 275. A widower, Mr Buckel had no one to call since his only family was back in New York. Finally, Detective Rogers put him up for the night and, early the next morning, filled the car up with petrol and drove Mr Buckel all the way home himself. He even paid his own plane fare from Tampa back to Miami.

'You've got to do what your heart dictates,' said Detective Rogers. 'He's a nice, sweet man and when we crossed the bridge into his own county, he began to cry. I was just glad I could help him.'

All over St Petersburg and Tampa, the winter crowd are

telling this story. Somehow it is not one that they expect to hear about a policeman in New York.
Date to follow **Linda Blandford**

Simla, but different

Paul Theroux, it is true, fell asleep as soon as the train pulled precipitously out of Kalka. And V. S. Naipaul followed the old tonga road to Simla by car; a mistake unless, like the horse-drawn tonga, the car is open to the sky and the shifting peaks from Monkey Point, above Kasauli, to Jakku, above Simla.

'Ah, Monkey Point,' I said as the railcar lurched around a bend of the narrow-gauge railway line on the edge of a green precipice and disclosed the bare brown flanks of the first of these peaks. From Monkey Point you can look to the south and see Chandigarh in the plains of the Punjab; look north at range on range of Himalayan mountains.

'You have been here before,' said the Sikh sitting opposite. Yes. Chandigarh wasn't there then. Nor was the dish aerial on the side of Monkey Point, cupped towards China. As boys we watched through the month as the December sun set closer and closer to Monkey Point, and we crossed days off our home-made calendars inside the lids of our tin trunks until the sun at last dropped behind the peak and the last day was crossed off and the time had come to go home to the plains for Christmas, some to Bangalore, some to Calcutta or Delhi or Mysore, some to Lahore or further through the Sind to Karachi. And there were the orphans who stayed at school and had not been crossing off the days.

'Yes,' I said. 'Forty years ago.' The Sikh's laugh was pure pleasure. 'Then you are a true hillman,' he said, 'not like me.'

No question, the haul up from Kalka is one of the great railway journeys of the world. 'A fair land – a most beautiful land is this of Hind – and the land of the Five Rivers is fairer than all,' said Kim; and Kipling's description needs no amending:

> *the wandering road, climbing, dipping, and sweeping about the growing spurs; the flush of the morning laid along the distant snows; the*

branched cacti, tier upon tier on the stony hillsides; the voices of a
thousand water channels; the chatter of the monkeys; the solemn deodars,
climbing one after another with down-drooped branches; the vista of the
Plains rolled out far beneath . . .

You arrive at Chandigarh by air, or at Kalka itself by the night mail from Delhi, armed with a nine-inch square document to which you have appended your signature or thumb print and which entitles the pass-holder to first-class travel with 70kg of luggage and half for each child, plus 'one attendant in second class with 50kg of luggage'.

At Kalka, there is tea and biscuits to be taken in one of the long cane chairs that are a legacy of the British, anyway in the officers' waiting room. Then you can make the six-hour fifty-mile trip to Simla in a train or a railcar. Either way, from late February until May you can lean out of the window and pick spring flowers from the *khud* side as the train winds up through Taksal, Gumman, Koti, Jabli, Sonwara, Dharampur, Kumar Hatti, Barog, Solan and Solan Brewery, Salogra, Kanda Ghat, Kanoh, Kathlee Ghat, Shoghi, Tara Devi, Jutogh, Summer Hill, Simla.

The names are as redolent as Addlestrop, and the little station buildings are a version of English wayside halts, each with a station *mali*, white-haired, clad in khaki drill, erect as soldiers, tending neat little lawns and borders of snapdragons and marigolds; gardens with eucalyptus trees with the bottom four feet of the trunk white-washed, standing sentinel at the perimeters of the stations against the pines and deodars of the precipitous hillsides.

At Barog, the train may pull in to a siding so that you can have breakfast. You start by washing in what used to be the rest room of the Viceroy, then a meal of cornflakes with hot milk and jam, an omelette, curried vegetable cutlets, toast, and tea. Or if you are later, lunch at Salogra, where the *mali* may present you with flower and fern elegantly bound together with cotton.

'What kind of flower is this?'

'Buttonholejai.'

The railcar has the advantages of glass all round and swivel chairs in the rear, and the disadvantage that the railway's chief engineer is inordinately proud of the sound system he has

152

installed so the hills are alive to the sound of Muzak.

Half a century and more before the railway was built in 1904 the hills were already the only place in summer for a lady, though not all ladies immediately appreciated it. Young Emily Eden, sister of Lord Auckland, Governor-General of India shortly before the Mutiny, wrote peevishly: '. . . if the Himalayas were only a continuation of Primrose Hill, or Penge Common, I should have no objection to pass the rest of my life on them.'

Without the British, Simla is still less like Penge Common, though the rhododendrons are indigenous, wild, and grow into trees. The railway authority has labelled the station signboard 'Shimla', which is how Indians have always said it but to the evident distress of the tourist authority, which wants British tourists to remember Simla as the imperial summer capital it once was.

Now in the daytime Simla is a glorious great bazaar clinging to the ridge and its precipitous slopes. At night it looks like a fall of stars. Either time cars are banned from most of the narrow roads; they make up for it on the hair-raising hairpin bends of the Kalka road to the South and the Hindustan-Tibet road towards the Shipke pass in the North, out towards the tourist bungalow forty miles away of Narkanda, set, even in summer, at the snow's edge.

Simla teems with the faces of the hillmen of Himachal Pradesh, Mongol faces, Pathan faces, faces from Tibet; drivers from the plains waiting to load the fabulously painted and chromed lorries with the market produce of the hills, seed potatoes, cabbages, mushrooms, apples; shepherds in retreat from the encroaching snowline and in town for supplies, wrapped in hill blankets and wearing on their heads, not the turban or pugree of the plainsman but the round grey shepherd's hat of the Kulu Valley, embroidered at the front in scarlet and gold thread.

The Mall stretches along Simla ridge, taking in Kipling's Scandal Point, between the Viceregal Lodge at one end and the slightly comical lime-washed Christ Church at the other, beneath Jakku, Simla's highest peak crowned by the tin-roofed temple to the monkey god Hanuman, and alive with some of that army of monkeys that helped Rama to recover his consort Sita from the demon king of Sri Lanka.

Along the Mall, the Gaiety Theatre is still there ('small and hot, and somewhat dirty, but it does very well' – Emily Eden) where the Viceroy might go to watch his friends in *Floradora* or *The Mikado* or *The Geisha*.

Ask around and you might find someone, too, who remembers where the room is that was described by E. Marion Crawford where 'it appeared as if the walls and the ceiling were lined with gold and precious stones; and in truth it was almost literally the truth . . . every available space, nook or cranny was filled with gold and jewelled ornaments, shining weapons, or uncouth but resplendent idols.'

This was the room inhabited by the fabled Mr A. M. Jacob, the Armenian freed from slavery in Turkey as a youth who made a fortune as a dealer in rich jewels, was possessed of magical powers and, not much translated, became both Lurgan Sahib in *Kim* and the eponymous hero of Crawford's first and forgotten, dated but charming novel of Simla, *Mr Isaacs*.

Mr Jacob died in 1921 but the trade lives on in the Mall and in every Indian town, where diamonds and rubies, sapphires, pearls, cornelian, lapis lazuli, and the Punjab jewel black as night but with a hint of moonlight in it are loved for themselves as well as for their value as in no other country.

Away from the noise and smells of the bazaar is the Viceregal Lodge, on a plateau commanding the most spectacular view in Simla of the eternal snows, built for Lord Dufferin in Elizabethan Renaissance style (allowing that the Elizabethans had no verandas) in hard blue limestone and soft grey sandstone, with a great central tower and enormous mullioned windows and the great hall panelled with Burmese teak and the staircase constructed of deodar and walnut, and furnished throughout by Messrs Maple, of Tottenham Court Road.

There were hangings of velvet and silk, and Japanese paper, and Curzon added damask in sky blue and crimson and pale green with yellow in the long ballroom overlooking the Great Himalayan Range: Ghataran, Ghata Kanda, Gushu Pishal, Kand Mahadev and around a hundred and fifty peaks of about 20,000 feet, mostly unnamed and unscaled. In the Viceregal

Lodge were held the State balls and levees and the scores of dinners every season and at last, in this building in June, 1947, Mountbatten gave Nehru the timetable of independence.

Like that meeting, the silk and damask hangings are history. The rose pergola blooms, the lawns are trim, but there are no more garden parties. Dufferin, Lansdowne, Elgin, Curzon, Minto, Hardinge of Penshurst, Chelmsford, Reading, Irwin, Willingdon, Linlithgow, Wavell, Mountbatten dispensed more power and patronage than princes and emperors, but their portraits and armorial bearings are gone, replaced by Gandhi, Nehru, and Vinobha Bhave, and the Viceregal Lodge is the Rashtrapati Nivas, home of the Indian Institute of Advanced Study.

> *Cast out your swarthy sacrilegious train,*
> *And give – ere dancing cease and hearts be broken –*
> *Give us our ravished ballroom back again!*

Curzon hated the town, the officials, the wives, the gossip, and he spent as much time out of it as he decently could under canvas at pine-scented Naldera, a hill he loved so much that he gave his daughter Alexandra one of her names after it; and he created there a nine-hole golf-course with a slope up to the last green so steep as to break the heart of a Ballesteros.

And at Chail, the Maharajah of Patiala, expelled from Simla for the impertinence of giving the Viceroy's daughter a lift along the Mall on the back of his horse, built his summer palace so that its lights could be seen by the British in Simla.

It could be a country house transplanted from the Cotswolds, but across the lawns and beyond the scarlet japonica is the world's greatest land barrier; and the independent rajas of India lasted scarcely longer than the Viceroys so that Chail Palace is a hotel now, with princely rooms and service by bearers caparisoned in pure white. Out in the garden is the one man who remembers the old days: the *mali*, an old man now, clips back the bushes and patiently shows visitors his domain. He wears his turban tied evenly in a double crown each side of his head. Patiala style, just as it has always been.

Near Chail, on the way up, I met a thickset, pale-skinned former officer dressed in a light suit and silk tie and handker-

chief that might have come from Bond Street, trim white
military moustache, polished brown brogues, clipped Sand-
hurst English. He had fought with the 15th Punjab Regiment in
Burma, North Africa, and Italy, and was still known with
affectionate respect as Colonel Sahib.

'How about a nice cold beer, when we get to Solan Brewery,
eh?' he said, and slapped me on the shoulder. He, of course, had
never been to England, was a teetotaller and vegetarian, kept an
image of Siva in his bedroom, and intoned hymns and prayers in
the back of the car on the half-day journey to his wife and long
stone house deep in the Himalayas above the gorge where the
infant Sutlej flows through from Tibet to the Punjab plain.

He was the honorary village headman whose wife ran the post
office, who employed labour to mill the villagers' corn and saw
their wood, who was helping to pioneer the cultivation of apple
orchards as a non-subsistence crop. Before I visited him or knew
any of this, I had explained that my return to India was in the
nature of a sentimental journey. 'Ah,' he said with a wide smile.
'Then you are a true hill man. Not like me.'

2 July 1983   **Michael McNay**

From a village in the Himalayas 1

The government had abolished slavery, Vijay whispered to his
fellow-untouchables, and all bonded labourers would hence-
forth be free. The richer farmers denied the rumour. Vijay was
trying to stir up the untouchables again, they said, but he would
fail. The headman, whose own fields were worked by bonded
labour, said he had heard nothing from the government.

But Vijay had an ally among the landlords. The other untouchables warned him against trusting the high-caste rajput,
but Vijay was sure he could rely on Ram Singh. Hadn't they
grown up together? Ram would never eat food touched by
Vijay, but at least he hadn't beaten him when they were children
or expected him to work for nothing when they grew up.

When Vijay came back from the government school – the only
educated untouchable in the area – the landlords recognized him

as a threat to their power and tried to intimidate him. But Ram Singh was impressed by Vijay's accounts of government plans to emancipate the outcasts.

Ram hoped to become headman himself one day. He would need the goodwill of government officials who were supposed to see that untouchables got their rights. He took Vijay's side.

He had helped Vijay to stop the rite of buffalo-baiting, the annual festival during which the villagers chased the hapless creature through the fields and hacked him to death. Now he promised to help again.

About a third of the sixty or so families in the village were untouchables, the landless labourer caste which has for centuries served the high-caste rajputs and the brahmin priests. There was no work to be had except from the landlords, who paid a pittance. The untouchables lived from hand to mouth, perpetually in debt, segregated on the lower slope. The only way out was for one man in the family, usually a younger son, to become 'bondj'. He would work for the farmer without pay, just two meals a day and some clothes, until he had worked off the family debt. He rarely succeeded.

Either the family borrowed more, or the farmer – who kept the accounts – would claim that the bondsman's labour hadn't even paid the interest on the loan. The labourer, illiterate, couldn't argue. Often the debt would pass from father to son. So would the bondage.

In the mid-Seventies, long before I came to the village, the government cancelled all such debts. But the headman kept the news to himself. Vijay asked him repeatedly about the new law, but to no avail. Ram Singh, with his eye on the headman's post, released his own bondsmen. He told his fellow-landlords of the three-year prison terms and the huge fines which the new law imposed on bonded-labour masters. The farmers began to take notice.

A canny brahmin landlord, Joshi, joined the Vijay-Ram alliance. He had applied for a government contract to build an irrigation canal, and thought this was a way to get it. Then Vijay recruited a couple of youths who had been chafing under the stern rule exercised by the village elders. They were ready to defy the headman.

157

The all-caste group set out on a march through the hills to tell the untouchables about the new law. The landlords tried to keep them out of the villages. But the marchers found shelter among the outcasts on the lower slopes. The bondsmen were curious, but distrustful. Where was the assurance, they asked, that the Government would protect them if they deserted their masters? The marchers gave them government leaflets listing the labourers' rights and their masters' obligations. But the untouchables couldn't read them.

The landlords threatened to break the agitators' bones. The marchers held meetings secretly to protect the bondsmen from the landlords' anger. Ram Singh, tall and sturdy, made sure that his fellow-rajputs did not invade the meetings. The farmers had said that labourers who repudiated their bonds would make the spirits angry. But Joshi the brahmin former-priest assured the untouchables that the gods had no objection to the new law.

In one village a gang of rajputs forced its way into a meeting held at dead of night. 'You swore a solemn oath to repay our loans,' the gang-leader reminded the untouchables. 'No government can annul your debt. If you default, the gods will send calamities to punish you and your families.' They threatened the untouchables with misfortune, disease, even death.

Ram Singh thundered that it was the landlords who would be punished, by the government. Vijay told the untouchables that they were free men. They must report to the authorities any attempt to retain them in bondage.

The bondsmen were bewildered. The authorities were far away, and officials hardly ever set foot in the village. But the landlords were on the spot. Their power, unchallenged for centuries, rested on tradition, religion, and sheer force.

'Let's wait and see,' the untouchables said.

12 December, 1982   **Victor Zorza**

Trash trail

In the mid-Seventies, I joined a party of Swiss climbers en route to the Everest base camp. Their leader had climbed there two years before, and he was horrified at the change: 'Look at the garbage. There'll be road cleaners on Everest in ten years' time.'

It hasn't taken that long: the Nepalese government has just announced that any future group on the Everest trail must take with them ten extra porters to bring back their rubbish.

It must be very bad by now: then, there was only an eighteen-month queue to climb the world's top mountain. It was very odd, on the way to the ultimate outpost of human life, to trip over beer cans and boxes, and to see azaleas flowering at 15,000 feet – only they turned out to be face tissues and plastic bags.

Unfortunately, a diet of yak and potatoes and tea with melted butter instead of milk does not keep you regular, and what is bio-degradable at 5,000 feet is preserved for posterity at 15,000. Even for the Swiss, who responded morning and evening to some communal inner call and rushed out together into the freezing dark to queue at a tented hole in the ground, there are only a limited number of flat places to dig holes.

The Sherpas had made good use of some of the detritus left behind by Western civilized industrial culture. The sixty-degree landing strip at Lukla was marked out for the pilots of incoming aircraft with the shells of broken planes, frozen for all time.

Disconcerting though, to stand like stout Cortez . . . and look down on the back of some huge hawk hovering thousands of feet above its prey, and hear Frank Zappa throbbing from above as a young Sherpa walks by with his pocket radio at full blast.

There are more far-reaching pollutions, too. VD, unknown three years before, had become a problem since large numbers of American tourists had passed through. Colds and flu can kill the locals – antibiotics, apparently, are not as effective over 10,000 feet.

There were, of course, the commercial effects of hundreds of thousands of tourists en route to the experience of treading where so few had trod before. Most monasteries, even then, had *the* authentic Yeti head or hand, reddish and bristling; smiling

Sherpa women moved ahead of you along the path and spread their curios and souvenirs; Beer like Back Home in the Everest View Café.

As we all queued at Lukla for the tiny plane back to Kathmandhu, a man tried to flog the petrified body of a bear, the size of a child, as a souvenir of the trip of a lifetime.

What was already becoming clear in the mid-Seventies, when trekking was in its infancy, was that the young Sherpas wanted no more of that hard, high life. They wanted the bright lights of Kathmandhu, rather than the struggle to clear the stones from terraces of earth snatched from the mountainsides to grow potatoes.

There was an old man there who had translated the whole of *Paradise Lost* into Nepalese. He was full of memories, nostalgic for the past, hating change. 'Nothing good will ever come of them,' he said, of a group of young and eager visitors photographing Everest for future reference.

All that garbage clogging the path to the unknown proves him right. It's ironic that when civilized man tries to escape his civilization, he pollutes everything he touches.

31 January, 1983   **Jane McLoughlin**

From a village in the Himalayas 2

The policemen sent from town to prevent fights on election day were on edge, because in another village a candidate for headman had been killed in a quarrel. They watched uneasily as the tension rose between the two groups outside the polling station. Each man who came out of the village school after voting joined one group or the other, and soon complaints and insults flew across the grassy patch between the two.

The untouchables suspected they were being cheated of victory. The police had told Vijay to keep his followers in check, and he had done so, but now he was beginning to wonder. Several of his supporters had not been allowed to vote. Someone had made sure, he told me, that their names would not appear on the voters' roll. Who?

Only one man was in a position to do that, Vijay said. The Patwari, who kept the land records, was also responsible for the election register. He had hinted that those who voted for Vijay need not expect him to take their side in quarrels over land ownership. The untouchables were vulnerable. The ownership of fields allocated to them under the land reform was often disputed. Vijay could afford to lose some votes, because the untouchables in the five villages outnumbered the outcasts. But not too many.

He appealed to the senior policeman to restore his supporters' names to the register. The officer went into a huddle with the Patwari and with Vijay's rival, Ram Singh – and blandly informed the untouchables that it was all their own fault. The voters' register had been posted for some time in a public place, as required by law. They had been given every opportunity to ensure that their names were on it. Of course, he said, mistakes could happen, and this no doubt accounted for the missing names. But it was too late to do anything about it.

'How could I have checked the list?' a man shouted. 'I cannot read.' Vijay remonstrated with the police officer. Hadn't he been sent to the village to make sure that the untouchables were not cheated? If it was a mistake, how did it happen that only Harijan names were missing? The untouchables yelled their approval. The high-castes threw insults back at them. The two groups moved forward, menacing each other, but were kept apart by half a dozen policemen.

By the end of the day fourteen untouchables had been turned away from the polling station – but so had a couple of high-castes. This proved, the Brahmins said, that they too had suffered from mistakes made in compiling the list. No one had deliberately discriminated against the untouchables. But Vijay had his own explanation. The two high-caste names had been omitted on purpose, he said – to shield the perpetrators of the deception.

The ballot box was carried for the count to the district centre, under police guard. Vijay and Ram Singh, each with a group of supporters, followed close behind to make sure that no one would bribe the policemen to slip in false ballot papers. Dozens of other such parties were converging from the hills on the district centre. In half of the fifty or so constituencies the candidates – all high-caste – had been returned unopposed. In the other half, high-caste candidates for headman had been challenged by untouchables.

Now they all stood in front of the government office in the district centre, waiting for the returning officer to declare the results. As he read them out, the cheers came only from the high-caste groups. The returning officer called out the name of our village. Vijay bent forward, tensely. Ram Singh – 177 votes, the returning officer intoned. Vijay – 100 votes. He had lost.

So had all the other untouchable challengers. But this was the first time any untouchable had stood for election in this area.

Ram Singh approached Vijay with hand outstretched. He wanted to be friends now, and invited Vijay and his whole party to join him in the teashop. But Vijay put his hand behind his back, and turned away without a word. His supporters hesitated. One or two followed him. Others went with Ram Singh. They couldn't afford to antagonize the winner.

Word of Ram Singh's victory reached the village before his return. Untouchables as well as high-castes came out to meet him and accompanied him to the temple to give thanks to the gods.

Vijay didn't come back. Ram Singh said he had been humiliated and dared not show his face in the village. Vijay's supporters said he had gone to the city to complain that he had been robbed of victory, and to demand a new election.

31 January, 1983   **Victor Zorza**

Quarks, leptons and beyond

Are particle physicists the schoolmen of our time? Asking the question does not imply the answer yes, although it does, we fear, breach the unwritten rule against any interference in what is going on. There are two sound reasons for the rule. First, no one understands particle physics except particle physicists themselves, and since for the most part they know what they are doing, the question why they are doing it is not one which they find occasion to pose. Secondly, for the rest of us it must smack of philistinism to enter the arena at all, as though one who was tone-deaf should cast doubt on a performance of *The Ring* at Bayreuth. However, there is a difference. Even those who do not readily identify with Wagner recognize (a) that he had a certain aim in mind in composing the score, and (b) that that aim is accomplished whenever the work is performed. As to (a) it is not clear what aim the particle physicists now have for themselves, and as to (b) there is therefore no knowing how the accomplishment of the aim, if there is one, would be recognized and applauded if it came about.

For instance, some 200 sub-atomic particles have been discovered in the last two or three decades, and whereas in the early days each particle was the occasion for a press conference and an announcement that we were now approaching the very building blocks of matter, that practice has now been discontinued. Each building block has turned out to consist of other building blocks, and as they became smaller and more elusive the gigantic machines needed to detect them when they turn up (they don't always) have increased in size. In the vast circular tube built for CERN near Geneva, particles will be caused to collide at enormous speed and without touching life at any point. Quarks, leptons, mesons, and charmed particles will be thrown off in all directions, but will the cosmos be disturbed? Alas, or perhaps thankfully, no.

Last week a symposium was called at Cambridge to discuss six of the 200 particles which are, it appears, partly matter and partly not-matter. (That does not mean that they are anti-matter, which is a different thing entirely, as we should soon be aware if we came into contact with any. We should disappear in a puff of particles – or anti-particles as the case might be.) For want of a better term, the physicists have called them glue, because they apparently hold quarks together inside protons, but any similarity to the known world is purely coincidental. But the Cambridge colloquium does raise some terribly naive questions which someone has to be fool enough to ask. And the sort of questions which occur are: when are we going to get to the bottom of all this? What is the aim? Can a philosophy be built on these 200 interim quarks, leptons, glues, and hermaphrodite particles? If not, how many more sub-particles will it take? Will anybody understand, particle physicists apart, when it is all over? We ask because, pleasant though it is to have a highly intelligent, if expensive, science with no military application whatever, it would be comforting to know that there is a purpose of some kind that can, even dimly, be discerned. Pure mathematics is one thing: a brain at one end and a pencil at the other. But a science that exists, or so it seems, simply to go subdividing particles at ever-increasing technological cost, would be embarrassed to find that it was only proving a tautology and might lose its audience in trying to settle how many leptons dance at the sharp end of a quark.

15 November, 1982   **Leader**

Funny peculiar

Current notions of the comic in fiction often strike one as bizarre, if not downright hard-hearted. Hilarious, delightfully witty, a feast of fun, the blurbs and review quotes tend to call themes and narrative sequences that would make Strindberg blench.

Wider Pools ('sparkles with mordant humour', the jacket promises) deals in all manner of human abuse, deprivation, sexual exploitation and assault, with baby-stealing and an attempted suicide thrown in. Even the swimming pool which forms a key part of the locale has dry rot, which can at least be readily identified as a sort of mordant joke. True, Ursula Holden's style, while far from frivolous, is conspicuously sprightlier than her material, a contrast from which she derives much of her distinctive effect. The main characters are four women, all sorely abused by life, all revealed with a merciless clarity in their struggles at the deep end. No doubt they are waving rather than drowning but you can never be sure; there's always a hint of hidden depths, a final turn-up, the last joker in the pack.

Dangerous Pursuits is Nicholas Salaman's second novel and the blurb calls it hilarious, an overworked and often misused word which my dictionary defines as 'mirthful, joyous'. I'd say this book is a number of good things but hardly that. It is notably well written and well composed, if a shade overplotted. It is knowing, disquieting and – yes – funny, in a distinctly mirthless way.

An ex-combat soldier who has clearly gone round the bend decides that London life is a continuation of jungle warfare, dedicating his deadly techniques to tracking down an American who has offended his stern moral code and rescuing a pure English rose in the process. The man is as barmy as Quixote and has a gift for aphorism. Sex, he ruminates, has been the ruin of our civilisation; in one generation 'we have exposed what it took a thousand years to obscure.' He is a puritan with a vengeance.

Salaman has a curious knack of switching his style like a costume change, from the sleaziness befitting most of his characters to the prim, shadowed air that suits his haunted and haunting hero. If this is humour it's dark, if not black, and nobody is going to be surprised at that. Perhaps the surprise is to find any at all. We need an updated Bergson to explain how laughter currently operates. Contorting our facial muscles, taking them by surprise, bending them in ways they don't in the least expect to go – what is it in itself but a form of violence? If we didn't laugh we'd cry.

In *Author From a Savage People* ('brilliantly funny and poignant picture of a woman on the verge of sanity') the gifted Bette Pesetsky starts with a mugging and flings us round the demented city streets where people talk to their cars, watch vandals at work and generally carry on the sort of normal lives that have the analysts gibbering.

The heroine is a ghost-writer planning to blackmail a client who has won the Nobel Prize with her work. She is hopping mad and you can understand it. She wrote the stuff; why should he get the fame and the loot? You could laugh like mad at this but what you could hardly be able to produce would be a smile of human recognition.

The same applies, I'd say, to the hero of Todd McEwen's first novel, *Fisher's Hornpipe* ('outrageously funny and original'), who falls heavily on his head in the opening pages; this conditions all that happens to him. The stunned fantasy is impressively handled but doesn't mix too well with the more orthodox humour of misadventure; the book seems a bit at odds with itself as well as a shade repetitious. The musical motif is original though left undeveloped. Fisher owns a violin named Mr Squeaky, which is not encouraging, but the hornpipe promised in the title never gets played. Also – surely a first ever – there is a house haunted by a ghostly string quartet.

The book that achieves a smile, the human communication signal, is one that doesn't set out to be funny at all; not, at least, as a primary target. *Apprentice* is a series of linked stories in which Tom Gallacher presents the adventures of a learner in the Clydeside shipyards. Humour abounds; it emerges from the characters and their situations. There's the impassioned arguer in the dockside pub who pounds the table with one hand while carefully holding his glass steady with the other – he's funny, I'd say. And Gallacher reminds us, in this excellent book, how amusing naturalistic dialogue can be.

30 June, 1983   **Norman Shrapnel**

Worlds apart

My new play has opened to quite a furore. Critics have told me how little I understand my subject, how poor my construction is, and – this from the *Sunday Times!* – how perverted my values are. Some others have mercifully been kinder, and to them I am grateful. My biennial run-ins with the British press are no less depressing for being so predictable. But in this case they throw ironic light on the play's theme.

A Map Of The World takes its title from Oscar Wilde's saying that 'A map of the world which does not include Utopia is not worth even glancing at.' But it also alludes to a line from the play's central character, Victor Mehta, an Indian novelist who complains that we only notice those things which fit in with what we already believe. For 'everything that suits us we place upon our map.' The play's notices provide vivid illustration of this truth.

Mehta comes to a Unesco conference in Bombay in order to

deliver a keynote address. But first he is asked to read out a trumped-up statement, drafted by a committee, on the nature of fiction. He refuses, citing the writer's absolute freedom to say what he wants.

His position is countered by an African politician who objects that such freedom is frequently abused, and particularly by the Western press in their reporting of anything that has to do with the Third World. He describes the hurt of having the life of your country only ever reported in the political terms of the two great blocs.

This point of view is put by a character called M'Bengue in a ten-minute speech at the centre of the first act. It is acted by John Matshikiza, a South African-born actor of exceptional power. It is not often in plays that ten-minute speeches go by entirely unremarked. Yet it is as if nobody from Fleet Street has seen or heard this actor at all.

The whole of James Fenton's long review in the *Sunday Times* does no more than re-state Mehta's position before M'Bengue speaks. Nowhere does he refer to the fact that countervailing arguments exist, whatever he may think of them, nor to the fact that both sides' arguments are extensively modified in a later debate.

John Matshikiza returns as M'Bengue in the last scene – though once more you have only my word for it, for apparently whenever this actor appears the press find urgent business elsewhere. This time he is in a scene with Martinsen, the boss of the conference, who is seen to be pushing aid to Senegal on terms which will effectively destroy the economy of the country.

Throughout the play, the giving of aid has been presented as an apparently good thing in itself, yet now M'Bengue reveals that not only must a price be paid in political loyalty, but that the World Bank and the IMF both seek to dictate the social policies of those countries to whom they give help. By accepting aid, Third World countries become either political colonies of the aid-givers, or they have to abandon social policies of which the monetarists at the IMF disapprove. This international scandal, which is the climactic reversal of the play, is again something which goes right by the theatre reviewers at the pitch of a dog-whistle.

The critics, in other words, concentrate only on those things in the play which confirm them in their own prejudices, apparently unaware that they are themselves thereby becoming a spectacular demonstration of the play's basic argument. Michael Church, the third member of a Rupert Murdoch formation hit-team, nevertheless concedes in a review of the *South Bank Show*, which discussed the play, that I talk well about cynicism and maturity because, of course, these are the very subjects which most appeal to him. Milton Shulman, in a generous piece in the *Standard*, notes that I give the best arguments to the right-wing figure. He does not consider that perhaps they only seem to be the best arguments to him.

The reviewers also present themselves as thoroughly confused by the device in the play whereby a film is shown to be made from the original events in Bombay. When *A Map Of The World* was premiered at the Adelaide Festival, this device caused the Australian critics and audiences no problems at all. Yet for some reason it throws the home team into mass confusion. Shifts in reality, and of time and place, have been so much part of the language of film for so long that only people completely ignorant of modern cinema could find such changes difficult.

Five years ago, with courage, Peter Hall presented my last play, *Plenty*, which opened to what the National Theatre press office assure me were much worse reviews. For a couple of months we were hurt by this. But slowly, by word of mouth, our audience built and the play ran eight months in repertoire.

Plenty opened in New York last October and is still full. I have no idea if *A Map Of The World* is a good play or not, I only know it has not yet been judged. The audience will judge it, and from an extraordinary mass of letters already sent to me – more, and more various, than I have ever received – their judgment will be rounded. For I still have the unfashionable belief that critics should try to see plays as they are, in their fullness, and not concentrate solely on those parts which flatter their prejudices. In this case what the press has chosen to report and what to ignore seems to me especially significant.

Like motorway catering, theatre criticism in the main has been so dismal in England for so long that hope of overall improvement often seems to have gone. Higher standards are as likely as a new Trust House Forte sausage. On Sunday I collected £10 from an actor in the cast who had bet on good reviews for the play. The actor, I need hardly say, was not English.

3 February, 1983   **David Hare**

Grope and gore at the drive-in

In the land of the urban cowboy, where chic is a bashed-up old Chevvy, a long-necked beer bottle in the back pocket and a night out groping at Gillies or the drive-in cinema, there is a new hero. He is the anti-intellectual, the antithesis of the East Coast film critic, a red-neck who never shows himself but is famed throughout the Lone Star State.

Joe Bob Briggs is the US's first drive-in movie critic. His weekly reviews in the *Dallas Times Herald* have spread his reputation far and wide. The makers of low budget films from Los Angeles to New York love him. He is seen as a breath of fresh air in an industry in which the accolades usually go to directors with foreign-sounding names and accents who edit their films in a cellar somewhere, preferably hiding from the watchful eye of the KGB.

Joe Bob makes no concessions to art in judging a film. His standards are the same as his audiences: 'Blood, breasts, and beasts.' He gives extra stars for special effects, such as a good beheading. He writes nostalgically of the classic blood-lust films such as *The Texas Chain Saw Massacre*. His top rating goes to films in which 'anybody can die at any moment'.

Those who read his column know that Joe Bob stalks the drive-ins in his 1972 Oldsmobile Tornado. He usually takes along one of his woman friends, Wanda Bodine, Cherry Dilday, and May Ellen Masters. He describes them as 'dumb as the rocks'.

His column mysteriously stopped for three weeks last year after he went to gaol in Bossier City, Louisiana. He confided to readers that his sojourn was caused by a run-in with a mechanic who had stripped down one of his cars and run off with Mary Ellen. Despite his colourful life, Joe Bob Briggs keeps a low profile. He never answers requests for interviews, especially if they come from the 'wimps' of the New York or San Francisco press.

Indeed, there are some, including film critics on the rival *Dallas Morning News*, who doubt that he exists. Lengthy news agency reports have appeared speculating on the true identity of Joe Bob. But his identity remains as enigmatic as Deep Throat.

The descriptions in his reviews leave little to chance. *Evilspeak*, a film about devil cults, 'has more and better blood' than *Nightmare*, a film about a psychopathic murderer. Of *Parasite*, a science fiction film, he writes: 'Everything in this one. One kung fu scene. Eight corpses. Excellent slime monster. Hands roll. Heads roll. Three-and-a-half stars. Joe Bob says check-out.'

He hates the trendy. He regularly preaches against 'wimpola' (a Joe Bob conjugation of wimp) such as aerobic dancing, punk rock, car emissions standards, universities, Communism, drugs, and surfing. A pet dislike is public television, with its output of British, cultural, and political fare, and no advertisements.

His fans love him even though he has never been spotted. At a recent drive-in, a crowd gathered around a hot-dog kiosk led by a man wearing a 'leatherface' mask from the character in *The Texas Chain Saw Massacre*. 'We want Joe Bob,' they yelled.

13 November, 1982   **Alex Brummer**

Structuralist Diary

Professor Colin McCabe, the matinee idol of the Structuralist Years, recently welcomed the thought that postgraduates might study *Coronation Street* as part of a new course he is helping instigate at Strathclyde University.

A taste of the kind of work involved in such a project is contained in a *Coronation Street* teaching pack for fourth and fifth formers which has just been issued by the British Film Institute.

'Some of the work,' it warns in an introduction, 'has tended towards the notion of a text being a fixed unit of meaning which is organized by an underlying structural system of binary oppositions. Or to put it less technically' – (if you wouldn't mind) – 'and on more traditional terms, all texts contained basic themes which are shaped through the texts' language and which exist in a series of oppositions.' Through this, it says, students will come to an understanding of the specificity of *Coronation Street*.

An example of the approach: students are shown a slide of Dennis and Elsie quarrelling. The teacher's note runs as follows: 'The classic opposition across the frame of the dominant standing figure and subordinate (in this case, only for a moment) sitting figure. It might be interesting to ask students to consider here the difficult question of body gestures and of how we are able to read meaning from them.

'For example. Elsie here, arms folded (and along with all the other interpretative clues we have available to us) clearly connotes aggression, staying her ground; but *why* folding the arms in women should so signify is by no means clear.' Something to do with underlying structural systems of binary opposition, maybe.

27 May, 1983   **Alan Rusbridger**

One distant Tuscan cheer

Warm congratulations, puzzled though they may be, are owed to the buffer. As regular readers of this column may know, the buffer is the functionary of the Post Office, now approaching retirement, whose last professional ambition is to uphold and if possible perpetuate the ½p. From time to time we have questioned the value of this work to society at large, especially as the ½p is worth less than was the farthing when it made its ascent, many years ago, to the numismatist's Valhalla. Earlier this year the Post Office conceded that the new first-class letter rate should be 16p and not 16½p, and an inattentive observer might have thought that the buffer's resources had failed. That was not so. They were being marshalled. The result which has emerged is a stamp of hitherto unknown and unsuspected value.

The advent of the 3½p stamp is remarkable not, of course, because it contributes to another first-day cover, for that event is now so commonplace as to make the serious philatelist weep over his tweezers. The quality of the stamp lies in the absence of any use for it when the cheapest post is 12½p and stamps already exist in the ½p, 1p, 2p, 3p, and 5p denominations. So far from detracting from the buffer's achievement the failure of the 3½p either to meet a need or to create one enhances it. It takes a high degree of self-assurance to father forth so genuine an anachronism. Nor does the 3½p stamp in any way mark the completion of the year's toil. To replace the now redundant 19½p stamp the buffer has introduced another, not at 20p but at 20½p. Between 19½ and 20½ there is to be no happy, sloppy medium. (There is also a new 31p stamp, rather than the more obvious 30p, but that is not strictly relevant since whole numbers do not fall within the buffer's jurisdiction.) The buffer brooks no compromise. He is his own man. It would be churlish not to salute him.

18 April, 1983   **Leader**

Brief Chatline

For well-informed, stimulating conversations, one naturally turns to readers of the *Guardian*. And so did British Telecom, which chose this newspaper to announce its admirable new Chatline service.

'Ring Chatline on 01-555 0321 any day, any time to join in a live discussion for up to fifteen minutes. As many as nine people can talk on this new British Telecom London service,' said the announcement on the Personal page of yesterday morning's edition. Before the winter dawn broke – one imagined – the lines would be buzzing with animated discussion of the morning's leading articles; the detailed news coverage would be compared favourably with cheaper competitors, and provocative pieces on sport and the arts would be analysed as they are, daily in all the important saloon bars.

Alas, the line was silent. A similar advertisement had been

placed in Tuesday evening's edition of the *Standard*, a three-and-sixpenny newspaper circulating in the London area. The *Standard* announcement was available to its readers from around midday on Tuesday. By early evening, according to a British Telecom spokesman, conversation was progressing amiably, if not quite up to Parkinson standard.

'I listened in for a time and it all seemed quite innocuous to me. People were talking about what sort of jobs they had and where they lived, and what their interests were,' he reported. Moreover, the style, if not the content, of this illuminating dialogue was suited to polite society. The spokesman heard only one four-letter word.

Sadly, as the evening wore on, British Telecom monitors checking the new service were horrified to hear jokes, obscene suggestions and language which could only be described as tabloid. At 10 p.m., only ten hours after the service had started, and at least eight hours before *Guardian* readers could be expected to raise the tone, the plugs were pulled and Chatline was abandoned.

'We started it mainly with the aim of helping lonely people,' said the Telecom spokesman. 'They could have rung this number and talked to other lonely people. If they didn't want to continue the conversation they could have rung off. It seemed to be going very well in the early stages but, unfortunately, later on in the evening it was spoiled by a number of people whose conversations were unacceptable.

'We were monitoring the service because we wanted to note the number of calls so that we could have provided more lines if needed. But now Chatline is ended.'

23 December, 1982   **Derek Brown**

A country diary: The Lake District

Between the rain clouds sweeping across Mardale Ill Bell I can see from my study window the snow patches in Hall Cove and there is much more of it, unseen from here, on the north and east slopes of the fells – halfway through May. But this is nothing unusual. Sixteen years ago there were two inches of new May snow on my lawns one morning; and the following evening, as we were trooping into the Mary Wakefield Festival concert, the blizzard returned, quickly coating the Kendal pavements with three inches of wet slush, so that some of us sat through the music with damp feet. The festival is with us again this week and the farmers' weather forecast has already hinted at snow showers in the north. Snow is my perennial delight – but not new snow in May or June when we expect dry, sunlit fells and warm rocks. I remember June 1975, when there were quite heavy snowfalls so that it looked high summer across the green fields, the blossoming hedges and the thick woodlands but mid-winter on the backcloth of the fells with snow down to 1,500 feet and the summits more alpine than in December. Earlier that month I had kicked steps in hard snow up Cust's Gully on Great End and the previous September seen visitors snowballing each other on the top of Helvellyn. We have had a lot of snow on the fells this winter, with an excellent skiing and winter climbing season, but also a great deal of rain and miserable, cloudy weather. Indeed, since our return from Canada last September we have had more rain in these parts than I can remember in any other year and the fells have never been more persistently saturated. Perhaps all this foreshadows a blazing summer.

16 May, 1983   **A. Harry Griffin**

A Leveller

Anyone who thinks Tony Benn is a ranter should listen to his quiet persuadings. Anyone who thinks he is a looney should listen to his lucidities. But, for all that, he does appear to be a man convinced that if you are not for him you are against him, and probably want to blacken him into the bargain.

The other day at his house in Holland Park we had been talking about Divinity, the Levellers, the Declaration of Independence, the Chartists, and the betrayals of Ramsay Macdonald and David Owen. We talked about Mr Benn's father, who was forty-seven years in Parliament, and was once Secretary of State for India. We talked about Mr Benn's uncle, Sir Ernest Benn, who was as convinced and active a capitalist as Mr Benn is a Socialist, and once wrote in one of his many polemical books that he had failed to discover any material benefit which had ever reached mankind except through the agency of individual enterprise.

We talked – he a bit edgily – about Mr Benn's diminishing and then vanishing *Who's Who* entry. He told me, though I did not inquire the exact amount, that his private income amounted, after tax, to only £5,000 a year. He had of course talked about the sinful rewriting of political history, and about the 'bland fascism' of Mrs Thatcher's government. It was all most amiable.

Then, after about an hour, Mr Benn said that his constituency surgeries in Bristol, which used to be quiet chats, were now tragic. He told me the story of a man who had telephoned him saying he was out of work, that his wife and one of his children were ill, and that the Electricity Board had told him that unless he paid his bill of £78 he would be cut off and it would take £300 to re-connect him. He did not have £78. Mr Benn phoned the Electricity Board, got through by accident to the chairman, whom he happened to have appointed, and all was well.

I said, 'Three cheers for a good constituency MP.' It was a remark very much in the tone of our previous conversation, but Mr Benn changed at that moment.

'No,' he said. 'No, don't say that.'

We looked at each other, and he then began to speak passionately. I give the passage in full:

'People,' he said, 'are absolutely *desperate*. And unless somehow – this is an appeal I shouldn't perhaps make to you – but unless these issues are dealt with in the public media and in Parliament in a way that shows people are *concerned*, and not just about what happens in the sort of personality conflicts that are so beloved, then this country is going to descend into a major tragedy. Now I can't persuade you, and I mustn't try like Mr Gladstone to address you as if you were a public meeting, but what do you think, if you stop for a moment? Because you've asked me a lot of deep questions about *Who's Who*, and my father, but what do you think I am? Why do you think I've changed in my life? Do you think I suddenly read a book? Don't you think it's probably because I've been round the country and seen people whose lives are being destroyed?'

This was a question which expected no reply. Mr Benn continued, headlong:

'And yet, having said that, I did try for many years as a minister to make the old system work. I was a very *conscientious* Minister of Technology: I was trying to make the SDP's current policy work. I had doubts about whether it would work, but that was the consensus – that we'd help, we'd assist, we'd protect. And it failed. And I'm fifty-eight. I'm getting on now. What do you think in the middle of life makes me change? It's that I've seen people's lives being destroyed, and it burns me up. Now if I say this, if you really want to understand me, look at what I've been in my life – that I've tried and I've failed. You've picked in this very clinical way round me, like a post-mortem, but what do you think chewed me up, what do you think made me what I am? What do you think makes a guy in middle life become a Socialist, much to his surprise?

'It's the *circumstances*. I've seen the motor industry destroyed. I've seen the motorbike industry destroyed. I've seen Merseyside destroyed. I've seen Clydeside destroyed. I've seen South Wales destroyed. I'm seeing in Bristol a growing cancer of unemployment and hopelessness in a prosperous city. I was at a meeting the other day where a black family was present. The police had kicked their door in at four in the morning, got them out of bed, stripped them, made them stand against the wall. . . .'

Where? 'In London. It happens all the time. When they rang the local police station the next morning they'd never heard of it. It turned out that the police (of the night before) had got the wrong address. I mean, there are bookshops being burned. This isn't reported. And what's going on in the black community? I don't know whether any synagogues are being burned, but I mean . . .'

This broke the spell. I asked if he knew of a single synagogue being burned. 'Well I don't know. There have been attacks. I was saying I don't know . . . But attacks on left-wing bookshops are going on all the time, and the police are harassing people in West London, Asians; it's a serious problem.'

This was not Mr Benn's public meeting style, which is pretty cool. Nor was there a shred of acting about it. He was angry, and I thought he was close to tears of anger.

Now, to put this in context, back to what had gone before. On meeting, small talk about his American clock in the hall, a nineteenth-century, factory-made clock, very pretty, sent here, he said, at a dumping price. The first clocks to be dumped. The clockwork had failed and he had replaced it with a battery. Then we talked about his grandfather, the publishing Benn who was made a baronet and served eighteen years in the Commons, and then about Mr Benn's father, William Wedgwood Benn, a younger son who therefore did not inherit the baronetcy but went into politics and in 1942 was created Viscount Stansgate.

He sat first as a Liberal, was Whip in the great Liberal Government of 1910 in which Churchill was Home Secretary, then in 1927 joined the Labour Party and resigned his seat the same day, a principle which Mr Benn thinks should apply to all, including Labour defectors to the SDP.

Between 1928 and 1931 he was back in the Commons and became Secretary of State for India, which is arguably a higher office than his son has ever held. The young Benn, then aged five or six, met Gandhi, expecting magic but finding only a kindly man sitting on an hotel floor. He met a Maharajah, a cruel man, who talked to him about tiger hunting and was later assassinated.

William Wedgwood Benn lost his seat in the landslide of 1931, and set off with his wife to travel to America, Japan, China, Russia, and round the world.

Anthony was left alone in London, perhaps for a year, perhaps only for a few months. He cannot remember, but it seemed a long time. He and his brothers were looked after by a nurse, who is still alive and whom he visited the other day. She is now eighty-three. She was born on January 1, 1900, so it's easy to remember.

At the age of eleven, he bought and partly read *Mein Kampf*. At Westminster School he won the Toplady Prize for Divinity, for an essay touching on the role of the prophets.

Ah, I said, I believed it was one of Mr Powell's ideas that one of the functions of a parliamentarian was to *speak forth* as a prophet.

Mr Benn did not like the association. 'I have very different political views, but I do think we have corrupted politics in recent years by associating them more with the tasks of management than with understanding, representation, and education. As I get older, perhaps because I've had my span of life in managerial politics, I'm more interested in understanding what's happening, in speaking to people, and giving them confidence to do things for themselves, rather than inviting them to have confidence in me.'

Did this mean he did not expect to hold office again? He had no ideas about that.

Then to other relatives. Margaret Rutherford was his father's cousin. His father's elder brother Ernest, the second baronet and a publishing magnate, was a Manchester School Liberal who would have been very pleased with what was happening now. In spite of the deep political breach, between his father and uncle, the family used to go to Sir Ernest's at Christmas. The young Tony Benn played chess with the arch-capitalist.

Just before the war William Wedgwood Benn was elected equal first to the Labour Shadow Cabinet. In the war he and his eldest son, Michael, joined the RAF. In 1943 Michael was killed, and his father, though by then aged sixty-six, was so moved by this that he used his rank of Air Commodore to get himself on several flying missions, before the RAF caught up with him.

Tony Benn trained as a bomber pilot in Rhodesia, but the war ended before he could see action, and he returned to England where he went up to Oxford and became president of the Union. He also went across America as one of the Union debating teams. Hadn't he said he always felt very much at home there?

'America did recreate in its own foundation some of the principles which were blanked out here. If you look at the Agreement of the People in 1649, of course it reappeared in the Declaration of Independence, and had some influence in creating a society which an English radical would find agreeable.'

With the Agreement of the People we were back to the English Levellers, who, with the Chartists, are Mr Benn's favourite people in history. He believes that, as you go back, you find men facing the same problems as you do now, and they are your roots. At times, reading about a man long dead, it is like recognizing a relative. He says the Levellers saw the earth as common treasury, an idea that recurs in the ecology movement, and which came originally from St Francis of Assisi.

When I said the Levellers weren't much known these days, Mr Benn replied: 'It's the privilege of the victors to extinguish the memory of the vanquished, and yet they don't succeed. I suppose you could say that the New Testament story ended with failure, that Che Guevara was interred with his bones, that Trotsky, having been murdered in Mexico, was a figure of total failure. . . . But you can't suppress ideas.'

It seemed to me that the pickaxe through Trotsky's skull has been the instrument of his apotheosis just as surely as the Cross has been Jesus's, but, not wanting to return to Divinity, I asked instead why the ideas of the Levellers had taken so long, 125 years, to find expression, as Mr Benn believes they did, in the American Declaration of Independence.

'It depends,' he said, 'whether you accept the Wilson view that a week is a long time in politics. I very often like to quote what Mao said when he was asked to assess the influence of the French Revolution on world history, and he replied "It's a bit early to say." '

Did Mr Benn believe that? 'Of course I do. Much too early to say.'

And Mr Benn believed, in spite of manifest evidence to the contrary, that all men were created equal?

'I believe there's an inherent right to equality, which you don't have to earn by your own effort: it's inherent. And I think that is the moral basis of socialism.'

A right to life, liberty, and the pursuit of happiness? 'Let's say peace and jobs and freedom. You can interpret it in different ways: . . . but a right to a full life, and that right is where equality lies.'

We then came to the various forms of Mr Benn's name. His unwilling inheritance of the Stansgate viscountcy and his eventual disclaiming of it by means of an Act which incidentally changed the course of political history by allowing Lord Home to become Prime Minister, are well known, and shall be left aside here.

But what about his entries in *Who's Who*? For years these had been routine. He was the Hon Anthony Neil Wedgwood Benn; the Rt Hon when he became a Privy Councillor. His places of education were given as Westminster and New College, Oxford. Then first his public school and then his college disappeared, and his education was stated to be 'still in progress'; then in 1976 his entry was reduced from thirty-eight lines to three, and in 1977 disappeared altogether. Now what was the point of all this, when anyone could look him up in other reference books, and, in most detail, in the current Debrett, under the Stansgate peerage, where even his honorary doctorates of Strathclyde, Ashton, and Bradford were given?

He did not at first answer directly, but then said he supposed *Who's Who* was a symbol of the Establishment and he did not want to be in it.

So, I said, he was now Tony Benn. His old nurse, and friends at Oxford, had called him Anthony. Mr Crosland had called him Jimmy.

(He said this was because his mother always called him James, and still did.)

But what was there in 1975 or 1976 that had suddenly determined him to cut his *Who's Who* entry?

He didn't answer this. He did say: 'May I put this to you? *Tony* Crosland. *Jim* Callaghan. Charles Anthony Raven Crosland. James Callaghan. The truth is there's nothing to it. These comments were not made about Charles Anthony Raven Crosland. I don't mind if you want to, and I dare say the article could centre round some deep psychological explanation of this. I sign myself Tony Benn. And, all right, I did it at a particular time, progressively, but all my friends have called me Tony all my life. . . . At the end of his life my father was made a peer like George Brown, or Joe Gormley. Even if I was the eighteenth duke and owned all Yorkshire it wouldn't make any difference. People would have to judge you on what you said and did. That's all.'

About here I used the word 'populist' purely descriptively, but Mr Benn demurred, saying he was no demagogue. In his speeches he tried to analyse and explain, so that people should feel there was more they could do themselves, rather than putting their faith in political leaders.

Wasn't it strange for a man who had spent his life in politics to tell others not to put their faith in political leaders? 'Well, look at them. Just take them. Take Ramsay Macdonald, take George Brown, take David Owen. Take Roy Jenkins.'

Not a bad lot? 'They're people who climbed into power on the back of the movement and kicked the ladder away, and they betrayed the people who put faith in them. They didn't resign their seats. That's why I'm so proud of my father, who resigned his seat the day he changed his party.'

We touched briefly on Peter Tatchell, whose treatment at Bermondsey, said Mr Benn, entitled one to ask whether the democratic process was now working properly, since no man should be so vilified. We touched on Bevan, of the Left, who had been wrong to ask, in the matter of nuclear disarmament, whether he should go naked into the conference chamber; and on Gaitskell, of the Right, who had been wrong to say, on the same issue, that he would fight, and fight, and fight again. Mr Benn said he no more wanted American bases in England than he would want Russian bases.

Then we came to the bland fascism which Mr Benn believes is being introduced by Mrs Thatcher's Government. First he defined fascism, which in the 1920s and 1930s had meant the creation of a corporate state, the suppression of parliament, democracy, trade unions, and socialism, and was, he said, anti-women and anti-homosexual. These ideas were still in circulation, and in a society in deep crisis would have an appeal.

'If you want,' he said, 'to preserve the present pattern of power and privilege, then you are driven to unemployment, and the Establishment has to have plastic bullets, and then CS gas, and then a Police Bill which now allows the police to enter any house.'

Why did he say *bland* fascism? 'I must make myself clear. If you have a very severe economic crisis, then the Establishment has to develop ideas to make people accept that it's their fault. It has to persuade people that they've lost their jobs because they were greedy, that they were not productive, not competitive: that they are not entitled to have health care unless they can pay for it.'

Surely no one had said that last thing? 'Well, the idea now is

181

that all these things must be "won by individual effort." . . . It is already a very centralized, and secretive, and rather corporate society.'

I asked where this fascism came from. Did he mean from Mrs Thatcher? From her government? From the petty bourgeoisie in the constituencies who were to the right of the Government? I did not get an answer. It is my reading that Mr Benn is so thorough a collectivist that he will not recognize merely individual responsibility if he can help it. He says he advises people not to attack Thatcherism as such, because if Mrs Thatcher were to go tomorrow there would be Pym-ism, or Whitelaw-ism. He asked me to uncouple names from ideas.

He believes this is a cruel government. When I said cruelty implied malice, an intent to hurt, he would not accept that, and it was agreed that he meant there was an indifference to suffering.

It was here that he called his constituency surgery a centre of tragedy, and, changing his tone to one of the greatest intensity, spoke the words reported at the beginning of this article.

The conversation couldn't be maintained at that intensity, but it did not become relaxed again. Mr Benn mentioned the women at Greenham Common, over whose bodies he said the police had trampled. 'How,' he asked 'does it differ from what's happening in Poland?'

I began to answer, but Mr Benn must have seen that I hardly thought it worth an answer because he said, 'Gaoling the dissidents here wouldn't agitate you like gaoling Lech Walesa? I feel that actually when we do talk about these things we live in very different worlds.'

He thought people in this country were afraid, and fearful, and said: 'If you take the view I do, that you're bound to try and reverse government policies—, when I do that the language is used, that I am hard-Left, that I am extreme. It's none of these things. I should like to see a society where people have a better deal, and it's so simple, so moderate, and so modest in its objective. To want people to have work, homes, and schools, health, and dignity in retirement – that's not extreme. And it is the achievement of the media to present these modest demands as destructive of society. . . . Clearly a way has to be found for change, but change can be set back if those who advocate it are blackened and discredited, distorted, harassed, and abused.'

Could he name a single Socialist society which had not become a tyranny. 'Yes, London . . . the London of Livingstone.'

But a nation? 'Why a nation? Where is socialism to be found? It is to be found in those little pockets of our life where we have protected decent human values from the ravages of violence or market forces. Every hospital in the National Health Service is a pocket of socialism, and every comprehensive school.'

Then, at the end, he said he believed it was not socialism but democracy that was controversial.

Democracy? 'Oh, of course. I mean, look at the Labour Party. What people are really afraid of, in power, is having to share it. The reason that the climate of Labour Party discussion in the years since 1979 has got so hot is not because Socialist rhetoric changed. It is because people said "We want to share the power more widely". What we suffer from is not too much democracy but too little.'

And there speaks a leader who passionately exhorts people not to put their faith in leaders. There speaks a man who says he has tried, and failed, and now sees people as desperate. And it's the *circumstances*. And he was a very conscientious minister.

25 February, 1983   **Terry Coleman**

Our bloody little scribbler

Having told Trotsky he was wrong about the international revolution, been George Orwell's officer on the Aragon front in the Spanish Civil War, helped organize the American Auto Workers' Union, Bob Edwards then wrote a pamphlet entitled *War On The People* about the coming of the atom bomb. That was in 1943. 'It will mean race suicide,' he wrote, two years before Hiroshima.

'I was writing a column on American labour news for *Socialist Leader*, and I took all the US union journals and read about this strike of miners in Colorado who were digging for some stuff I'd

183

never heard of called uranium. So I started doing some research, and felt I had to write the pamphlet. Never underestimate the power of a pamphlet,' says Edwards, seventy-seven this year, sharp as a button and reselected by his Wolverhampton constituency.

There is a move among MPs to start an oral history programme in the House, putting its elders before a tape recorder and getting them to reminisce. When it starts, Bob Edwards has to be top of the list. A despatch rider for the TUC in the General Strike of 1926, he is a walking history of the labour movement. It was at Bob's meetings in the streets of Liverpool that Jack Jones learned to be a socialist, and when Bob led one of the first hunger marches from the 'Pool, young Jack strode in the ranks. When he recalled chatting with Mao in Moscow in 1926, the Chinese denied their Chairman had ever been there until they checked, found Bob was right, and honourably made amends by inviting him to China.

'I was meant to go in 1926, to help Sun Yat Sen's revolution, but when the Russians found I was in the Independent Labour Party, and not a young Communist, they stopped me. Just as well. The entire delegation of seventy was wiped out by Chiang Kai Shek.

'Trotsky was the most impressive speaker I ever knew, he could lift us all off our feet, but he was a womanizer, a bit lazy. And Stalin was right about the need to build socialism in one country. I had a row with Trotsky when he said that the defence of Russia lay in the imminent revolutions in Britain and Germany. I'd just come from the General Strike and I knew it wasn't on.

'Still, he gave me a copy of his book *Whither Britain*, and signed it for me. I know where that is, but I'm not sure where my letters from George Orwell and Ernest Hemingway are. I used to call George our bloody little scribbler, but he was too brave. The Spaniards with us would never take cover under fire, and George would stand up with them to save their Spanish dignity.

'I was an elected officer, elected when our first one wanted to have a couple of batmen. We soon got rid of him. But having been an officer in a foreign army, they wouldn't let me into the British Army in World War Two.

184

'I'm still an internationalist, solid Labour but I'm a great believer in Europe. We'll have a socialist EEC next and we'd be daft to come out. I never wanted to be a Minister. I'd been general secretary of my union, the Chemical Workers and chairman of the ILP, and an MP and I never wanted to be anything else. And then we merged the union with Jack Jones's T&G. I was brought up a socialist, christened in a socialist Sunday school. When I was seven my dad took me to a meeting with Keir Hardie.'

12 February, 1983   **Martin Walker**

Oh lucky John, he goes on and on

'A new row is brewing over the Falklands. A war of words. Not the Argies this time. The trouble comes from the nitpickers in this country.'

This warning – this stark warning – was issued this week by the *Sun* newspaper. The threat, it said, came from 'intellectuals', 'sneerers', and the Left in the highbrow Press. 'What,' it demanded, 'do the any-country-but-my-own brigade argue? They swallow any whopper which blots Britain's record.' Had such people been heeded, of course, we would never have fought for the Falklands at all. 'We would have been seen as softies . . . the Russians would have drawn their own conclusions.' 'These twits' a headline proclaimed 'are a blot on Britain.'

No *Sun* staff chap wrote this piece. It did not even spring from the pens that gave us 'Gotcha' (when the Belgrano went down) and 'Up yours, Galtieri'. It came instead from the booklined cloisters of the University of Bristol, dreaming amidst its ivory towers. It was the work of Professor John Vincent, Professor of Modern History in that university, and until recently better known as author of *The Formation of the British Liberal Party, 1857–68*; *Poll Books: How the Victorians Voted*; and (with A. B. Cooke) *Governing Passions: Cabinet Government and Party Politics in Britain 1885–86*.

Long ago the Professor dipped his toes into journalism with

185

scholarly pieces in *New Society*. He wrote then from a position which seemed sympathetic to the Liberal Party, though he was not afraid to give it trenchant and outspoken advice. 'The Liberals,' he once counselled, 'should forget proportional representation, forget about strenuous attempts to become a country party on a minute scale, and just sit and wait for the other chaps to make mistakes.'

In those days the Professor would regularly write a sentence of a hundred words or more. Nor was he ashamed to pepper his work with uncompromisingly intellectual, if not necessarily leftish, words like 'persona', 'modus vivendi' and 'déclassé'. Yet he was usually pungent and pithy; and still more so when he began a regular column for *The Times* last year. Quirky, sharp and combative, it nonetheless managed to blend tastefully with the wallpaper at New Printing House Square.

But elsewhere in the Murdoch empire, keen eyes were by now trained on the pungent Professor. The polysyllables were forgiven in the light of the Thatcherite tint they carried. The Professor was asked to launch a second front: a regular column in the *Sun*. Instantly, the 'let's-face-it,-you've-got-to-hand-it-to-Maggie,-the-girl's-got-guts' school of British journalism claimed another victim. Effortlessly, the highbrow from Bristol adapted to the modus vivendi of a newspaper which never says in half a dozen words what can somehow be rammed across with only two, or, better still, two fingers.

'Another smear going the rounds on the Left,' the *Sun*'s page six boy wrote with relentless pungency this week, 'is that the war cost £1 million for each Falklander. I sniff exaggeration here.' What a restful change it must be from the dreary old academic disciplines where people expect you to check such points, instead of simply sniffing and passing on! Still, even the sneerers have to admit that the column is unfailingly pungent and pithy. Indeed, Professor Vincent, pithy in *New Society*, pithier still in the *The Times* and pithiest of all in The Paper That Supports Our Boys, may deservedly come to be recognized in 1983 as one of the supreme pith artists in modern British journalism.

8 January, 1983   **Leader**

Force fed on pidgin pie

That old newspaper speciality, printer's pie, over-seasoned with literals, can be indigestible fare, to be sure, but as a long-time practitioner in the words industry what I find much harder to stomach these days is the pidgin being served up more and more by television and radio as well as the press.

Only Canute's courtiers would deny that language is a living thing which has been adapting organically to changing needs and mores since personkind's first Neanderthal grunt. But the increasingly rapid spread of what I can only describe as Engloid throughout the all-pervasive communications media fore-shadows an anarchy that must eventually defeat the whole object of communication – to understand and be understood.

Chaucer put his finger on the problem 600 years ago when he declared:

> *ther is so great diversitë*
> *in Englissh and in writyng of our tongue*
> *so prey I God that non myswrite thë . . .*
> *that thow be understonde,*
> *God I beseche!*

That diversity was because he and his contemporaries were just beginning to meld two languages and a score of dialects into one coherent national speech. Today the process is being put into reverse. The modification of sound, spelling and meaning which once proceeded over centuries at the ox's pace has been speeded up electronically in the last two decades and exacer-bated by the growth of sub-literacy among post-war generations taught by 'progressive' teachers for whom grammar, syntax, spelling and standard pronunciation were anachronistic relics of Victorian discipline, like the cane and the ten-times table.

As a Scot I was dismayed to read recently that in Scotland, traditionally the guardian of English grammar, a professor of education had dismissed students' glaring lack of it as mere 'verbal infelicity'. But the defensive attitude of such academics ignores the long-term implications for our now universal lan-guage, an international medium of cultural, political and econo-mic influence if ever there was one, unless our schools make a sound knowledge of English at least as important a part of the curriculum as facility with the computers now being installed in primary schools.

To get back to Chaucer's point: good communication depends on both parties knowing precisely what the other means. This demands agreed grammatical forms that eliminate ambiguity. It isn't a question of pedantic nit-picking but of accuracy. Take the growing misuse of 'prevarication' (lying) for 'procrastination' (putting off decisions etc). No less eminent an exemplar than Mrs Thatcher condemned Argentina's *prevarication* in one of her broadcast speeches during the Falklands affair when the context plainly implied she meant the junta was 'stalling'. One wonders what effect this may have had on Galtieri . . .

It is difficult to know whether mistaken usage, garbled syntax or misleading punctuation is doing most harm to clarity of thought and the transmission of ideas and information, but the sum of the solecisms is greater than the whole because of the dual influence of the printed and broadcasting media. In the same week that I heard a participant in a radio programme about *writing* refer to 'the two mediums' and 'the media has' in almost the same breath I was discomfited to find the neologism 'discomforture' in the *Guardian*'s splash. It seems the grating intrusive 'r' as in 'Indiar is' is infiltrating the written word: 'torturous' is now common journalese.

If you think I'm unnecessarily alarmist I must warn you that many of the new race of graduate journalists have a very shaky grasp of the basic tool of their trade. Not all believe, like an otherwise very bright one, that 'plummet' means to shoot upwards, but most, like the lad who writes the greengrocer's tickets, think the apostrophe's only function is to indicate plural's, if you see what I mean. For them agreement of subject and verb is as pointless as the hyphen (hence all those vice chairmen and vice principals, who presumably organize vice rings). As one replied defensively, 'There's hundreds of examples in the papers every day'. And it has to be admitted that the qualities are no better than the pops in this respect.

Further, the heavies are becoming even heavier by the increasing adoption of the uglier aspects of German-American English with its overlay of sociological jargon and advertising copywriter's cant. This invasion takes several forms. Most common is the US habit of never using one word when two or more can be pressed into service, however tautological. For instance, the insertion of superfluous prepositions behind verbs: consult *with*, meet *with*, separate *out*, calculate *out*, drown *out*, lose *out*, not to mention the whole corpus of numbing clichés – low profile, scenario, parameter (wrongly used as a synonym for limit or framework).

Infinitives are now being split so wide it takes a Teutonic syntactical sense to bridge the gap, as in 'to actually, in the light of experience gained from the pilot scheme that will precede it, modify the final project.' Then there is that other transatlantic importation (as we now call an import), the long-winded vanguard that is ousting the qualifying clause: 'the recently hoped for but now increasingly doubtful end of the review period decision.'

The very catholicism of radio and TV, broadcasting voices from every social and regional group, has made yesterday's oral 'vulgarisms' today's norm, from the universal 'secketary', 'Febuary', 'libry' and 'opra' to the shifting of stress in words now pronounced like distri*buted* and *pro*tested. This metathesis knows no barriers of class or rank. While Mr Norman Tebbit declares there will be 'no in*crease*' in NHS pay, David Coleman tells us that Seb's hamstring is 'sus*pect*'. The differentiation between noun, verb and adjective is following 'whom' into linguistic limbo, all nuance lost.

Another oral innovation introduced by Australian broadcasters, whose Strine has American undertones, is the revival of final vowels long muted in Brit'n but increasingly pronounced as by an infant reading from his primer – Brit-tain, writ-ten, sud-den, cot-ton etc. Placenames are equally subject to this offence against euphony: the A-von now sounds more like a peddled cosmetic than the noble Swan's bourne, and *Coal*chester suggests one of Mr Scargill's constituencies. Again, our betters know no better – Mr Pym invariably refers to the Leban'n as Leba-non, acknowledging America's sovereignty in the matter.

The contagion is deep-seated, within a Catch-22 context. Only a radical revision of the method of teaching English will reverse the trend to sloppy anarchy. But, to paraphrase Justinian, who will teach the teachers? Until someone more sensitive to the problem than Sir Keith Joseph tackles it I can only recommend that all communicators make it a new year resolution to get hold of Gowers's *Plain Words* and Michael Temple's admirable little handbook, *A Pocket Guide to Written English*. Study them, I beseche ye!

13 December, 1982   **Tom Baistow**

For all you geeks out there

It's like the bitchenest, like neatest way to talk, I'm sure, totally. It's so awesome, I mean, fer shurrr, toadly, toe-dully! To the max! Come onnnnn-bag your face, you geek, you grody totally shanky spaz, if you can't talk like a total Valley Girl, rilly, I'm shurrr. Gag me with a spoooooon! Ohhhhmigawwwd! OK: Valspeak is, I meannnn, wow!, the funnest, most totally radical language, I guess, like in the whole mega gnarly city of Los Angeles? Fer shur-r-r-r!

English as she is mangled in America contains so many astoundingly inventive dialects that students of sociolinguistics in California think they've died and gone to heaven. Valspeak is the latest teentalk craze to surface in the real world, brought to adults' attention in the usual way: a hit record, *Valley Girl* by Frank Zappa and his fifteen-year-old daughter Moon Unit, is a five-minute soliloquy on the ValGal lifestyle, from school to mall and back again.

Zappa has always specialized in obscure outrages like *My Guitar Wants to Kill Your Mama*, and has never before had a hit single. *Valley Girl* started out as a typical riff 'n' mumble Zappaism, but then Dad asked daughter to step into the studio 'and just babble – ramble on about nothing, basically,' Moon has recalled. The hilarious result has sold a million copies and pushed Zappa's forty-sixth album, *Ship Arriving Too Late to Save a Drowning Witch*, into the upper reaches of the charts.

Valspeak is principally girltalk, depending as it does on an infinite variety of gurgles, squeaks and squeals. Exclamations

190

are drawn out and sung through several octaves. Declarative sentences have a way of sounding like questions. To understand, you have to watch how the hand flips the hair, how the foreleg stands akimbo, how the upper lip twitches. Conversations tend to the antiphonal: 'I'm sure' (meaning yes) suggests the reply 'I'm sure (meaning no). Sarcasm and put-downs are essential to any dialogue, as ValGals sort and grade their possessions and impressions according to that day's prevailing standards.

To Valspeak, 'You stick your jaw way out until it's almost as if you have an underbite,' Moon Zappa has advised. 'All the muscles in the neck must be straining to pronounce each word. With the buck-jaw, there is the ear that is epoxyed to the shoulder and the frantic lever-type action that finds the hair being constantly flipped back. The shoulders seem to wobble as though the person is riding a horse – as though shocks of electricity repeatedly jolt the body.'

Moon's clever babble brought shrieks of recognition all up and down Ventura Boulevard from Encino to Burbank, the heartland of the sprawling nouveau middle class San Fernando Valley. The place is commonly referred to as the Valley, as in 'Tell me you don't live in the Valley.' It is often said of Los Angeles that 'There is no *there* there,' and the Valley is one of the least *there* places in L.A. It's a huge continuous suburb that lies to the north of all the nicer parts of town.

The Valley is the home of more than a million stucco-dwellers who see no need to cross the Hill to Sunset Boulevard – they have everything they want right there in the Valley. What they want most is to shop, and where they want most to shop is the Sherman Oaks Galleria. In a land cursed with almost continuous sunshine, The Galleria offers sheltered shopping and guaranteed uniformity of styles. Whatever you buy at the Galleria, you won't have to worry about looking any different from all the other Vals.

The Valley Girl, well-heeled with time on her hands, suburban and middle-class, is, first and foremost, a consumer. She gets about $50 a week spending money and she puts her billies into anti-zit make-up, tanning oil, pedicures, Van Halen tapes for her Walkman, ruffled blouses and miniskirts for formal occasions and designer jeans for caj wear, pointy-toed slippers for school, metallic belts and bracelets, Harlequin bodice-rippers for beach reading, upmarket fast food, Heinies and Lowies for brew, pot of the odd bud sesh, and gas for Daddy's BMW, which she can drive any time she wants as long as she doesn't total it.

The Valley Girl is named Andrea, Cynthia, Roni, Tani, Jayme, Cori, Kelli, Kim, Keri, Kristi, Michelle, Stacy, Tracy, Trina or Tricia. If her mother named her Mary, her friends got so barfed out she changed it to Merri. She goes for a really tubular type of dude, the kind of hot babe with a cute butt who isn't all hairy and gross but isn't any nerdy zod either. The Valley Guy drives a make-out van with sheepskin seatcovers and one little window shaped like a teardrop. If he isn't behind the wheel, the Valley Guy is working at Hamburger Hamlet to scratch some readies, which is mondo cool, 'cause the Valley Girl stoops 'n' scoops at Haagen Dasz ice cream, just across the aisle at the mall. She doesn't need the billies but she makes the scene to eye the guys and just generally be a soc. As the *Valley Girl's Guide to Life* by Mimi Pond advises, 'Being popular is important. Otherwise, people might not like you.' Fer Shur–r–r–r!

A GLOSSARY OF VALSPEAK

Awesome (adj.) good.
Bag your face (interjec.) expression of disagreement.
Barf (v., n.) vomit.
Barf me out (v.) to disgust; interjec., expression of disgust.
Billies (n., plu.) money.
Bitchen (adj.) good.
Brew (n.) beer.
Bud (n.) marijuana.
Buf (adj.) desirable.
Butt (n.) posterior.
Caj (adj., abbr.) (casual); good.
For sure (interjec.) expression of either support or scorn.
Gag me with a spoon (interjec.) expression of disgust.
Geek (n.) undesirable person.
Get away (interjec.) expression of disgust.

Gnarly (adj.) good.

Grody (adj.) unspeakably awful.

Gross (adj.) really unspeakably awful.

Heine (n.) Heinekens beer.

Hot (adj.) very good.

Kiss my tuna (interjec.) expression of superiority.

Lowe (n.) Lowenbrau beer.

Major (adv.) very.

Max (n.) maximum; (v.) to score high.

Mega (adj.) powerful, large.

Mondo (adv.) very.

Nerd (n.) insignificant person; good student.

Oh my God (interjec.) expression of surprise, enthusiasm or disgust.

OK (interjec.) please pay attention to the following statement.

Radical (adj.) very good.

Scarf (out) (v.) eat greedily.

Sesh (n., abbr.) session.

Skanky (adj.) unpleasant.

Soc (n., abbr.) (socialite); sociable person.

Spaz (n., abbr.) (spastic); undesirable person.

Totally Tubular (adj. interjec.) very good. (adj.) orig., in surfing, descr., a well-curved wave; very good.

Val (n.) Valley dweller, usu., fem. under 18.

Vicious (adj.) extremely desirable.

Zod (n.) insignificant person, usu. also ugly.

26 October, 1982   **Bart Mills**

Say it again Hrusev

Tsortsil, Gete, and Gamlet are all old friends in unfamiliar disguise: they are the standard spellings of Churchill in modern Greek, Goethe in Bengali, and Hamlet in Russian. We don't quite know how Thistlethwaite would go into Thai, but the question is bound to arise one of these days and the answer will probably be surprising, perhaps contentious. So it is not at all strange that the United Nations should have called a conference to try to reach agreement on transliteration. It has hit a snag over

Russian, though the Soviet delegation has mildly suggested that its proposals should be held over until everyone has had a good think.

What the Russians would like all users of the Latin alphabet to do is to substitute for each cyrillic letter or sign one Latin letter or sign only. This has obvious attractions, not least to German headline writers for whom the man they know as Chruschtschew and we know as Khrushchev would dwindle into Hrusev. Then there are the benefits of uniformity. The trouble is that the succinctness of Hrusev depends on a diacritical mark or twiddle over the 's' which modern printing technology is less and less able to provide. With the best of goodwill, we should ourselves be unable to supply some of these twiddles. And that might lead to awkward mix-ups.

Transliteration can also have odd long-term consequences. In their bluff early days the British in India spelt local names in what they took to be English phonetic equivalents. So they took the name of the hamlet from which a great city grew and wrote it 'Calcutta' to rhyme with 'call cutter' – accurate enough in its reproduction of vowel sounds and stress. But with time all that changed; the first 'a' came to rhyme with 'pal' and the stress shifted to the second syllable. Then the French in their ruthless way pronounced the word as if it were French; by way of a pun too elaborate to explain, this led ultimately to the nude revue *Oh! Calcutta!*. Perhaps the UN conference had better remain adjourned indefinitely.

7 September, 1982   **Leader**

A touch of the high life

After nearly two decades of unremitting controversy about the oceans of money spent on its development and the ensuing catalogue of operating megalosses, Concorde has at last come into its own, just as we were despairing of ever being able to find a decent way of ditching it. There is something ineffably British about the idea of redundant British Airways crews chartering the elegant white elephant and taking it round the country's

194

unemployment blackspots to give the jobless a taste of the high life at a modest £40 to £50 a time. Just think of it: you too can experience the cramped delights of the frontier of technology for just two weeks' basic unemployment benefit or one fortnightly Girocheque from the Department of Employment (champagne, Vat 69 and VAT not included).

The plan is to make circular flights round the blackspots, setting down and picking up passengers on each hop. The 125-mile trip from Merseyside to Tyneside would last all of fifteen minutes. On this basis, the experience would resemble nothing so much as a ride on a lavishly appointed artillery shell, with the passengers on their backs for the first half of the trajectory and burying their noses in the back of the seat in front for the second half. The idea opens up all manner of possibilities for giving those out of work a fleeting taste of the kind of thing they would have been no more able to afford when they were working. What about packing the royal yacht Britannia with crates of tepid brown ale and a couple of dole queues for a mystery tour round Morecambe Bay – one week's benefit ought to be more than enough for that. Or by dividing the hours of darkness into fifteen-minute minishifts, a single bed at Claridge's could give a taste of luxury lodgement to forty-eight people every night, with a ten per cent rebate for those prepared to share a double bed. Apparently the Concorde enthusiasts were inspired by the fact that 50,000 people turned out during the bank holiday weekend to watch the aircraft make its first stop at Newcastle airport. The jobless jaunt cooperative has obviously overlooked two aspects of this misleading enthusiasm. The display did not cost £50 a head; and it is entirely possible that the 50,000 had nothing better to do.

1 September, 1982 **Leader**

Pinter's sleeping beauty

Harold Pinter obviously believes in saving the best till last. The first two plays in his new triple-bill at the Cottesloe, *Other Places*, are strange, comic and fascinating but you would know

195

they were by Pinter if you met them in your dreams. However the third play, *A Kind of Alaska* (which strikes me on instant acquaintance as a masterpiece) moves one in a way no work of his has ever done before; and it gets from Judi Dench a performance that will brand itself on the memory of all those lucky enough to see it.

The play was inspired by Oliver Sacks' book *Awakenings*; and it is about *encaphalitis lethargica* (or sleeping sickness) which claimed some five million victims in the years from 1916 to 1926. What we see is a girl-woman, old in years but young in experience, coming to life again after a twenty-nine-year coma. She was struck still like marble in the act of putting down a vase at the age of 16. Now she wakes in a white bed in a high-windowed room unable to recognize either her sister or the man who has watched over her. She is sad, bemused, fretful, questioning, conscious of having been on a strange journey but unable to get her emotional bearings.

It is a perfect theatrical metaphor for Pinter's fascination (which runs through the whole triple-bill) with the no-man's land between life and death. Most people have at some stage had the feeling that family, friends, lovers are phantoms in some dream; and this play uses an uncommon instance to tap a common experience. But it is also particular, moving and direct. It harks back to a lost upper-class world. It shows the weird comedy in being warmly greeted by relations you don't recognize ('you've aged – substantially,' the heroine abruptly says to her grey-haired sister). It also, crucially, says that with this disease the watchers suffer more than the watched.

Never before have I known a Pinter play to leave one so emotionally wrung through; and much of the credit, in Peter Hall's exact production, belongs to the incredible Judi Dench. Her great, sad eyes roam the strange room seeking comfort. She struggles to walk, arms extended like a condor's wings, as if motion were a human miracle. Yet through her performance comes a sense of recollected gaiety. Face glistening, she cries: 'Of course I laughed. I have a laughing nature'; and Ms Dench, an actress to her fingertips, gives one a sense of a deep, buried happiness. To convey a feeling of being re-born is a rare achievement; and it is reinforced by the amazed, compassionate

196

stillness of Paul Rogers and Anna Massey as the unrecognized relations.

But if this play deals emotionally with the theme of half-life, *Family Voices* (already heard on radio and done as a platform performance) handles it on Pinter's more familiar comic-metaphysic level. Two characters, a mother and son, sit on chairs framed against a vellum background. She hungers for contact with her seeming-dead child. But Pinter treats the idea of the great chasm between kith and kin by highlighting the son's occupancy of some eccentric lodging-house complete with homosexual cop and landlady's lubricious daughter catching buns between her toes: it is a funny play (nicely acted by Nigel Havers and Anna Massey) about a tragic situation.

And a reminder that Pinter is also a born revue-sketch writer comes with *Victoria Station*, in which Paul Rogers plays a flat-capped foul-mouthed controller of radio-cabs desperately trying to make contact with an aberrant driver hunched over the wheel of his Ford Cortina. You could see it as a study in power and panic; or you could take it as a return to Pinter's early surrealist sketches.

Either way, it means you will never sit in a radio-car again without having an image of some god-like figure trying to control traffic from his glass-booth. And it contributes to an extraordinary evening that shows Pinter's gift for pinning down the dream-like oddity of all waking existence.

15 October, 1982   **Michael Billington**

An interesting condition

One of the most curious passages in my research into fatherhood is watching men become pregnant. 'I've got this feeling of fullness in my stomach all the time,' said a Bristol dockworker to me in a puzzled voice. His wife was six months pregnant, and he did not connect the two matters. A young computer engineer (wife twenty-four weeks into pregnancy) certainly did: 'I've put on three-quarters of a stone since Sally got pregnant. I'm keeping up with her all right.' Other men talk about visiting the doctor with mysterious stomach pains – and yet nothing is diagnosed.

There are a dozen such symptoms, from broken sleep to back ache, and it is called the male couvade. That is the term that anthropologists have used for over a century, when they have observed fathers in tribal society imitating labour, wearing women's clothes, or pretending to be delivered of a stone or a doll.

I suspect that what the anthropologists are observing is a claim to paternity: an identification of who is and who will be responsible for a child. What I am hearing and seeing here may be different. At its best you might call it sympathetic pregnancy and at its worst, green-eyed jealousy. And in-between lies a good deal of anxiety. No: this is not tribal magic, but the behaviour of man today. Because this happens in the midst of our computer age we naturally try to quantify it.

In my research, I find around seven per cent of first-time fathers experience the couvade and perfectly well know that they are doing so. I would predict that this figure will steadily rise as more men become aware of their state (and some come to seek it). Around another forty per cent, in my experience, clearly enter the couvade and are unaware of what is happening to them. Other researchers have published papers reporting figures of over fifty or sixty per cent. I would guess the truth touches the higher rather than the lower mark.

But what is it all about, and why do I spend endless hours analysing men's reports of what it is like to become a father? As to couvade, I am now fairly clear that there is a significant but extremely minor element of envy. Man can do everything, except bear a child. Simultaneously there can be a more diffuse sense of tension: and that can come out in odd ways. I listened to one man who told me how he got up at three o'clock in the morning to go out to do his marathon training. 'I've got to get fit for the baby,' he said, as if there was an obvious connection. But dominantly there is another note. Men mostly want to be involved with their child from the beginning. Much more so than *their* fathers. Just as all the bees in the hive are, in one sense, a single-fragmented being; so the couvade can be seen as a male yearning for unity with the woman and the unknown child.

198

Yet that does not explain to me why I am researching into fatherhood. For me it began with action research on what happened to the child if the mother went out to work. I focused on childminding both as a symbol of this conflict, and as a vital service whose quality was not difficult to raise in dynamic ways. Now the National Childminding Association looks after its own future.

Fine for working mothers, but in the course of it I was again and again challenged by women who quietly said 'Why should I go out to work? What's wrong is the status of motherhood.' This was the gut and general response. Not really the view of articulate feminists. Those pointed more towards a future in which an equal proportion of women as of men worked and children lived in a world of crèche and nursery. Kibbutz rules OK? I have always taken and practised the view that a woman should have the choice to work or be with her child. But listening to those defiant statements (I'm a mother, and none of your fancy-dancy); I am no longer sure that my reply goes deeply enough. Nor do I think it is more than a part of the future.

For if women should ideally have such choice, why should not men? That sounds like elementary social engineering: one item on my agenda for the Second Welfare State. But immediately it brings up the fact and nature of fatherhood. And that is partly why we are beginning to explore or articulate the unknown male experience. So I am absorbed in two collections of valuable academic papers, re-reading them and taking notes, precisely because of what, in shorthand, we might call the new politics of the family. No longer can we write with the confidence of that most distinguished enquirer John Bowlby only thirty years ago: 'Little will be said of the father-child relation: his value as the economic and emotional support of the mother will be assumed.' Poor dad. Even Dr Spock had to offer him a token place in the last edition. He deserves better, and will demand more.

Maybe by the end of the century we will know a little more about this strange creature in the family. The facts ('does he come home in time to put the children to bed?') will be slow, but not intrinsically difficult to gather. Do not despise our academic anthills. New policies – like paternity leave – can be campaigned. But ultimately all rests on knowing what fathers feel about the child and about the mother. Some are still dismissive of childbirth ('for a start it killed our sex life') and shelter in the old routines. But more and more seems to echo Aristotle's old phrase ('in everything natural there is something marvellous') – and wonder what they have been missing. Listening to fathers may be deceptive, but it gives me the feeling that they might help to utterly change the quality of our grandchildren's lives – just as childhood has been both discovered and then as astonishingly altered over the last two centuries.

It may be so. But – like the male couvade – I feel that with future fatherhood I am exploring very strange territory indeed.
7 December, 1982   **Brian Jackson**

Trouble at t'workplace

Dear Mary,
Josh took me out to dinner yesterday. I didn't much want to go: what with one thing and another I've rather given up food. All that fuss seems so dated – fine in the 'sixties, okay in the 'seventies but definitely passé in the 'eighties. I'm simply not into the cookety-cook lark anymore, nor into the noshety-nosh neither. Besides, watching the baby apply food to his person like a hot poultice three times daily is enough to take the edge off Nero's appetite, never mind mine. That infant works as a sort of symbolic vomitorium: one look in his direction and whatever you've just swallowed is making its dash for freedom again.

I'm taking vitamin pills instead and even that seems too much effort. What I'd really like is a nice restful intravenous feed administered in beddy-byes by an apple-cheeked district nurse or, possibly, a sort of food pill that acts like that contraceptive: a nutritionist inserts it under your skin and it leaks meals into your bloodstream at appropriate moments throughout the month. Think of it. No more shopping or banging about with saucepans or washing up. Just occasional small surges of taste-bud sensation and the odd psychic burp.

So when Josh suggested eating out, I said why not order a takeaway kebab and have it here instead? But he looked in a shifty manner at Ben, Jane, the baby, Judas and the Woolly Mite milling about and said with unnecessary fervour no no no *no*. Then he went on about this marvellous little place he'd discovered, really Martha you'll love it, it'll remind you (and here, I swear, his eyes went misty) of our Very Own Perigord caff, remember Martha, remember? So, sighing, I put on my wellies and we sloshed off into the rain.

Why do the English look down on everything French and then go bonkers when they find they can cook a perfectly ordinary French dish? The place was one of those hysterically casual little bistros called something studiedly unchic like *Service Non Compris* where the owner puts you through an exam in Food Appreciation and you can't crumble a piece of bread without him springing from the wings for a round of applause. So tiring.

For Josh's sake I did my best to live up to the demanding role of four-star gourmet, smiling myself silly and saying *très bien* at every bite to the boring patron, who was no more French than I am, under his quivering moustache. Anyway, at last we reached the coffee stage (beam beam, clap clap, *c'est formidable* Monsieur Fred) and were finally left in peace as Monsieur Fred darted off to knot his cordon bleu round another customer's jugular. And then Josh leaned towards me, cleared his throat and said Martha, I need your advice. It is a problem of sexual harassment in the workplace, will you help? Oh Josh, of *course*, I said. Mary, I was really moved. All those years of talking were not wasted on him after all. Josh had understood. At last he empathizes with the woman's dilemma. Whose sexual harassment? I said in a low and caring voice. Mine, he said. Me. I'm being touched up at work. Martha, and I don't know what to do.

Well you could have knocked me down with a *rognon de veau au vin blanc avec herbes de Provence*. *You*, I said, staring. Yes, he said, miffed. 'And who's the lucky lady,' I said. Martha, he said, you reveal with that remark a deeply sexist attitude that I would not have expected in you. Irene, he said. Irene? I shrieked quietly, scalding my tongue with *le demi-tasse*. A short interlude followed in which I rolled in the aisles. What does she do, Josh?

Run her fingers round your turn-ups? Tweak your braces? Get you behind the filing cabinet and loosen your cuff-links? For heaven's sake, you're a foot taller than Irene even counting her beehive. What are you, a man or a Mickey Mouse?

I see you have not grasped the implications, he said coldly. Irene is my boss. She can make or break me at the Department. There is no fury, Martha, like a woman scorned. Laugh if you will but when I get fired, you'll be laughing in a caravan park in Neasden, how does that grab you? An icy hand clutched at my heart as I wiped away the tears and glimpsed a bleak future. Me and the baby reduced to penury, our little blue chilblains throbbing, our little tummies empty of even a draught of Vitamin C, all because of a sex-crazed harpy storming down the corridors of power after my poor Josh.

Then the voice of Josh said it's all your fault, Martha. None of this would have happened if you hadn't left me. A man in my position needs a woman to protect him. Irene thinks I'm fair game and without you, Martha, I am. Complain to the boss, I said. She *is* the boss, he said. Well, the Minister, go to the Minister, Josh. Sir John? he said. Sir John becomes overheated if he reads the word 'she' in a brief. The word 'brief' is almost too much for him. If I complain to him he'll think I'm gay and have me followed. There'll be security checks, confidential files will be withdrawn, men will edge away as I unzip, your letters to Mary will be opened and possibly leaked to the *Guardian*. I shall end up wishing I *were* homosexual – at least, then, I'd have some friends in high places. Oh Martha, I beg you, make an honest man of me or we are all undone!

Or words to that effect, Mary, that went through me like a knife. What am I to do. Where is the Sex Discrimination Act, now that I need it? Write with advice immediately, in the old school code. – Oursay,

Thaymar
Jill Tweedie

31 January, 1983

Darcy goes mad

There is a touching convention in European professional golf that if a player picks up a club belonging to someone else and likes the feel of it, then the owner is honour-bound to let him have it, against a tacit promise that one day, if the thing proves to be any good, recompense will be made in cash or kind. It is a form of *droit de seigneur*, and I myself had a superb sand wedge commandeered in this high-handed manner, a bit strange in view of the fact that I am not even a member of the Guild of Lightfingered Tournament Golfers.

Eamonn Darcy had already appropriated woods to suit his highly individual swing when he walked into the St George's Hill workshop of Barry Willett, the sorcerer who breathes magic into the clubs of all sensible tournament players. Darcy picked up a club which had just been given the Excalibur treatment and remarked: 'This feels good; I will take the entire set of irons.' Because of the unwritten tribal law of pro-golf, Willett was powerless to prevent what you and I would very properly regard as a breach of the Larceny Act of 1925.

When Michael King arrived some days later to retrieve the new set of irons he had deposited for supernaturalizing, he was miffed to learn that they had been expropriated by Darcy. Because of the sacred code of the circuit there was nothing King could do about it except to resolve that in due course he would sting Darcy for the full retail value plus VAT.

Two weeks ago Darcy idly plucked the putter from the bag of Charlie Cox. Since it was the same Ping O – blade model with which he had turned water into wine for eight years, his hand immediately became firmly vulcanized to the grip. A blow torch would not have separated Darcy from his newly acquired ally.

In the first round of the State Express Classic at The Belfry, Cox scored eighty-five and if you cared to presume that he was lost without his favourite putter then there is nothing I can do to dispel your evil thoughts. For his part Darcy had twenty-seven putts in a round of seventy-one.

In the second round Darcy, who had a watertight legal title to precisely one of the fourteen clubs in his bag, to wit the sand wedge, went mad, a technical golfing expression meaning that he could do no wrong. He cannot even remember whose driver it was that split the fairways of The Belfry. King's irons were wands in his hands. Cox's putter performed prodigies on the green for a total of twenty-five putts. To be fair, he did use his own sand wedge once, to save his par at the third, and it all added up to a communal effort of nine birdies, his sixty-three lowering the course record by two strokes.

8 July 1983   **Peter Dobereiner**

True grit Willis

Bob Willis is not the first number eleven to captain England – but he is certainly the worst batsman. Come to think of it, his famous curtain-rail forward defensive – angled blade speculatively seeking contact as it slides, as if on runners, from square leg to cover point – is probably the worst shot ever to have been regularly displayed in any arena of Test match cricket.

Willis is in fact the only genuine number eleven to have captained England. Three have previously done so, but, in Guyana in 1948, Gubby Allen was injured, as was Farmer White when he preceded the roller at Melbourne in 1929. The other skipper to have sloped in at the very rear was none other than Lord Hawke at Cape Town in 1898. His lordship was actually not at all a bad bat and his self-appointed place in the order had a definite *Hauteur* about it, rather in the manner of those village green squires these days: 'I'm only here to preside over the rustics having a jolly good game.'

On the other hand, Bob Willis is certainly the best fast bowler to have captained England. With luck, he may yet prove to be one of the very best captains to have captained England. It is going to be one of the fascinations of the winter to see how he makes out as leader of what he admits is 'not the greatest side to have left these hallowed shores.' Then he adds with that blazing, faraway glare of his, 'But it's not to say we will not all be doing our very darndest for Queen and Country.'

Bob is given to releasing such quaintly old-fashioned press statements. On the page or on the radio they often come out as flat and humdrum clichés, as if he is knowingly giving us what we want. In fact, there is usually attached a marvellously appealing glint of irony or humour or even anger and menace in his eyes when he so utters.

After his first Test as captain this summer he answered some bland routine questions of mine with an even more bland and routine answer, then paused to change his deadpan, monotonous tone to a twinkling 'That all right for you then, dearie?' A remembrance of my occasional late-night bar stool lapses into theatricality on previous tours together. In Bombay this time last year he christened me 'the lounge lizard of Farringdon Road', but fortunately it didn't catch on.

Willis is, in his own words, a 'Grauniad decipherer'. He is the third of the last four England captains regularly to take the *Guardian* and in India last winter Willis's father Ted, a retired journalist, sent his son out a weekly batch of cuttings. 'You've been at it again, you lounge lizard!' Alas his father, who had always been a great encouragement, died in the spring just weeks before Bob was called to the Palace for his OBE, and then called to the colours to captain the old country.

When working in Manchester, Ted had taken Bob to his first cricket match, to Old Trafford in a push chair with his baby's bottle. By the time the family moved to Surrey, Bob and his elder brother were padding up in their garden greenhouse before going out to play imaginary Test matches on Stoke D'Abernon 'rec'. Bob was Snow at one end and Statham at the other. At Guildford GS rival schoolboys found his rib-ticklers most unfunny and he graduated to Surrey Colts.

After school he thought of having a concentrated cram for university or being something in the city or following his father, then a BBC newsroom sub-editor, into journalism. But in 1969 Surrey invited him for an extended trial.

Ted recalled last year: 'I had my misgivings. Many are called: few are chosen. But I was convinced a lad who pored over Wisden as if it were a spy thriller must have another dimension. The boy assured me he would play for Surrey, and one day for England. A light seemed to burn within him.'

The ungainly, long-limbed laddo played five championship games in his first summer, taking seventeen surprising wickets.

When Ward broke down in Australia that winter, captain Illingworth and vice-captain Cowdrey were at a loss for a replacement. 'Send for young Willis,' insisted John Edrich. Illy had never even heard of him but knew his doughty gum-chewing opener only spoke annually, when there was something to say. Willis was a revelation: of a sudden he was opening the bowling with, not as, John Snow. He took twelve wickets in four tests, fielded with the ferociousness that he was later to V-sign Mr Packer, and his zestful contribution to team spirit is still talked about with pleasure by Illy.

Bob's first room-mate on that tour was Basil D'Oliveira. The young man would even bring the old boy his breakfast in bed. He recalls:

'I would bring it up and sit on my bed, listen to his words of wisdom and drink it all in. If John Edrich told me something on that tour I would think to myself, "He must be right, he's been playing all these years." Was it wrong to be so starry-eyed? But I firmly believe that listening to such experience and watching every bit of Test cricket I could manage helped equip me mentally.

'On the 1979 tour some of our young players confessed themselves bored after ten minutes' play in the Tests; they wanted to go and play tennis or walk around the ground or something, rather than watch and learn from men like Lillee. I was amazed and disappointed. I felt frustrated: I was vice-captain, yet Mike Brearley did not want me to interfere with anyone's technique. Players who did not like nets were not made to go in them and work. It may be all very well saying that a bloke selected for his country should be able to sort out what is wrong with his game, but on that tour I felt there was a lack of pride in performance and of application.'

At the beginning of that 1978 tour, over dinner in Sydney, Willis, the new vice-captain, had his first friendly row with Brearley. He was concerned about the dashers and flashers in Englands brittle batting order. Brearley recalls: 'Like rugby forwards irritated by fancy play among the backs that has them traipsing back to their own corner flag, fast bowlers have scant sympathy with batsmen who specialize in pretty twenties.

'On this occasion, I remember, Bob's targets were Randall

and Gower, who he felt were not applying themselves. His pet phrase was: "They've got to be spoken to." ' Warily, Brearley did speak to the delicate duo.

Again, at Headingley in 1981 on the afternoon Botham went gloriously potty for 149, England were in effect twenty-five for eight when Dilley was out. Old, a notoriously fragile bat, was next man in. Willis, eyes blazing and imploring, demanded of Brearley 'Make Chilly play!' Old and Botham added sixty-seven crucial runs and so set up the heroic finale for Willis himself.

In Sri Lanka this early spring, when England were demoralized and ready to throw in the towel against the unbelieving debutante islanders, Willis lost his cool at lunch-time on the third day. 'I can't believe it. Damn me,' he sneered, 'here we are, the so-called pride of English professional cricket, happy to be beaten by Sri Lanka and we're still whining on about the local umpiring. Let's go out there and do something about it!' They did just that in next to no time.

The grapevine flourishes in cricket and I fancy that short sharp shock administered to ten cringing Englishmen won Willis the captaincy for the summer when May was busting out all over. 'Yes,' he admits, in that self-deprecating way he can manage when he feels like it, 'I recall I did take it upon myself to give the lads a bit of a gee-up' – and then he throws back his head, digs you in the ribs, and lets out a marvellous great warm belly laugh of satisfaction at the memory, not so much of his withering exhortation but of the victory it lead to.

What pleases him most in his long love-hate affair with the press is that Fleet Street, not to say Farringdon Road, has totally written him off several times in the past decade, and now he is captain of an Ashes tour, the very peak of ambition, not to say power.

He admits he has the gaucheness of a camel, that he is a carthorse, an 'effort' man compared with, say, Holding or Lillee, but the knees have not mended just by accident. Six-mile runs at dawn are no fun, the mental concentration – not the glazed, agonized, almost self-hypnotized stare when he's bowling well – is obviously no picnic.

He had not come off his manic high a long time after his eight for forty-three and the first time he consciously realized what he had done at Headingley was fully five hours later when Henry Blofeld's dotty dulcets informed him on his car radio. Bob had to pull up to let it sink in.

As captain he seemed to get his own bowling spells pretty much right this summer. He will be very much a leader; he is good at being alone, yet he is never aloof. He is a fine companion. He is compassionate towards the weak and confident with the strong. He is a star turn at charades and one of these days should be a regular panellist on *Give Us A Clue*.

He could also sit in the hot seat and answer questions on the life and works of Jane Austen or P. G. Wodehouse or Bob Dylan or the zany wit and wisdom of Jim Cumbes.

He knows by heart some of the sketches of that satiric recording *The Secret Policeman's Ball* and he is not sure whether Mahler is more of a genius than Shostakovich but knows that Chopin and Mozart are even better in full flights of fancy than Don Bradman or Vivian Richards could ever have hoped to be. No matter, his reading this winter might have to be *Henry V* or Winnie's *Dunkirk Determinations* or even Mrs Thatcher's *Falklands Factor*. The fact is that England's cricket team have a very singular captain who has – for all his stubborn views, quirky flights, amiably argued presumptions, or silences as long as his limbs – a deep affection, reverence even, for the chivalries necessary to the profession he has chosen.

Don't worry about the formality of the press statements, think of the glint in his eye as he utters them. But a pity about his batting. . . .

16 October, 1982   **Frank Keating**

On the stump

Bob Willis, hardly happy and victorious, arrived back from the Antipodes with no excuses and a modicum of plain talk about the elements of refurbishment that might be needed to take England off the bottom betting spot for next summer's cricketing World Cup. Even the Queen Mother weighed in with some advice while congratulating Brian Johnston for his commentaries.

There was no such hoo-ha when the *Guardian* CC returned, equally unable to point to much in the way of winning glory, from its tour of South India and Sri Lanka. But we did beat the Combined Press of Sri Lanka (well, Colombo anyway) by eight wickets in the first match. Four defeats and two draws later, we had clearly forgotten the knack.

Bob made no excuses, apart from the umpiring, the length of the tour, injuries to Botham, etc., etc.; so why should we, apart from the fact that every team we met seemed to expect a good few ex-county or Lancashire Leaguers in the side as well as a sprinkling of ageing and rather portly journalists.

But the way they insisted on putting class bats in when the tail was due, and reserved their canniest spinners for our own non-batsmen, could be thought a mite unsporting. They seemed determined to teach us ex-colonials a late but effective lesson. We were just determined not to collapse in the heat.

The *Guardian* being what it is, however, we were vouchsafed some special privileges. We were given the choice of forty overs, fifty overs or an ordinary one-day match – the third alternative allowing us at least the possibility of a face-saving draw. In Madras we were accorded three matches within a week on the lordly turf of the famous Chepauk Test Stadium. And we were told, now and then, that we did jolly well under the circumstances.

The Hindu newspaper, generally known as 'The Guardian of the East', only beat us, very graciously, in the last five minutes, having given this writer a heaven-sent chance to alter the result with a catch in the deep which he dropped. 'Never mind, you nearly caught it,' said the bowler (the wiley *Guardian* freelance Timeri Murari, who lives in Madras). But as captain of the team, the fielder is still having nightmares, presaged by the words 'If Only' blazoned in blood across the night sky.

Other *Guardian* regulars acquitted themselves more nobly, like deputy sports editor, Roger Alton, who despite an attack of food poisoning and a dreadful blow in the midriff, batted on to be twenty-two not out against Kurunegala, the ace Sri Lankan outback team. He also got sixty-two in more comfortable style at

Madras. Then there was David Lacey, football correspondent, making a blinding stop and quick throw-in which had the Tamil Nadu State players, practising on the boundary at Chepauk, bursting into spontaneous applause. That's the stuff of dreams too.

Naturally, at the end of it all, I had to make a statement at the airport, though there was no one in particular there to record it for posterity. 'The boys,' I said, 'did well under very trying circumstances. But there will have to be improvements in batting, bowling and fielding if we are to retain our reputation as the best national newspaper side in the UK. I shall remain captain for as long as the paper wants me, though perfectly willing to serve under anybody else bar the rest of the present team.'

3 March 1983   **Derek Malcolm**

Matchmaking the minorities

American sports are often battlefields in which not only teams clash like armies but fans express hostilities that are usually kept hidden. This is an invaluable outlet in a tense period like the present deepening recession and undoubtedly saves a great many violent clashes in the streets.

With nearly twelve million Americans officially out of work, the worst hit groups are the leading minorities, the blacks and the Hispanics. As both groups often compete for the same bottom-rung labouring jobs, there is an intense rivalry between them. This is usually kept under control, often by directing a mutual hostility against white groups, but this weekend both minorities found the perfect setting for a confrontation in a World Championship junior middleweight boxing match in which one boxer was black and the other Hispanic.

Thomas Hearns of Detroit and Wilfred Benitez of the Bronx (and Puerto Rico) became much more than boxers in battlefields across the United States – like the massive Armoury in the Bronx borough of New York. They were champions representing their group like ancient gladiators. Two hours before closed circuit film of the fight filled the huge screen in the Bronx Armoury (the actual fight took place in New Orleans), the big elbow-to-elbow audience chanted its allegiance.

On the crowded right side blacks were in the majority and it took a courageous supporter to cheer for Benitez. On the crowded left the position was reversed, and a Hearns fan had to be foolhardy to openly boost his man. Great cheers went up every time Puerto Rican flags were carried down the aisle. Enough beer was being drunk to sink a ship and clouds of bitter marijuana smoke soon wafted up from both sides. Bets were made and macho threats exchanged. If the fight was close, the result disputed, war might break out in the Armoury.

It ended early Saturday morning, New York time, and luckily Hearns won easily on points. Benitez's army of supporters had to swallow it, though there was a rush to get out of the Armoury as exploding bottles at the rear began to express the mighty Hispanic frustration.

Outside in the early morning darkness, ranks of police, on horseback and on foot – all armed – prevented any fights from breaking out. Blacks clearly had a sense of triumph but were very cautious about expressing it. Hispanic crowds filled the streets, stopping traffic, their defeat all the more galling because they couldn't dispute it. An angry motorist who shouted that Benitez had been 'robbed' was moved on by police but no one in the passing crowds seemed inclined to fight over it. And blacks wisely didn't wait around to crow but were first on the buses and subway trains.

The blow to Spanish pride could easily be understood. In one section of the Armoury crowd, eight out of ten were unemployed with five on welfare. This was as far as they had got in realizing their American dream. Yet even life on New York welfare payments is often better than the life many of them left behind in Latin America. That is why Hispanics are the fastest growing group in the United States, with over a million legal and illegal immigrants a year expected over the next decade.

Conscious of being on the bottom rung of the American ladder, they need something of their own to crow about. Benitez was carrying not only their bets but their pride. When he lost, they lost a boost to their morale in the welfare lines, a greater sense of identity in this still alien country.

Many can barely speak English and are in no hurry to learn. Yet they are clearly in the US to stay and are spreading through the country, rapidly changing the image of American society. They followed President Reagan's recent trip to Latin America with pride but also with scepticism. On the whole the Hispanic immigrants are from the poorer classes and bring with them Catholic and more radical beliefs.

They join the great American underbelly of alienation with almost fifty per cent of the voters not voting in Presidential elections. If they and the other alienated groups, notably the blacks, ever join together in support of a presidential candidate, they could change the whole American political picture.

The Hearns-Benitez fight in this context was instructive. The confrontation between black and Hispanic champions was not nearly so financially profitable as the fight earlier this year between Larry Holmes, a black champion, and Gerry Cooney, a white challenger. Blacks and Hispanics then were on the same side in the Armoury and far more white fans attended than turned out for the Hearns-Benitez battle. This shows what can happen when different groups in American society have a common cause. Their racial and other differences blur.

At the welfare office on 14th Street, the day of the fight – and the day the latest unemployment rate (a post-war record of 10.8 per cent) was announced – all the people except about three waiting in line were black or Hispanic and all the welfare clerks were the same. The blacks, with older roots in the country, were not so desperate for a win for the sake of group pride but backed Hearns in the hope of putting down their welfare competitors. One black angrily told a Hispanic in the middle of an argument, 'Go back to Puerto Rico.' The heated reply was 'You go back to Africa.' Only the Hearns-Benitez fight could decide such an argument.

Of course it didn't decide anything. It merely let out a little of the frustration as both sides roared for their champion. But perhaps that was the difference between a bearable level of frustration and an explosion in the streets.

Let those who wish to abolish boxing remember that American sports serve a social purpose as well as being part of show business. There would be far more clashes between opposing groups in American society but for such events as the Hearns-Benitez fight.

6 December, 1982   **W. J. Weatherby**

Testament of an Ibsen girl

When she approached through the crowded foyer of the Lyric, Hammersmith, the heads that turned, turned not from recognition, but from simple pleasure. The fine gold-bronze hair was worn as a waist-length shawl. The mini began, and ended, not very far below. The sweater had 'Fit . . . Fit . . . Fit . . .' knitted all over it. She looked like a very pretty drum majorette in mufti.

She did not look much like Cheryl Campbell. Or like the haunting kitten-woman of Strindberg's *Miss Julie*, which opens at the Lyric tonight. But after her Nora in the RSC's *A Doll's House*, a performance hugely admired and for some time to come, definitive, she has taken on nothing less than Strindberg's bitter riposte to Ibsen's play, and to his championing of women's equality.

Julie, the tease who will provoke her manservant Jean first to seduce, then to reject her, is one of the next generation, the daughters of Nora who in Strindberg's raging prediction, will apply sexual equality to disastrous purpose.

Cheryl Campbell sees her as mercurial, quixotic in her relations with Jean, and pitiful, and at one time felt she could not like her. But finally she felt, it was not Julie's fault.

'No one has shown her any example as to how to behave. She doesn't know how to behave as a lady or as a peasant. She doesn't know how to care for anybody, how to love anybody, or how to be loved. She is in a terrible mess. In the end I didn't want to write her off, but I had to find a way to make her plausible.

'The problem was, as I worked on it, I came to feel it wasn't a play about Jean and Julie, but about Strindberg, because it's based so much on his own personal experience. He's the one in

213

the terrible mess. He is a mixture of Julie and Jean. You can try and pin it down and analyse it, but sometimes all you can do is express it, through emotional pyrotechnics, and somehow you have to do it so that it is credible.'

The apparent source of the plot was the relationship between the woman from whom Strindberg rented rooms in an old castle, and her bailiff – the woman, without any real title, called herself Countess. Strindberg presumed they were lovers. But the bailiff turned out to be, not the woman's lover, but her illegitimate half-brother, a fact they kept secret to protect the family reputation.

Yet that experience may just have crystallized Strindberg's own troubled relationship with his wife. He was the son of a servant girl, his wife was a baroness. They were divorced two years after *Miss Julie* was first staged in 1889.

Playing Julie, who is twenty-five, a virgin, and in some emotional ways, a spoilt child, has presented Campbell with a totally different task from the one she faced in *A Doll's House*. Julie's emotional pyrotechnics are exactly that. Nora's are usually a way of misleading her husband. Campbell's aim, she says, was to 'make the beginning and the end homogeneous'. Nora has to change from a woman prepared to manipulate people within the terms of a male world into a woman demanding equal power and equal responsibility.

'It appears to be a sudden change, but of course it isn't. There have been a lot of small signs, but you can't make too much of them, because she doesn't realize herself.'

You have to remember, she says – and she is clearly talking not just about Nora, but about the art of reconstructing emotion – 'you have to remember what it is like in life. You can't remember the experience of pain. If women could remember pain, they wouldn't go on having babies.' So how is the experience recalled? 'By trying to think, by trying to remember. Eventually it will come back.'

Nora and Julie are prime women's roles from almost the only period of modern theatre to produce them in any numbers. While Ibsen and Strindberg set up their domestic battles in Scandinavia, Shaw did it here. Campbell was in the production of *You Never Can Tell* that reopened the Lyric a few years ago, but she has no real enthusiasm for Shaw – the thought of *Major Barbara* or *St Joan* does not stir her.

She started as an ASM at Watford Palace, then reluctantly went to train at LAMDA, was at the Glasgow Citizens, whose increasingly extrovert style did not suit her, and worked with Birmingham Rep. Still widely unknown, in 1977 she was cast as the schoolteacher turned criminal in Dennis Potter's mould-breaking television series, *Pennies From Heaven.*

'It is the only time I've been up for a part where I felt that if I didn't get it, I would write to them and tell them they had made a terrible mistake.' She felt, and was, totally right for the role. She did not work for seven months after it hit the screen.

A year or so later she went to another audition, feeling dispirited because her voice was tired and rough, and not cheered by finding, as she read through the script while she was waiting, that the character started off age eighteen. 'So I thought, well that's it. I'm far too old for it, and a young, dark-haired girl was waiting to audition too, and I thought, well it's her, she'll get it, of course.'

Campbell went in and did a pretty good reading in her tired voice, but just as she was leaving, they asked her how tall she was. 'So I said, five foot two, and I thought, well that's the end, she's probably supposed to be five foot eight, so I'm too short. I rang my agent and told her I hadn't got it.' Two days later, her agent rang her and told her she had. The series was *Testament Of Youth.*

Pennies made her reputation, but playing Vera Brittain in *Testament Of Youth* made her a television star, and she has done a lot of screen work since – serials like *Malice Aforethought*, Agatha Christie's *Seven Dials Mystery*, films like *Chariots of Fire* and *McVicar*. So she began to worry. 'I'd always thought of myself as a stage actress, but I was doing my best work on television.

'Television eats material. It eats people, like a hungry animal. You're not offered that much variety of roles – I've been incredibly lucky to be offered so many different ones. I was afraid I wouldn't be able to get back to the stage. I thought I might get stage fright. I'd never had it, but people do get it.

'I saw someone with it once, at a read-through she was

shaking like this.' She demonstrated the woman's hand shaking a full inch as she tried to hold the script. 'I thought, if I ever get like that, I'll give up.'

So after filming the Christie, she took a deliberate rest. She started salvaging a garden from the rubble round the house she had just bought, her way of relaxing.

The only cheering fact after five months was that the offers were still rolling in. Then Adrian Noble rang from the RSC and offered her Nora. She says that she had always, from the days of her drama school *Hedda Gabler*, thought of herself as an Ibsen girl.

She once said that acting was a way of expressing the gregarious side of her nature. She is reticent about the other sides, except that like Julia she is mercurial, and that she has 'a very keen sense of the ridiculous', a handy attribute she shares with Stephen Rea, who plays Jean in this production. She also confesses to being a giggler.

But there is also, observably, a kittenish aspect, a slight luxuriance about the way she folds her small bones into a chair, or swirls her mane round her shoulders. Maturely kittenish – though interviewers are not told her age or many other details of her private life.

While I wondered what more an interviewer might profitably ask, she unconsciously answered the question. 'They ask . . . They ask things like what you like to cook.' So; what does she like to cook? 'Food!' she cried cheerfully. 'Anything. Any kind of food, I'm a human dustbin.' But all I could see was a sweater with 'Fit . . . Fit . . . Fit' written all over, and plenty of room in it.

17 January, 1983   **Hugh Hebert**

Iron market, silver bullet

A misprint much to the point occurs in the chapter on Haiti in Graham Greene's *Ways of Escape*. Petionville comes out Pietonville. The letters should be transposed in the real world too, because almost everybody there is walking.

But then all the towns are pietonvilles. Hardly any cars, petrol, money or work: naturally everywhere in Haiti most of the people are walking. In the country too it is a phenomenon, the sight of such large numbers in rhythmic file on the verges of the roads. The idiosyncratic buses called tap-taps are packed, but the real business is feet.

They cover great distances. The women have always walked, with bundles and baskets of produce on their heads for the markets, being trained to do so from the age of four. (It is beneath the dignity of the men to carry in this way, they prefer handcarts, though you do see a few breaking what is nearly a taboo.)

The women manage twenty-five kilometres at a stretch, and when night falls they lie on the side of the road and do the same again next day. All the way into the very main avenues of the capital others set up mini field-kitchens, with oil drums sizzling full of pigs' fries, little fishes in batter, banana fritters, tripe . . . So they're supported until at last they fetch up at the great Iron Market in the centre of Port-au-Prince, there to sleep like half-filled sacks among their heaped-up piles of pulses and rice and fruit.

Markets are most sinewy and fascinating in nations of small-holdings, and in Haiti the holdings are very small – an acre or so. The variety is prodigious, but it can't be efficient. Looking back for the causes of Haiti's distress beyond the nightmare years of Papa Doc with his Tontons Macoutes that isolated Haiti, and the more relaxed but still selfish control of Baby Doc since 1971, with his crack palace guard The Leopards, one might see in the Iron Market a metaphor for the original wrong turning.

Ironically the mistake was made by the most benevolent of Haiti's plenitude of autocrats, friend of Bolivar and satrap of the south, the patrician mulatto Alexandre Petion. He revoked the plans of his sometime commander, the liberator Toussaint L'Ouverture, and democratized land tenure, carrying to extremes this *laisser-faire* policy.

Still, the market's energy spills out of the metaphor, as the goods do from the covered hangar, and has to be seen. Fat live chickens go for four dollars, dried snake for more; spice and veg, voodoo urns, Afro masks and gewgaws, tin baths and batteries

de cuisine, cloths and clothes, umbrellas and toothpaste poach
on each other's territory in Rabelaisian profusion.

All around are the most impressive of the metropolitan
organs. Item, the Cathedral of St Trinité, from which one of
several beggars, a woman with an arm shorn off at the shoulder,
fell in step with me for some distance – the sick and the
mutilated are the charges of their families.

Item, the Presidential Palace by the Champ de Mars, white
against a background of hills, and the dark statue of Toussaint.
Item, the mustard-coloured barracks, a smart trot away.

Item, the art centre, a starting point for enquiry into the naif
painting of Haiti, for which the American Selden Rodman, who
still lives in the southern port of Jacmel and defends Haiti from
slurs in the foreign press, first achieved international recognition in 1947.

Bright, whimsical and charming examples of this naif tradition can be picked up from roadside displays for picayune sums,
but I did not find among them, nor in the galleries of the capital
and the second city, Cap Haitien, any recent works charac-
terized by that inwardness of the imagination and escape into
African dreams that gave such a charge to Patrick Leigh Fermor
thirty years ago. Those would now run into hundreds of dollars.

Nor can one readily dip into the contemporary pool of Haitian
writing. A Haitian doctor suggested some novelists, headed by
Edrice Saint-Amand, but to have found any of their works in the
Rue des Miracles would have been miraculous. The bookshops'
staff had never heard of any of them.

By contrast with Havana's, stocks were pathetic – some
ornate, sentimental poetry which is never in nor out of fashion
anywhere in the world, translations of adventure stories and
elementary text books were the staples. Some seventy-five per
cent of the people can't read: sad reminders of this come from
'guides' who are foxed by street names.

On the other hand the libraries are richly documented on the
stories of the making of the first black republic. Haiti can muster
astonishing chronicles of the protagonists, but this past is hardly
an escape from the present, with massacres and treacheries and
executions to parallel the excesses of the French Revolution.

The noble head of Boukman, the maroon Jamaican first

leader, finished on a pike. Toussaint, a pure Negro, was betrayed by Napoleon to a cold death in a cell in the Jura; Dessalines the Emperor was shot down by his own people; Henri Christophe, who as king pressed 200,000 labourers into raising the impregnable Citadelle on the heights above Cap Haitien, whose vertiginous tracks are scaled today by tourists on muleback, ended his fantastic life with a silver bullet.

It is not often, in latter days, that the visitor can remark, like Ronald Firbank planning a trip, that 'they say the President is a perfect dear.' In Firbankian mood they say of the President today, 'It's a pity wizened little Papa Doc pumped his son up with steroids; a pity, that is, for the ladies.' When his Lady, Haiti's Evita, nails that one, they'll say. . . .

But the independent traveller won't move in Presidential circles, even if they do say in Haiti anything can happen. I own to a slight *frisson* when I took stock of my quarters in Habitacion Leclerc, thinking I was alone, and a sibilant voice in my ear murmured, 'I am Jean-Claude. I am your servant.'

And they did take me along to see the family tomb of the late President. The Great Divide is the smallest interval I would ever want between us. There is a satisfying hefty volume of monumental masonry over him, preventing any Baron Samedi from raising him up as a zombi.

There are many handsome graves in that well kept cemetery. In this part the dead are better housed than the living. The nearby Rue Dessalines, bordered by a disused rail track that serves as footway, intermittently penetrated by open sewers, is a long thoroughfare through fearsome slums.

On both sides runs a jumble of single and two-storey buildings, matchboard mostly with corrugated iron roofs, crowded in their deep dark recesses with people day and night. Here and there dilapidated colonial villas stand aside in consternation, and small modern houses in pink plaster like suburban residences appear aloof and genteel, calling themselves banks, or establishments for teaching English, or lottery centres.

There are beerhouses and cafes selling meals of goat or fish for a dollar or so. Among the field kitchens and clothing stalls, people squeeze by one another with their baskets and basins and their handcarts of bottles or bones. Occasionally one is enveloped in a ripe stench, so sudden and thick and local that one almost expects to find visible edges.

I passed what the army calls a honey-waggon, an open truck with some three tons of ordures aboard, and men swinging more up from the street with pitchforks, some of its oozing off to leave a double trace of its passage. I saw a woman cool her baby in one of those stagnant pools. Infant mortality in Haiti is 150 to the thousand, five times the next highest figure for the Caribbean.

These are the notes of a principal highway in a city of more than a million people, a fifth of the population of the western third of Hispaniola. I should not omit an important exception to this indigo impression. It is lightened by the schools. Those I saw were rather like dame schools, in having all ages in a common assembly, but the boys in their uniforms and the girls in their pleated skirts and ankle socks looked universally cared for. (I saw only two cats in Haiti – one was in a naif painting and the other, no doubt its model, was a stout school pet.)

Every which way a regular Grand Prix of 'tap-taps' tears along the pot-holed streets. These are the public transport of Haiti – trucks, half-trucks, camionettes converted into buses. On their forehead they bear pious protective legends: *L'Eternel mon Berger*; *Le Cercle de Dieu*; *Tout à Dieu*, and the odd daringly familiar address, like *Dieu mon Copain*.

All along their sides they carry a fantasticated and brilliant assortment of decorations on cream surrounds, of flowers and fruits and birds, and some more elaborate of smiling suns, nudes with bulbous breasts, angels, lions and zebras, or idealized young lovers. Travelling in one is a hot and sticky ride, but cheap, on benches set about the sides, with often a curtain at the back, through which you plunge into a passenger load with no apparent limit.

To the casual eye they seem to be another spontaneous expression of folk art, like the naif paintings, but in this case a frivolous release rarely showing on the faces of this docile, courteous people. But it soon was obvious to me that there was a stylized similarity about their execution which suggested a controlling atelier.

After much trouble, I located it among a tangle of side streets, and the boss man, a burly, surly figure called Jean Baptiste

Apollon. A minatory sign before his workshop advised '*Pas de credit, surtout pour vous.*' Son of a Cuban exile, unable to read or write, he has built one of the few prosperous outfits around, and the gear on the backs of his artisans, carpenters and painters, shows it.

They were customizing some twelve vehicles a month, he said, to add to the 3,000 in circulation. A good finished article would be worth $19,000. To own one for most Haitians, with an average annual per capita income of $300, is an impossible dream. The cachet of achieving one is enormous. For the rich, whose every dream is possible, Apollon has a sideline in speedboats. But that is another world, and another story.

21 August, 1982   **Alex Hamilton**

How dangerous is the duopoly

The whirligig of time brings in its revenge. Twenty years ago, when I first became actively involved in theatre, the fashionable progressive cause was the establishment of big, permanent, subsidized companies. The National Theatre and the Royal Shakespeare Company, then in their infancy, were held to be a Good Thing: organizations that could begin to rival the great foreign institutions like the Moscow Arts and the Berliner Ensemble and rescue the British theatre from decades of commercial sterility. There was even bold, brave talk of the right to fail.

Now in 1983 with the economy in recession, people are talking about a dangerous theatrical duopoly. Commercial managements bitch about the national companies' ability to put on popular classics and musicals like *Guys and Dolls* and their seduction of box office writers like Ayckbourn, Directors of theatres like Hampstead, the Royal Court, the Bush, the Half Moon, and the Stratford East Theatre Royal join forces to condemn the 'privileged' position of the National and the RSC. On all sides, I hear talk of a return to the situation that obtained from 1662 to 1843 when Covent Garden and Drury Lane had Letters Patent giving them a monopoly of legitimate drama in

London. Championed once by the Left, the National and the RSC are now the butt of Left and Right alike.

Much of the criticism (doubtless intensified by the news that the National is to receive nearly £6.4 millions and the RSC £3.6 millions in the coming year) savours of paranoia. The comparison with the Covent Garden-Drury Lane situation of the past is patent rubbish. Outside the Barbican and the National, there are currently some forty mainstream theatres open in London and another thirty-to-forty lunchtime and fringe venues. Times may be hard; but we have not yet reached the point where a night out in London means recourse to one of two venues.

I also have minimal sympathy with the criticism from the commercial sector. Those managers who have long pinned their faith in new writing (such as Michael Codron, generously praised by both Tom Stoppard and Michael Frayn at last week's Standard Awards), who have done their best to win over new audiences (such as Ian Albery who bulges with incentive schemes), and who are keeping the classical flag flying in the West End (such as *Triumph Apollo* at the Haymarket) are maintaining their heads above water.

But the 'we wuz robbed' cries that periodically emanate from the commercial sector fall a little tinnily on the ears of anyone who remembers what London theatre was like in the 1950s when the profit-men held sway: on the whole, it was safe, cosy, predictable, star-orientated, writer-starved and, in the classic phrase of Arthur Miller, 'hermetically sealed off from life'.

I have rather more sympathy with hard-pressed regional theatres and London neighbourhood playhouses, struggling to make ends meet on inadequate grants. One ex-director of a major regional company told me last week that he quit because he was fed up with always having to do small-cast plays. John McGrath informed me last autumn that 7:84, having put on a popular season of neglected Scottish working-class plays, hadn't the resources to mount any new work until the next financial year. Philip Hedley, the exuberant director of the Theatre Royal, Stratford East, announces in the current programme that he has a batch of sizeable new plays that he simply can't afford to put into full production: instead he is giving them public readings.

I can well understand the bitter frustration of someone like Hedley, able to pay his top actors only £100 a week, when he learns that the RSC have scrapped a public performance in The Pit to keep a chorus member of *Poppy* in rehearsal; or that the National have gone over budget by £15,000 on *Way Upstream* because of technical difficulties. To directors working on a pittance the recurrent cancellation of performances at the National and the RSC must be wormwood and gall – as it is to disappointed members of the public.

Even those of us who support the concept of the twin national companies also find there are things to question. I couldn't believe it when I first heard that the National this autumn plans to stage a new American musical by Marvin Hamlisch, called *Jean*, dealing with the life of Jean Seberg. *Guys and Dolls* was one thing. But is there really any case for public money being spent on a new musical which, if it flops, will be a costly waste and which, if it succeeds, will inevitably move to Broadway? And is the life of Jean Seberg really so compulsively interesting that it should command the Olivier stage when there is a bundle of world classics still waiting to be performed?

The RSC is also not immune from criticism. In London at least, it seems to me to have lost a little of the sharp, radical, cutting edge that made it in the seventies a palpable alternative to the National. David Jones once told me that the board policy was to leave the mainstream classics to the National and to concentrate on more neglected works. Thus in the heady days of the Aldwych in 1971 you find Shakespeare and Pinter balanced by Gorky, Etherege, Joyce and Genet. But ever since the runaway success of that middlebrow spectacular, *Nicholas Nickleby*, and since the move into the Barbican, the RSC on its main London stage has been investing in big 'shows' rather than rare classics and new works.

But – and this is a very sizeable but – my criticism of specifics is matched by a general belief in the absolute necessity for the continued, distinct existence of the National and the RSC. They are not, by foreign standards, hugely subsidized. They have not, in spite of understandable fears, put other companies out of business. And they have, in terms of local popularity and international prestige, justified their subvention many times over. I am all for their being closely monitored; but it would be insane to chip away at their existence.

Indeed, I would argue that the rage of people who run regional theatres, fringe companies, touring groups, neighbourhood playhouses should be directed not against the National and the RSC but against the Government itself. By great sleight of hand, it manages to convince us each year that the arts are being singled out for special treatment: the standard ploy is to spread news of gloom and doom in the autumn (a cutback, a standstill, a thin five per cent increase) and then to announce a slight improvement on the expected figure around Christmas. We are then apparently all meant to roll over on our backs with delight.

But the arts are still in crisis; and will continue to be either until we get an economic upturn or a Mitterand-like regime that recognizes the arts as both a sound national investment and a measure of a country's civilization rather than hush-money or a form of begging-bowl charity.

I certainly believe the National and the RSC, at a time of extreme hardship, should be alert to possible charges of over-spending and should not allow themselves to be turned into pre-Broadway try-out houses. But I also believe that constant mutterings about an oppressive duopoly are thinly substantiated and play into the hands of the philistines who would love nothing more than to dismantle the whole subsidized structure. We should all be lobbying for more cake: not quarrelling intra-murally and sourly about who gets which slice.

4 February, 1983 **Michael Billington**

Irish omelette

Recently, in my home area of Tyrone, a cousin was explaining to me how the Post Office where I grew up was raided after dark. 'You feel differently,' said Sean, 'when you have the cold steel under your chin.' His audience, both myself and some visitors from the South, savoured both the sentiment and the drinks; we were in a pub called Kelly's Tower (the night before I was in Adam Eves). 'Any notion,' I asked, looking around. 'Nothing for sure,' he said, 'but they had Protestant voices.'

Hugh Kenner would probably relish this as an Irish fact: a well-rehearsed anecdote to an audience as sympathetically irrigated as yourself. For he begins his new study* by demolishing two well-established Irish Facts. James Joyce was not baptized, as Professor Ellmann was led to believe, at the Church of St Joseph, Terenure, which was not built until 1904, the year of *Ulysses*, but (we learn from a footnote) at the Chapel of Ease, Roundtown. At three days old, Joyce had already begun to cover his tracks from American scholars!

And the same J.J. could not have informed Yeats on his fortieth birthday that 'you are too old for me to help', for the good reason that he was in Trieste, a thousand miles away. That beauty was invented by Oliver Gogarty for Bertie Rodgers and the Third Programme and sure who would blame them? Professor Kenner traces it all back to Swift who pronounced the premature death of the astrologer, Partridge. 'The type of the written Irish memoir is Lemuel Gulliver's', for 'no Irishman apparently addresses pen to paper with any intent save to produce a good yarn.'

So we stand warned: Kenner's aim is to give a pleasantly prejudiced account of the Irish Literary Revival. Though what they were reviving was never clear: of the major figures only the dramatists, Synge and O'Casey (and later Behan),had some Irish while Yeats could tie himself in knots over the simplest expression. Clooth na Bear is a poor disguise for the Hag or Cailleach of Beare, supposed speaker of the greatest poem in the early literature of these islands. And an actor playing Caoilte in an early play went through the evening being called 'Wheelchair', 'Coldtea', and 'Quilty'.

But Kenner is fully aware of the brilliant strategies of Yeats: he might rhyme ' "Eire" . . . indifferently with "Faery" and with "weary" ' but if you were a protégé of his you had to be good. Did he find Synge in the Latin Quarter and declare 'Give up Paris . . . Go to the Aran Islands'? Synge already knew some Irish and was recognised when he got off the boat because of a proselytizing uncle. Was he then paying off a spiritual debt, offering art instead of soup?

* A Colder Eye: The Modern Irish Writers, by Hugh Kenner

Kenner is brief but brilliant on him, mimicking a typically Yeatsian cadence with 'Synge, *it may be*, handled but the one story six times, a story of setting out and then dying, in which those who set forth have chosen better than those who choose to stay.' And adapting Eliot he compares Synge's yoking of ideas by violence to John Donne: the bed of love and the bed of clay are side by side. And of the end of *Deirdre of the Sorrows*: 'it seems beyond doubt that Synge's model was the death-scene of Cleopatra.'

So the quip in *Ulysses*, 'Synge, the chap that writes like Shakespeare', may have a basis? Outrageously, Kenner argues that Hamlet is derived from 'the Irish spelling of a decent Scandanavian name, Olaf,' but forgets that Lear or Ler was really the father figure of a famous Irish tale: *At Swim Four Swans*. At this point English readers might grow uneasy, except that he goes on to suggest that *our* national emblem is a sham rock. He is wrong about the recent ancestry of the wolfhound, however; I have known one so inbred that it was a hermaphrodite and another that had a heart attack every time he saw his wife. Delicate beasts, indeed, like their owner, the last of a noble line, Anglo-Irish, of course.

Nor can I go along completely with his claim that 'Ireland has the highest rate of insanity'. Not literary, anyway; having visited Roethke in Ballinasloe Mental Hospital and seen Berryman in the jigs in Dublin as well as a manic Lowell, I am inclined to regard even Kavanagh as near normal. Genuine Irish madness is Myles apart: Kenner is accurate on our satiric gnome, who despite being from Tyrone was a deeply upset man. With a scholarship to Bonn in Celtic Studies, he found himself stuck in neutral Dublin, a caged bilingual.

If I sound playful it is because *A Colder Eye* is a new kind of book, a study of an aspect of modern literature which presumes that we already know the scenario, and can relish an irreverent re-run. Kenner clearly enjoyed writing it, which makes for pleasant reading, although it is not as rich as *The Pound Era*, perhaps because George Moore had already stolen many of the plums.

Besides, Kenner has already written well on those godfathers of modern and Irish literature, Joyce and Beckett. I cherish an essay of his which showed how Yeats arranged his later poems into books, a tip I have found useful. While he does not, like the other Bloom, perversely maintain that early Yeats is best, he still sees 'The Wanderings of Oisin' as 'an astonishing debut', and even ranks the earlier 'Island of Statues' above 'Endymion'. He has a paragraph, indeed, on the Romantic Long Poem which would serve another scholar as basis for a book, just as he shows how Yeats solved the Romantic dilemma, the loss of inspiration lamented in Wordsworth's 'Immortality Ode' and Coleridge's 'Dejection', through his extraordinary renewal of abstract and even journalistic diction.

And can Modern Ireland extend the separate tradition so eloquently cerebrated here, or did Partition and partial Independence lessen us? When I came to Dublin after the war few spoke of Yeats but Joyce was adored by younger writers, the people I gathered in *The Dolmen Miscellany*. Kenner hints at 'the beginning of a new story entirely, the story of post-Yeatsian Ireland'. But the sons of Paudeen and Biddy ignored the North, where I came from, and yet Ulster Poetry is now so fashionable that it threatens to swamp recent British and even Irish writing. While admiring this takeover bid, in a spirit of local patriotism (like beating the English at Windsor Park) I hope it does not limit the vision that made Ireland a part of Modern literature.

28 July 1983   **John Montague**

The way I told it to Maisie

We lived a sheltered life in our Irish village, my sisters and brother and I. Though my mother was the local doctor and was always hurling herself and rolls of cotton wool into the car to attend home deliveries the facts of life never intruded. Billowing women sat in the waiting room every Wednesday armed with small sinister bottles of samples, but I never stopped to wonder how they could have got themselves into this odd condition. I must have put it all down to Divine Providence: I certainly didn't put it down to anything else.

So when Maisie, our eighteen-year-old maid decided to take

me into her confidence, it came as a complete shock to me and – as it turned out – to her.

Maisie was making soda bread in the kitchen and motes were dancing in a ray of sunlight coming in over the river when she paused in her pounding. I'd been watching her from the window seat, admiring the confident way she hurled herself at the dough. She was very pretty, with black curly hair and a blazning complexion. She was a great knitter and under her tuition I'd kitted the whole family out in an amazing array of striped ribbed jumpers for the winter. My mother only took a needle in her hand to stitch up terrible wounds after hurling matches; Maisie by contrast was an artist and for her I had all the respect due to this sparse species.

But the happy hours we'd spent together over the two plain, two purl jumpers had given me no warning of the other, darker side of her nature.

'Do you know, do you,' she said suddenly, 'how babies get in there?'

'Where?' I said blankly.

'Into their mammies' tummies,' said Maisie, resuming her siege after a sideways look at me.

'How d'you mean get in?' I said, playing for time. I was horrified at the turn things were taking; Maisie was looking excited. She wasn't at all the same Maisie who'd taught me how to turn the heel of a sock.

Maisie was in full flight. Leaning on the soda bread, quivering like a spy who'd managed to get the deadly blueprints out under a hail of bullets, she told me the lot. Sometimes, when her recital got too much for her she'd slap the soda bread, shoo the cat out from in front of the Aga, cough and say she thought she must be getting a cold. Looking back on it all, she was in a state of mortal fright.

If she was frightened, I was paralysed. At some stage I must have stopped listening, because when she finally sank exhausted down beside me on the window seat, I was ready for her.

'Desperate, isn't it,' said Maisie. 'What they do?'

'Not really,' I said, 'I never saw anything wrong with it.'

Maisie's mouth fell open. 'D'you mean you knew already,' she cried, 'who told you?'

'Nobody told me,' I said patiently, 'I saw it.'

Maisie's face was a picture. Of all the emotions that chased across her open rosy face terror was predominant. I could have been E.T.

'Where,' she whispered.

I gave her a distant look. 'In the surgery,' I said. 'Of course.'

Maisie was riveted. 'D'you mean in your mammy's surgery upstairs?' she asked.

'Yes,' I said, casually. 'I was reading behind the curtains when Mrs Mulligan came in with her husband.'

'Mrs Mulligan from Bawnbeg is it,' said Maisie who kept careful tabs on all the patients, 'what happened?'

I yawned. 'Oh, Mrs Mulligan said "Doctor we'd like to have a baby but we don't know how, would you ever show us how to have one?" '

Maisie was spellbound. 'What did your Mammy say?'

'She said Certainly Mrs Mulligan. Open your coat (a thick Donegal tweed) and lie down there on the floor with Mr Mulligan, it won't take a tick.'

'And did they?' asked Maisie, pale and practically at her last gasp.

'They did,' I said suppressing a shiver. 'They seemed to get the hang of it in no time.'

'And what did your Mammy do?' asked Maisie.

'She watched,' I said.

Maisie reeled. 'My God,' she said, 'I couldn't.'

'Well she's a doctor after all,' I said, 'that's her job.' (And welcome to it, I thought, as I saw my mother in her blue blouse, grey skirt and pearls, supervising the Mulligan's bizarre sex education.)

Maisie had moved away from me slightly on the window seat. She looked like someone who'd had a narrow escape from a car crusher.

I was exhausted myself after my major imaginative feat, fitting forerunner to the scientific studies of Masters and Johnson. If the Aga had exploded that minute I couldn't have run to save my life.

'Did Joe Mulligan get out of his wellingtons?' asked Maisie, after a long stunned pause.

'No,' I said. 'He said he was ashamed to take them off because he had holes in his socks.'

30 March, 1983   **Eithne Power**

The fortunes of Sutton Place

When J. Paul Getty died, reputedly the richest man in the world, the new owner of his house in Surrey found that some of the freshly installed panelling was made of plywood. The billionaire with the heart of flint had ensured that, if he couldn't take it with him, it wouldn't be worth leaving behind either.

That fits neatly with the fortunes of Sutton Place. Until this century it had been owned by a family as poor as church mice – Roman Catholic church mice, to be precise, since that probably explains why the family fortunes fell after the death of the house's founder.

Not that this was bad in the long run, because it meant that while other families were rebuilding their Tudor mansions to keep up with the Inigo Joneses, the Westons kept it as a fine example of early Tudor architecture (except that they forgetfully allowed one of its four sides around a college-like quadrangle to fall down).

Sutton Place was one of the first of the great mansion houses of England. Only a decade or so before great landowners were still building castles: soon after, the dissolution of the monasteries released unprecedented wealth for secular building. Sutton Place's builder, Sir Richard Weston, eased in just ahead of this. He had been one of Henry VII's trusted courtiers and, in 1519, was one of the 'sad and ancient knights' brought in to lend a note of sobriety to the court of Henry VIII.

He mastered the most important art of the age: survival. He accompanied Henry to the Field of the Cloth of Gold; he was one of Buckingham's judges on a charge of treason and the day Buckingham's head rolled he collected his reward of the Sutton estate; he was Wolsey's man but he survived the fall of Wolsey; he was the father of Francis Weston but survived even his son's disgrace and execution for allegedly sleeping with Anne Boleyn;

and the following year he was entrusted with escorting Anne of Cleves to London.

Some time between 1521, when Henry granted him Sutton, and 1533, when Henry came to stay as Sir Richard's guest, Sutton Place was completed, and the exhibition now showing there, The Renaissance at Sutton Place, celebrates the 450th anniversary of Henry VIII's visit.

Poetry aside, the renaissance in England was marginal; a few classical motifs often filtered through the temperament of Flemish artists and combined with the lingering gothic. So the Renaissance at Sutton Place is a note scribbled in the margin. The house itself is the main exhibit, and the house's medieval brick, tile, and style; but winged putti moulded in terracotta above the door and Italian patterning in terracotta around the windows are the signs that something new was in the air.

Not for a century yet would English builders follow in the footsteps of Palladio and Vitruvius. The court might fetch Torrigiano and a few craftsmen from Italy; it might have the good fortune to attract the incomparable Holbein; Wyatt and Surrey might bed down the Italian modes of verse in an English climate; but Henry's England, with its outbreaks of plague and sweating sickness, its population of less than two and a half million spread thinly through the countryside and taxed penally to pay for Henry's useless wars – this papal province on the outskirts of civilization was not rich ground for a classical renaissance.

Richard Weston had travelled; he had seen the great châteaux of the Loire in the building. But they too were more medieval than Renaissance, even Blois, where Leonardo spent his last days. So the mullioned windows of Sutton Place rise to cupped trefoils. There was a towering gatehouse (in the demolished side) just like Hampton Court. There are steeply pitched roofs and tall gables and courses of soft red and orange brick. There is sixteenth-century English stained glass similar, John Aubrey observed, to the glass in the Perpendicular chapel of King's College, Cambridge.

This is not to deny the beauty of Tudor architecture, from Hampton Court to Wollaton and Hardwick Hall. Sutton Place, Knole, Haddon Hall, Montacute were as English as the later landscapes of Capability Brown or the City churches of Wren.

231

But Renaissance? John Summerson has put it best: 'Paul van Somer, whose portraits hang happily enough in Hatfield or Audley End . . . would be absurd company for the architecture of Jones. The truth is that Jones's proper companion is Rubens.'

Still, for all King Henry's love of jousting and wrestling and gaudy courtly display – exemplified at the Field of the Cloth of Gold, for which there are designs in the Sutton Place exhibition – his toehold at Calais and his rivalry with and envy for François I laid his court open to continental influences.

The great masons and builders were English, but there were German silverware and stoneware, Flemish tapestry, glass from Murano and from Spain, stucco moulding from Italy, armour from Milan and from Henry's own workship at Greenwich, modelled on the fine continental example – though nothing quite so fine as the elaborately embossed and chiselled suit of armour made by Negroli for Henry II of France, sold for £2 million in the Hever Castle auction, and included in the Sutton Place show.

The indigenous work in the exhibition is often more homely – linstocks from the Mary Rose, one carved by the ship's gunners themselves into the fantastic likeness of a dragon, the other a clenched fist; from the Mary Rose too a cannon with a Tudor rose set among Renaissance decoration and the inscription, '*Robert and John Owyn Bretheryn Borne In The Cyte of London The Sonnes Of An Inglish Made Thys Bastard Anno dni 1537*'; pewter flagons, a candlestick, a tabor pipe, a carved wooden knife sheath.

If Henry needed anything more elaborate, like a triumphal arch for the coronation of his ill-starred Anne, he could always turn to Holbein: the arch is long gone, but the design for it is in the exhibition.

And if, in his constant rivalry with the French court, the lavish decoration of his own court fell short, then there were ways and means: from Hampton Court come two decorative bosses of the time of Henry VIII; they were run up of papier maché, gilded, and mounted on wood. At a distance in a candlelit banquet at Hampton Court, nobody would notice. And Getty would have approved.

27 May, 1983   **Michael McNay**

A country diary: Kent

At last a day of real warmth, the path through the hanger wood sunlit and dry. A time for just standing and staring and it was my good fortune that I did so, otherwise I should have missed a vignette of woodland life that would not have been out of place in a comic cartoon. A ripple running through the leaf litter turned out to be a weasel in hot pursuit of a wood mouse. The mouse ran or, rather, bounced in a succession of small leaps, clearing the ground flora like a hurdler. The weasel was gaining and they tangled together by the roots of an old beech tree. I assumed that was the end of the mouse, but the quarry proved very elusive and in the chase that followed even had the temerity to jump over the weasel. There was no paralysis of fear in this hunt. If anything, fear drove the mouse to even greater agility. At one point it crossed the path I was standing on, long tail outstretched, long, pointed ears in a high state of alertness. Then, unbelievably, it met the weasel again and the two ran past each other just like characters from a comic strip. The weasel turned sharply in its tracks, but too late. The mouse was away to some underground haven. The weasel, baffled, took up its stance on a large stone and raised its nine-inch body to the full extent to gain the maximum view of its hunting territory. Finding nothing in sight, it roamed back towards the beech tree, dived into the leaf litter and disturbed two more wood mice and they, too, raced away to different points of the compass in very swift and straight lines. The weasel lost them, too. Supposedly one of the more efficient killers of the woodland underworld and small enough to follow mice along their runs, the weasel hunts by day and night, especially with a young litter to feed. I have seen many a weasel out on patrol but never a display like this. The hunter has its problems.

27 April, 1983   **John T. White**

[*John Talbot White died at the age of fifty-seven, shortly before his final Country Diary appeared.*]

End piece

I tripped and fell flat on my back at the TUC last week. I must disappoint my detractors by telling them that the collapse of the stout party was literal rather than metaphorical and that the only recorded damage is the colourful imprint of coins and keys on the part of my anatomy which trapped the contents of one trouser pocket against the floor boards.

Lying there on the Congress House floor and staring at the Congress House ceiling as the thunder of my impact reverberated round the building I expected much of my past life to pass before me. But there was only one tiny incident that took shape and form in my memory. The image was so strong that it blotted out the voice of the Deputy Secretary reminding me that at the TUC they are not insured for self-inflicted injuries.

I suddenly remembered that (during the years when I was being brought up by hand) before I went out in a newly-mended pair of shoes, my mother worked on the hard and shining surface of the sole with a tin contraption that we called a 'nutmeg grater'. I am not sure how often in those days we grated nutmegs. But we always roughened the slippery patina of the recently hammered-on leather after the cobbler's work was done. It was an act of loving devotion.

For, five minutes with the nutmeg grater did more damage than the wear and tear of a full week's walking. Ten per cent of the new soles' value must have been scraped away in a few strokes. And we did not sacrifice even coppers lightly. Yet to reduce the risk of me breaking a leg or dislocating a shoulder we squandered several times each year the price of a seat in the back stalls at the Hillsborough Park Cinema. I lay on Congress House floor feeling deeply grateful.

We made a similar financial sacrifice on those frequent winter days when the Pennine snow had packed hard on our steep suburban roads. For then, the six-year-old ingrate was sent rebelliously to school with socks pulled on *over* his shoes to provide an abrasive surface between leather and ice and thus ensure that he remained vertical throughout his journey.

Sceptics may argue that the grey elastic tops were only pulled on after they had developed so many holes that they were past either wearing or darning. But in our house socks were never recognized as having reached that condition. The darns were darned. Advice was given about the foot on which a multiple-darned sock should be worn so as to avoid the special strain of big-toe tension on a particularly vulnerable patch of hand weaving.

At the time – too young to contemplate the psychological cause of my family's obsessive fears about the maintenance of my equilibrium – I simply regarded the over-socks as part of fate's conspiracy to make me look ridiculous. And although the roughened soles were mercifully invisible beneath my feet, every secure step was a reproach. For, although physically secure, the careful cosseting made me deeply uncertain about my incipient manhood.

At any rate that is how I felt about it at the age of nine. Forty years on, lying on the floor in Congress House, sole scraping seemed a thoroughly good idea.

Of course, in Sheffield we used to scrape our own as a by-product of our cottage industries. My father was a resident shoe repairer. It was all part of a determination to do it ourselves which overcame us long before do it yourself was invented. We baked our own bread, knitted our own pullovers, 'pegged' rugs out of old remnants of cloth, whitewashed, papered and painted, laid linoleum and mended our own shoes for reasons which owed nothing to the philosophies of Mahatma Gandhi or William Morris. We were disciples of Samuel Smiles. For self-help saved money.

My father mended shoes on Sunday mornings. He was a bad workman who, at least in this instance, had every reason to blame his tools – a hammer with a loose head which took lethal flight if it struck too hard, a pair of pliers from a 'Little Carpenter's' set which I had been given one Christmas, a steel rasp and my mother's carving knife. His hobbin iron (a heavy steel cobbler's anvil known in the south as a last) was not a tool in the proper sense of the word. Perhaps it qualifies for inclusion in the inventory. For it was certainly not a birthday present either – though it was masquerading under that description when my father received it.

His cobbling technique was simple. He first wrenched the

holey sole from its moorings with the aid of the toy pliers. He then picked out any of the remaining nails with the careful precision of a brain surgeon.

The soleless shoe was placed on a piece of leather that he had bought on his way home from work the previous day and a line was drawn round the welt with one of the 3B pencils that my grandmother used for writing letters to her sisters. Then, the putative sole was sawn out of the leather with the carving knife, nailed into place and rasped into something like the shape of the original welt. All that being done – and knuckles having been skinned, thumbs bruised, tacks swallowed and tempers lost – the pristine surface of his achievement was immediately defiled with a nutmeg grater.

I remembered all that thanks to some anonymous lady who polishes the floors at Congress House until Arthur Scargill can see his face in them and they become as slippery as the moral slope down which Narcissus slid when he became infatuated with his own reflection. Of course, the memory flashed through my mind in a second. And then I concentrated all my energies on considering whether or not to feel ridiculous. I decided against. Falling down is not half so bad as people think. I wish I had known that thirty years ago.

30 July 1983   **Roy Hattersley**

236

Index